Maximilian Sternberg, Frederick Richard Breeks Atkinson

Acromegaly

Maximilian Sternberg, Frederick Richard Breeks Atkinson

Acromegaly

ISBN/EAN: 9783744781336

Printed in Europe, USA, Canada, Australia, Japan

Cover: Foto ©ninafisch / pixelio.de

More available books at **www.hansebooks.com**

ACROMEGALY.

BY

Dr. MAXIMILIAN STERNBERG,

Privatdocent in the University of Vienna.

TRANSLATED

BY

F. R. B. ATKINSON, M.D., C.M. (Edin. Univ.).

CONTENTS.

		Page.
I.	History	5
II.	Review of the clinical appearances of the disease	11
III.	Pathological anatomy	13
	Supplement: Morphology and physiology of the pituitary gland	45
IV.	Symptomatology	53
V.	Development; course; terminations; types of the disease; prognosis	81
VI.	Relationship of acromegaly to other diseases and conditions	87
VII.	Etiology and pathogeny	95
VIII.	Diagnosis and differential diagnosis	99
IX.	Treatment	117
X.	Bibliography	120

ACROMEGALY.

By Dr. Maximilian Sternberg.

I. HISTORY.

In the year 1886 Pierre Marie, of Charcot's clinic, published an article under the title "Sur deux cas d'acromégalie, hypertrophie singulière non congénitale des extrémités supérieures, inférieures et céphalique." Therein, based on two observations of the author's, and some cases communicated under other names in older publications, a sketch of a new disease was given, of which the most striking characteristic consisted in a peculiar increase in the size of the extremities of the body—the "gipfelnden Theile," as more lately v. Recklinghausen has called it—namely, of the hands and feet, and distinctive sections of the head. The name ($ἄκρον$ = end, $μέγας$ = large) is intended to denote this appearance.* The enlargement in the hands and feet chiefly consists in an increase of thickness; in comparison with these bulky, clumsy parts, the forearm and lower part of the leg, which are not enlarged, but rather usually of feeble muscular development, offer a marked contrast. In the skull, the forehead markedly protrudes, the nose is increased in size, but especially the under jaw is powerfully developed, so that the chin widely projects, and its teeth overlap those of the upper jaw. A curvature of the spinal column is associated with these appearances, and in addition thickenings of the clavicles, ribs, kneecaps, and pelvis. In females, menstruation ceases at the beginning of the illness. The disease is entirely distinct (entité morbide spéciale); it has nothing to do with myxoedema, leontiasis ossea, congenital hypertrophy of a single part, or the osteitis deformans of Paget. Such is the original description given by Marie.

* Marie would have originally named the disease "Akromakrie," but chose before publication the above-mentioned name for the sake of euphony. (Souza-Leite: Revue Scientifique, 1890, p. 807.)

Already in earlier times repeated cases of this disease have been described. Some, as mentioned, Marie has made use of in his original work. Numerous others, communicated under the most varied designations, have only by degrees been brought again to light. Acromegaly has certainly a remarkable and instructive history. It shows with startling clearness the enormous difficulties, hardly dreamed of by the uninitiated and even by many physicians accustomed to research, with which the investigation into pathological occurrences has to struggle.

The oldest historical document on acromegaly hitherto known, is, as I have pointed out, the portrait of a "giant" of the court of the Elector of the Palatinate, Frederick II., preserved in the Ambras-Schloss in the Tyrol, painted life size in 1583 by his court painter. The oldest medical account[*] concerns the case of "Sieur Mirbeck," which Saucerotte (1772) and Noël (1779) have described as "accroissement considérable des os dans une personne adulte." Saucerotte succeeded, after the patient's death, in obtaining some of the bones from the grave, which were incorporated in the Musée Dupuytren. The distinguished dermatologist Alibert described in his lectures, which appeared in 1822, another case of this disease under the name "géant scrofuleux."

A short but striking description of two cases is contained in Magendie's lectures on the physiology of the nervous system, edited as a book in 1839.[†] The condition is therein described as "hypertrophy," of doubtful, possibly nervous origin.

[*] Possibly a giantess described in the year 1567 by Johannes Weyer (Lat., Wierus), the opponent of superstition and witchcraft, was suffering from acromegaly (no menses, "toto corpore torpida").

[†] Since this passage remains up to the present unknown, it may here be quoted word for word. We see the celebrated experimenter in the light of an acute clinical observer:—" Une activité extraordinaire de la nutrition est en général liée à un état particulier du système nerveux. État particulier c'est un mot bien vague ; mais je ne puis vous donner cette assertion que comme conjecturale, et par conséquent vous me permettrez de ne point me servir de termes trop positifs. Toujours est-il que j'ai dans ce moment à l'Hôtel-Dieu deux femmes offrant à son maximum de développement cette manière d'être de l'économie qu'on est convenu d'appeler hypertrophie. L'une est une vraie femme-monstre. Tête, membres, tronc, tout a un volume énorme ; sa langue a la largeur de celle du veau, ses doigts sont gros comme quatre des miens. Sa voix est celle d'un homme ; les sons en sont graves, pleins ; je ne doute pas que le larynx ne soit aussi hypertrophié.

The enlargement of the tongue in acromegaly, which Magendie rightly conceived as one symptom of the process, seemed to have produced an especial impression on Chalk. He published in 1855 a very characteristic case observed by himself, under the name " partial dislocation of the lower jaw from an enlarged tongue." Perhaps many cases of acromegaly may still be concealed under the older concise term " Macroglossia."

A special position in the history of acromegaly belongs to an observation of Friedreich (1868), which concerns the two brothers Wilhelm and Carl Hagner. Friedreich, owing to the condition met with in the osseous system, designated it as " general hyperostosis." We shall return to these cases later on.

Others were particularly struck by the alteration in the face. Verga described, in Italy in 1869, a case with the results of a post mortem examination as " Prosopectasia," Tarufti (1879) an old skeleton in the museum at Bologna under the same name. Verga's communication contained the first complete post mortem examination of a case of acromegaly. The narrator brings to notice as a specially remarkable discovery a large tumour, which had taken the place of the hypophysis, enlarged the sella Turcica, burrowed into the sphenoid, and pressed upon and pushed away the nerves. Tarufti's skeleton also showed, what many years later was established, a considerable expansion of the pituitary fossa.

Lombroso also described a case, in the same year as Verga, which he designated as " Macrosomia " (Gigantism).

In the year 1872, the anatomist Carl v. Langer, of Vienna, published an anatomical study on " giants." remarkable for the thoroughness of its details. He therein described two forms of giant skull. The one is well formed only somewhat enlarged (" normal type "). The other shows by contrast a very dilated pituitary fossa, huge lower jaw whose alveolar process everywhere overlapped that of the

---

L'autre femme est dans le même genre, seulement elle a un peu moins d'ampleur. Comme elle est plus jeune, et que chaque jour elle gagne d'avantage. je ne doute pas qu'avant peu elle ne puisse rivaliser avec son ainée. Rien d'ailleurs chez ces deux femmes n'explique cet accroissement énorme. Il est probable que le système nerveux y est pour beaucoup."

upper jaw, dilatation of the air sinuses, swelling of the processes for the muscles, deepening of the canals for the vessels, and contraction of many of the foramina for the nerves. The second form of giant skull he explained as distinctly "pathological." These giants with pathological skulls had also peculiarities in the rest of the skeleton, as exostoses on the vertebral bodies, deposits on the edges of the hip-joints, &c. From the extant portrait of the giant and from observations on a living subject, he showed that "degeneration in the soft parts" exists, especially swelling of the lips and nostrils, and enlargement of the tongue. From the enlargement of the sella Turcica he inferred a "degeneration of the hypophysis."

Henrot described in two publications (1877 and 1879) in a very careful manner a case with results of a post mortem, which he denoted as myxœdema. In this case also a large tumour of the hypophysis was found.

In the same year as Henrot's first communication appeared, Brigidi gave an excellent account of the results of a post mortem examination of the once celebrated actor Ghirlenzoni, which also contained the first microscopic examination of the tumour of the hypophysis. He brought into prominence the resemblance of the skeleton to that of the orang-outang, and was satisfied with the non-incriminating name a "peculiar deformity" (uomo divenuto stranamente deforme).

Cunningham published in 1879 an observation, in which the symptoms of diabetes and tumour of the hypophysis were conspicuous. He was particularly struck by the appearance of the patient, which he compared to that of a gorilla. Thomson (1890) was the first to recognise the preserved skeleton as belonging to a case of acromegaly. Probably many an old case in the literature of "tumours of the hypophysis" must have belonged to acromegaly. Unfortunately, owing to the larger part being deficient, no trustworthy conclusions can be drawn from the pathological descriptions.

Fritsche, in 1884, in a small book edited in common with Klebs, communicated a good description of a very severe case. Fritsche also for the first time attempted a grouping of similar cases in literature, and recognised in the affection a "very characteristic type of disease."

Klebs in the same publication treated the anatomical condition of the case with the greatest care. He defined it as "gigantism," and placed it, starting from general points of view, together with other most varied forms of gigantism in one group.

Unfortunately this view of the excellent pathologist was based substantially on a regrettable cursoriness in reading the work of Langer. Klebs believed Langer had pointed to the enlargement of the hypophysis in such giants whose giant growth represents "a simple increase of the physiological growth gradually and without special disturbance," while Langer, as aforesaid, has declared, on the contrary, this form of giant to be a pathological change. This misunderstanding not only prevented Klebs from the right comprehension of his case, but, owing to the influence of his opinion as expressed in his handbook, led later to an equally-to-be-regretted confusion on the part of French and Italian authors in the understanding of the relationship between gigantism and acromegaly. Klebs, moreover, also was the first to draw attention in this work to the enlargement of the thymus in his case, to which he ascribes the cause of the disease. But the communication of Fritsche and Klebs remained entirely disregarded by clinicians and pathological anatomists.

The same occurred to the communication of Hadden and Ballance who, in 1885, submitted to the London Clinical Society a case described as "hypertrophy of the subcutaneous tissues of the face, hands, and feet."

With this publication closes what may be termed the "prehistoric" period of acromegaly, for a year later the before-mentioned work of P. Marie appeared.

There are still a few odd publications of this time. There is one by Motais (1886), published as "a remarkable case of exophthalmos," another described by Lancereaux in his handbook of pathological anatomy, published in 1888, as "morbus Basedowii, with hypertrophy of the bones." Two further cases were communicated by Wadsworth (1885) and Tresilian (1888) under the name of "Myxœdema."

It was the treatise of Marie that all at once threw light on this dark region of pathology. Without prejudice to all earlier, and in some degree excellent works, Marie was the first to bring the disease out of the catalogue of the rare and monstrous into the domain of clinical medicine. His communication contains the first attempt to define the type of the disease and to make a differential diagnosis possible. Both these are necessary, in order to permit of a malady becoming well known in medical science.

The result proved that Marie made a successful hit. Immediately searches were made everywhere for analogous cases, and there appeared in quick succession a whole series of works on this new disease, "la maladie de Marie," as it is named by French writers, according to the proposal of Verstraeten. Amongst these there are some of greater importance than others. For instance, the description of the skeleton of one of Marie's cases by Broca; a very careful work by Erb, in which, amongst others, the case of the brothers Hagner was again described; a work by Freund, in which acromegaly was explained as an anomaly in growth, partly connected with atavism; an essay by v. Recklinghausen, who proposed the name "Pachyakrie," since increase in thickness is invariable; in addition, communications by Adler, Klebs, Schultz, Verstraeten, Virchow, &c.

Whereas up to this time cases of acromegaly had been published under other very varied designations, now, on the contrary, various other diseases were described under this name, and it was soon necessary to separate these from acromegaly, and, based on the newly gained knowledge, to define the type of the disease more accurately. Marie gave, in 1888, a copious grouping of the cases (2), then in a concise (3), and in a more detailed work in English (4) presented a new description of the disease. He laid stress on enlargement of the hypophysis as of regular occurrence in the complaint, which in the living subject calls forth various disturbances of vision, and through the expansion of the sella Turcica confers a characteristic appearance upon the bones of the skull.

He furthermore drew attention to the fact that a good many sufferers from acromegaly were of tall stature, and on that account many would be described in older observations as "giants." Nevertheless the majority of those affected with acromegaly are not by any means of giant size. The ordinary gigantism is an increase of physiological growth, acromegaly is a disease.

In the year 1870, Souza-Leite, a pupil of Marie, presented in an excellent monograph a representation of acromegaly, which also contained the collected cases in detail.

In both of these above-named works a number of cases are separated from acromegaly. Marie has grouped several of these into a new disease "Ostéo-arthropathie hypertrophiante pneumique," upon which he published a special treatise (5). He expressly insists that this new disease is not to be considered as a distinct disease ("entité morbide autonome,") but as a secondary process, which results from other affections, and is certainly connected with the respiratory apparatus, hence the adjective "pneumique." He classes with it the cases of the brothers Hagner, and in addition the observations of Saundby, Ewald, Fräntzel, Elliot, and Sollier. In this treatise and Souza-Leite's thesis the differential diagnosis is fully dealt with.

E. v. Bamberger had already shortly before set on foot clinical and anatomical investigations on the same phenomena. Soon literature brought numerous new contributions. It is now clear that this disease of the bones also occurs in other complaints, such as the lungs, and that the joints, judging by the anatomical examination of cases, show no essential alteration. The name "secundäre hyperplastische ostitis," proposed for it by Arnold (1), commends itself for general use.

It is tolerably generally recognised that this secondary affection is in no way connected with acromegaly: opinions only differ as to whether certain cases are to be included in one or the other class.

The brothers Hagner especially have been the subject of manifold discussion, which cannot even yet be regarded as ended. Fritsche had not included them in the consideration of his new forms of disease. Marie, on the other hand, at first considered them identical, but afterwards, owing to Erb's later exact description, separated them. Erb (2) denounced this separation as unjustifiable. Arnold (1) had the opportunity of making the post mortem on one of the cases ("Hagner I."), and gave a most careful report of it, in which he pronounced the case to be true acromegaly, as also in a second work (2), in which he called attention to a series of the conditions met with agreeing with those in other undoubted cases of acromegaly. Especially did he pronounce the want of change in the hypophysis as secondary. We shall return to this subject in Chapter VIII.

By means of Souza-Leite's work, which was also translated into English, the knowledge of acromegaly has been much extended, and the disease has quickly become of general interest. During the last years the flood of literature on the subject has swollen to almost unmanageable proportions. Whilst in 1890 Souza-Leite collected thirty-eight trustworthy cases, a year later Duchesnau, in his likewise excellent thesis, was able to add twenty-seven new cases from the literature, not counting one case of very careful personal observation with the results of a post mortem examination (Renaut).

Another collection of cases by Collins in 1892 brought Souza-Leite's number up to eighty-three cases. Among them certainly were some which did not strictly belong to acromegaly.* Since then a large mass of material has been added, so that whereas on considering the subject in 1894 I was able to refer to one hundred and thirty cases, there now exist two hundred and ten trustworthy examples.

Out of the abundance of names, we can here only mention a few of the larger or more important publications. Several have carefully studied the alterations in a single organic system, such as the organ of sight (Schultze, Asmus, Hertel, Denti, Uhthoff, &c.), the cardiac disturbances (Fournier). Others have directed attention to new symptoms, as mental (Pick), atrophy of muscles (Duchesnau), &c.

In 1894 I took up again the question of the relationship between acromegaly and gigantism, and have shown that the description of Langer of the giant skeletons with enlarge-

* These three publications, of which the two last mutually complete each other, contain those often very inaccessible cases up to 1891 in detailed excerpts, and their study is therefore indispensable for independent work on the subject of acromegaly. A good survey of a large number of cases, but in a much shorter tabulated form, is contained in Arnold's work.

ment of the sella Turcica are typical cases of acromegaly; further, I have drawn attention to a hitherto little noticed symptom of the illness, pain and parasthesia of the extremities, and also to the relationship of acromegaly to the "crania progenea" discussed by L. Meyer, and have introduced a new point of view to explain the hyperplasia of the thymus gland.

Simultaneously also Brissaud and Meige, as well as Massalongo, have worked at the question of gigantism, but both have believed, following the incorrect citation of Klebs, that Langer had seen "normal giants" with enlargement of the hypophysis, and have throughout adopted the identity of gigantism with acromegaly.

P. Marie (6) has recently, 1896, studied the hand in the subjects of acromegaly, and has now demonstrated two varieties, of which the one shows an increase in breadth (type en large), the other an increase in length (type en long). Numerous works have now placed the pathological anatomy on a broader basis.

Fresh light has been thrown on the etiology of the disease by Pel and Unverricht's suggestion of mental and bodily trauma.

As regards the treatment, which Souza-Leite considered hopeless, new points of view have been brought forward by observations which, carried on for a long time, have shown instances of authenticated improvements (*e.g.*, Denti, Schlesinger), as well as by the introduction of gland treatment (Brown-Séquard, 1893). Finally, we owe to the discovery of Röntgen a new method of clinical inquiry.

The knowledge of acromegaly has stimulated pathological and anatomical inquiry, since of recent years a great number of investigators have devoted themselves to the study of the hypophysis, and have brought to light much that is new regarding this remarkable organ.

In concluding this historical survey it may be mentioned, that acromegaly offers also some historical interest. Marie has shown it to be very probable (7) that the Franco-Italian type of clown, the hunchbacked "Punchinello," is one of acromegaly, so also Souques (2) for the English "Punch." Lastly, the relationship of acromegaly to gigantism throws new light on old tales and saws.

II. REVIEW OF THE CLINICAL FEATURES OF THE DISEASE.

Acromegaly persists for many years, in most cases as long as ten. The commencement is traceable to most varied causes; usually it is imperceptible. Very often the disease commences with pain and paræsthesia, affecting the arm and leg, often also the trunk or face, and may for a long time be misinterpreted. In females, cessation of menstruation is usually one of the earliest symptoms.

By degrees a change in the appearance of the face strikes the patient's friends, and finally also the patient himself. His nearest relations, even his mother, do not recognise him if they last saw him in good health. Figs. 1 and 2 show

Fig. 1.
Illustration of a man, about 24 years of age, before the appearance of the disease.

Fig. 2.
Illustration of case of Fig. 1, 33 years old, with well-marked acromegaly.

the change of appearance in an as yet unpublished case.* In some cases the patient feels nevertheless in good health, is strong, cheerful, and in good spirits.

* I am indebted to Primarius Dr. F. Kovács, of Vienna, for kindly handing me over the photographs and history of the illness.

But usually with the change in the countenance there is associated a whole train of disorders. Very often a peculiar change of character arises. Capable workmen, enterprising merchants, and active women become phlegmatic, vacillat-

FIG. 3.
Woman, 36 years old, with pronounced acromegaly.
(Hofrath L. v. Schrötter's ward.)

ing, languid, sullen, and irritable. Their hands become awkward, the legs feeble. Very often they are tormented by headache.

If the disease is developed, the deformity of the body is

in a high degree remarkable. At the first glance one sees the uncouth and dull features, the coarse and bulky hands and feet. The head sinks in between the shoulders, the back is curved in the upper dorsal region. Fig. 3 shows the woman Schlesinger demonstrated in 1894 at the "Naturforscher-Versammlung."* Looking more carefully at the head, one is also struck by the changes in the soft parts, as well as in the bones. The shape of the nose, lips, tongue, and lower jaw is typical. The nose is enlarged in every dimension, and snubbed, the lips much swollen, especially the under lip, which is very large and prominent. The tongue is much enlarged, often to such an extent that there is no room for it in the mouth, and protrudes between the open rows of teeth. The lower jaw is powerfully developed, the chin stands out for some distance. The alveolar process of the lower jaw with its teeth encircles that of the upper jaw. The whole face is lengthened and oval.

In many patients the change in the bones preponderates. The orbital curve is then strongly arched, the zygomatic arch prominent, and the horizontal circumference of the skull increased. If this is also brachycephalic, then the head with the powerful under jaw has a brutish appearance, similar to that of the anthropoid apes.

The hands are enormously large and broad, but not deformed: this depends upon an increase in all the structures. The furrows of the skin are deep, the folds puffy, the fingers thick like sausages, the nails proportionately small.

In the same way the feet are enormously bulky and flat, the toes thick and coarse. The change in the extremities is usually first noticed by the patient, when the rings, thimbles, gloves, or shoes become repeatedly too small.

With the curvature of the vertebral column there is also associated deformity of the chest. The lower part of the sternum projects as a swelling anteriorly. All the bones of the chest are increased in size.

Affections of the internal organs are added to the changes in the exterior form of the body. Among the organs of the senses, the visual apparatus is frequently very much damaged,

---

* I am indebted to Hofrath L. v. Schrötter for kindly handing me over the photographs for the illustrations of 3, 11, and 12.

exophthalmos constituting a striking deformity. Important for the patient is the injury to the optic tracts or to the oculo-motor nerves, caused by pressure of the tumour of the hypophysis, which causes repeatedly frightful headache. The hearing may also suffer.

The larynx shows in many cases increase in size in all its parts. The voice is unnaturally low and hoarse, so that the patients, especially women, often thereby attract attention.

Changes in the thyroid are usual: at one time one finds a goitre, at another the gland is diminished in size.

The appetite is often increased to an insatiable feeling of hunger. Thirst also may become extraordinary.

Serious changes may be experienced in the circulation. The heart is dilated and hypertrophied, the arterial system extensively diseased. Many patients show when at rest a slight cyanosis; the muscle of the heart is insufficient for any strong demand.

According to the degree of thirst, the quantity of the urine is, in many cases, increased. Frequently one finds an abundant secretion of sugar with the other phenomena which attend "true" diabetes, as boils, acetonuria, and separation of aceto-acetic acid. Hunger and thirst may also in cases be attended with a normal amount of urine.

The external genitals may also participate in the enlargement of the ἄκρα; moreover, there is frequently in men diminished sexual power; in women amenorrhœa is an early symptom, as above mentioned.

The disease may remain stationary for many years. Sometimes a very considerable abatement occurs. Gradually, however, the weakness increases; the muscles, in comparison with the powerful size of the extremities, always become weaker, breathlessness arises, weariness and drowsiness gain ground. Finally the organs of digestion fail in their function, or very often threatening symptoms due to the cranial tumour become prominent. If intermediate illnesses or complications do not carry off the invalid, he becomes worse, and is finally completely confined to his bed, until at last death, often sudden and unexpected, releases him.

III. PATHOLOGICAL ANATOMY.

Up to the present time the results of forty-seven post mortems of undoubted cases are to hand. Arranged according to the time of the first publications—many cases have again and again been studied—are the observations of: Saucerotte, Verga, Langer-Sternberg (two cases), Brigidi, Henrot, Cunningham-Thomson, Taruffi, Fritsche and Klebs, Marie-Broca-Marinesco, Lancereaux, Klebs, Duchesnau, Holsti, Bury, Wolf, Gauthier, Cepeda, Bonardi, Caton and Paul, Claus and Van der Stricht, Dana, Somers, Fratnich, Squance, Arnold (2) (woman Ruf), Boyce and Beadles, Linsmayer, Strümpell, Boltz (2), Tamburini, Dallemagne (three cases), Griffith, Hutchinson, Mossé and Daunic, Sigurini and Caporiacco, Bourneville and Regnault, Comini, Regnault, Roxburgh and Collis, Tichomiroff, Pineles, Hansemann, Uhthoff.

This large number of cases is certainly reduced by close examination.

Many of them are incompletely investigated, or only quite shortly, and insufficiently communicated. The pathological anatomy of acromegaly is therefore by no means to be regarded as settled. Much is not yet sufficiently explained, some questions especially are not as yet touched upon. Relatively best known is the osseous system, which was also the earliest to be investigated. Detailed descriptions of the whole skeleton have been given by Brigidi, Taruffi, Broca, Thomson, Langer-Sternberg, Regnault, and important particulars are to be found in almost all post mortem reports.*
Since, notwithstanding, incorrect statements regarding it still constantly appear, even in books, we must give a more comprehensive description.

The disease is generally symmetrical, but of a pair of bones, one may be more markedly affected than the other.

The deepening of the canals for the vessels, dilatation of the vessel foramina, and strengthening of the points of attachment for the muscles and ligaments are typical.

---

* Through the kindness of Hofrath Stadelmann, of Berlin, I had the opportunity of examining the bones of two as yet unpublished cases.

As a result of this, the bones acquire a coarse appearance, and the normal roughness of the surface is thereby increased. This change of shape exhibits a partial exaggeration of the normal proportions. Moreover, small exostoses appear on the outside of the muscular and ligamentous attachments. Minute consideration of the normal topographical relations is often necessary regarding these osseous deposits to distinguish them from the former. They are small, rarely prickly, and are placed most abundantly on the bones of the base of the skull, vertebræ, pelvis, and chest, very few on the bones of the extremities. They are far more scanty than the normal strong points and prominences. Prickly, warty, stalactiform exostoses are never found to any great extent in true massive acromegaly on normally smooth parts of the bones. Typical further is a peculiar growth of some bones (lower jaw, bones of the air sinuses, sternum). The tumour of the pituitary body produces in most cases special changes in the sphenoid bone. The extent of the changes depends naturally on whether, on dissection, the case is found to have reached an early or later stage.

The skull is frequently enlarged as a whole, often also thick-walled (see Fig. 10, p. 54), coarse and heavy, especially if the disease has lasted a long time. The circumference of the skull is, in a number of cases, considerably enlarged (size during life: Sigurini and Caporiacco 61·0, Unverricht 62·8, Holsti 63·5, Virchow-Möbius 65·5, Hàskovec 66·0, Schultze 67·0), in other cases normal. On the outer surface of the cranium the strong and very rough muscular tuberosities are characteristic, as the side view in Figs. 5 and 7 shows.

Frequently the occipital protuberance projects prominently (Fig. 7). The under surface of the skull, the site of the numerous ligamentous and muscular attachments, is extremely rough and jagged, the styloid process of the temporal bones most extraordinarily strong. The air sinuses are widened,* usually not all to the same extent. If the dilatation depends on inflation of their outer wall, the shape of the skull is thereby strongly affected, as also by the

* The frontal sinuses would be opened in acromegaly by a saw-cut through the usual horizontal plane of the skull, 1 cm. above the orbital curve, which otherwise is rarely the case.

arching forwards of the orbital curve (Fig. 5), or the whole forehead, the mastoid process (Fig. 5), or the antrum of Highmore. The bulging of those walls of the air sinuses, which are situated in the interior of the skull, naturally brings about changes in the surrounding parts. The orbit may

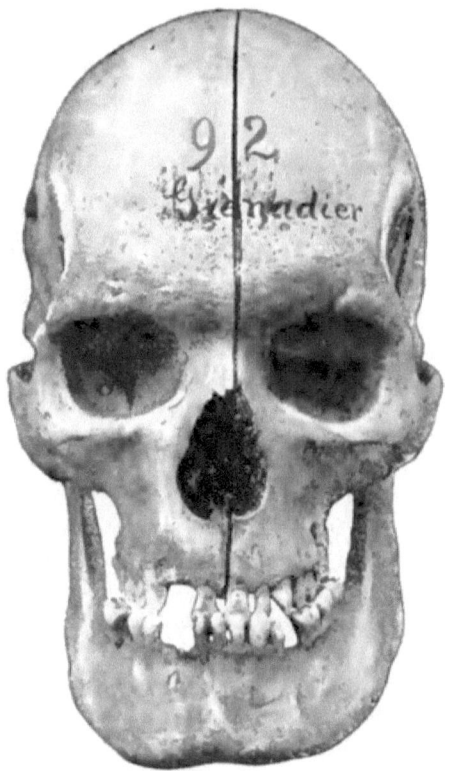

Fig. 4.—Front view of the skull of a case of acromegaly, 208·7 cm. high, from the Anatomical Institute in Vienna. Age about 30.

especially become narrowed through inflation of the ethmoid, of the lower walls of the frontal sinuses, and of the upper wall of the antrum of Highmore (cf. skiagraph, Fig. 10, p. 54). The inflated walls are sometimes thinned, even like paper, and transparent, but more frequently, and especially if the disease has lasted for a long time, there occurs at these points a thickening of the bones. The arching of the orbital curve and the mastoid process especially depends usually not only on a dilatation of the air sinuses, but also on the hypertrophy of the bones. The sutures on the roof of the skull often disappear early. (Duchesnau 45 years, Fritsche and Klebs 47 years).

The canals for the vessels are usually found hollowed out on the inner surface of the skull, the arterial and venous foramina

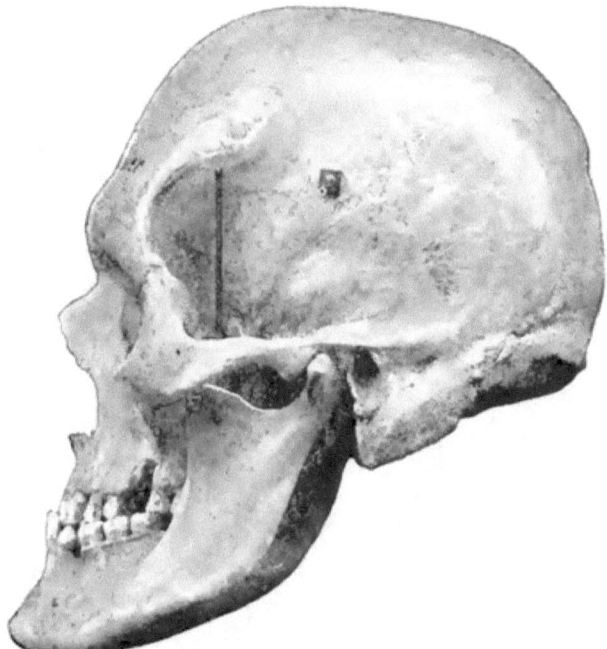

Fig. 5.—Side view of Fig. 4.

dilated. The facial bones, on which the zygomas rest, are greatly hypertrophied. The arches are expanded in every direction, thickened and more markedly curved (Figs. 4 and 5). The strengthening of the muscular attachments may cause these bones to assume still more extraordinary shapes. The alveolar process of the upper jaw may be also hypertrophied.

The body and rami of the lower jaw are hypertrophied, so that the bone may assume an altogether enormous size.

The alveolar process encircles that of the upper jaw, at times in a wide arch, as shown in plates 4—7 and the skiagraph Fig. 10 on p. 54. Corresponding to this, the crowns of the teeth are altogether abnormally situated, in very advanced cases the teeth do not meet each other.

Disturbances in the condition of the alveoli of the teeth may be associated with the morbid growth in the lower jaw, so that

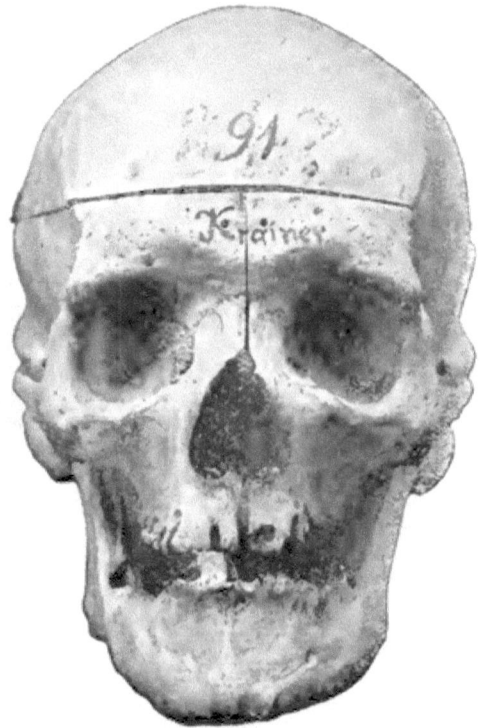

FIG. 6.—Front view of the skull of a case of acromegaly, 203.3 cm. high, in the Anatomical Museum of Vienna. Old man.

they become loosened and fall out. Single teeth undergo at times abnormal rotation on their vertical axis, even to 90°.

Owing to the hypertrophy of the jaw, the whole osseous framework stands out in front of the perpendicular of the forehead: prognathism. In addition, the alveolar processes of both jaws very frequently, especially when the teeth are retained, are arched forwards: alveolar prognathism. Fig.

5 shows such a formation with a very small Camper's facial angle.*

The protruding position of the lower jaw may be increased by a kind of subluxation of the joint, which is made possible

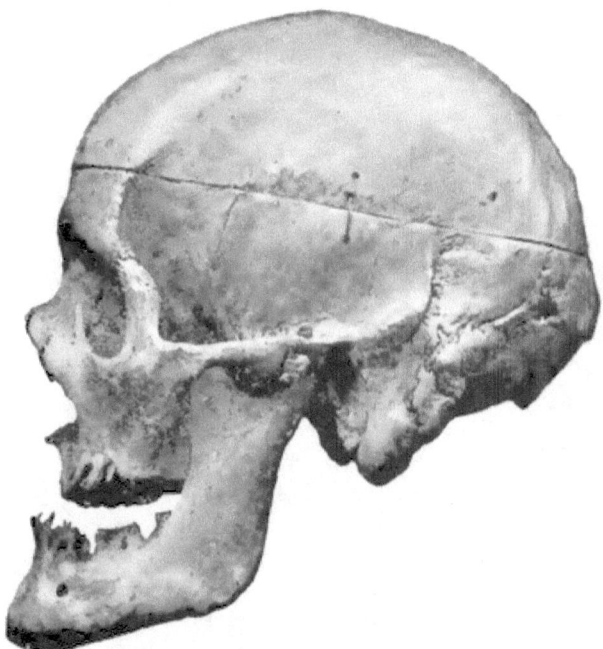

Fig. 7.—Side view of skull of Fig. 6.

by the enlargement of the glenoid cavity and shrivelling of the tuberculum articulare (Thomson).

This position of the lower jaw, its hypertrophy, and that

* In the literature of acromegaly a certain confusion reigns relative to the terms "prognathous" and "prognathism." The German anthropological and descriptive anatomists name those skulls "prognathous" in which the masticatory framework protrudes in front of the forehead (in contrast to "orthognathous"). The term is so used in the text. In the French publications on acromegaly, on the contrary, "prognathism" of the lower jaw is used in the sense of projection of its teeth over those of the upper jaw. The term "prognathism" is used in this sense also by many German writers, but this is incorrect. The right designation for this condition is that introduced by L. Meyer, "progeneum"; individuals with such teeth are called, after Zuckerkandl, "front chewers." For further remarks regarding this anomalous position of the teeth, which by no means only occurs in acromegaly, see Chapter vi.

of the upper jaw, malars, &c., increase the length of the face, and produce the long oval face which most patients with acromegaly possess (especially well marked in Fig. 4).

The hypertrophy of the bones of the base of the skull causes contraction, as a rule, of the nerve foramina. The optic foramina especially are laterally compressed, oval or angular. The narrowing is hardly ever sufficient to produce serious damage to the nerves.

The alterations in the temporal bones are important on account of their relationship to the ear. Owing to the swelling of the mastoid process, the osseous portion of the aqueductus vestibuli is lengthened and narrowed. Small exostoses in the wall still further injure the duct.

The sphenoid bone shows very varied conditions. In a small number of cases there exists no enlargement of the hypophysis, and consequently the pituitary fossa is found normal. In other cases, with relatively smaller uniform and slowly growing tumours of the hypophysis, the sella Turcica is widened in every direction. The surrounding bones are partly displaced, partly atrophied. Thus the dorsum sellæ is bent backwards and much thinned, the clinoid processes disappear. In the same way, the tuberculum sellæ Turcicæ and the middle clinoid processes disappear. The floor of the sella Turcica is bulged downwards, so that the sphenoidal sinuses are much diminished in size: at the same time it becomes like paper, and is often perforated in several places. If the tumour grows more markedly downwards, the thin plate of bone, which separates the pituitary fossa from the sphenoidal sinuses, becomes quite consumed. In most cases then the surrounding walls of bone give way on all sides to the pressure of the tumour and the bone is everywhere destroyed, something similar to the sternum and ribs before a forward growing aortic aneurysm. It may also attack the pharyngeal wall of the sphenoidal sinuses, so that of the whole body of the sphenoid only small thin trabeculæ of bone remain, which surround the fused pituitary fossa and sphenoidal sinuses. A similar condition is found if the tumour of the hypophysis directly infiltrates the bone. The growth then proceeds quite irregularly, the sphenoid is destroyed in the most varied manner, partly by

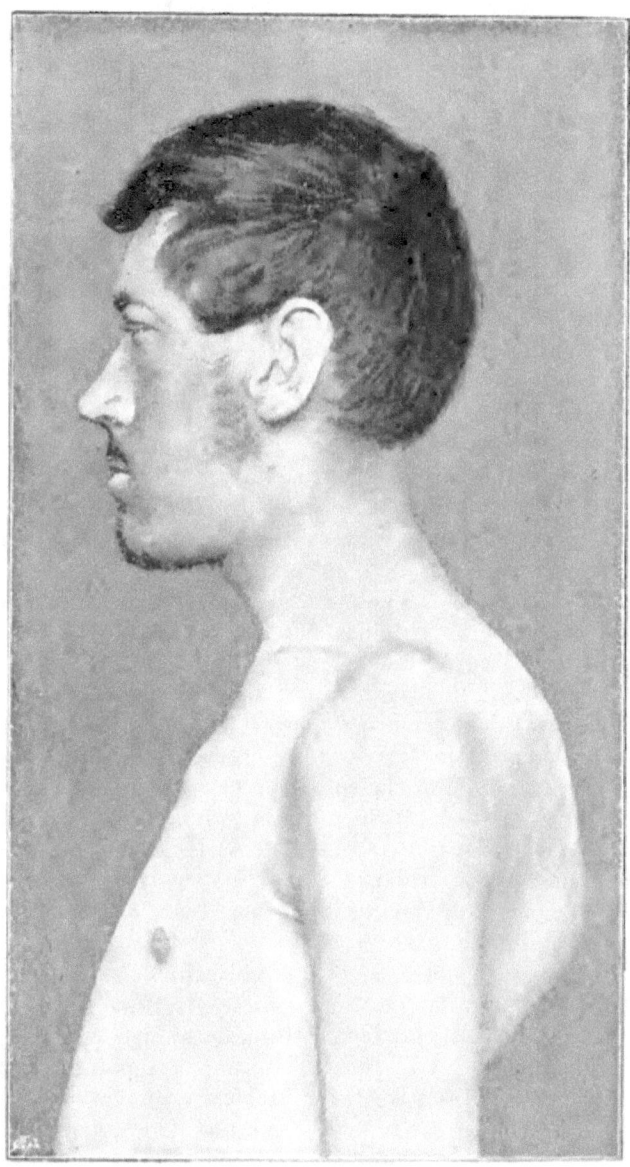

Fig. 8.—34-year-old man with acromegaly (same as in Fig. 2).

direct encroachment, partly through secondary growths in different places.

The upper surface of the sphenoid seldom supports true osteophytes: Brigidi has described two abnormally pointed and long clinoid processes (medii?). The body of the sphenoid also has no share in the hyperostosis: the canalis craniopharyngeus lateralis discovered by me,* which in the general hyperostotic skulls usually disappears without a trace, remains frequently in acromegaly partly preserved. The pterygoid processes are, on the contrary—as muscular attachments—hypertrophied and rough.

The vertebral column in advanced cases shows a kyphotic curve in the upper dorsal and lower cervical region, which is compensated for by a suitable lumbar lordosis. Lateral curvatures may also be present. The kyphosis is in many cases based on the shape of the vertebral bodies (Broca, Sternberg), since these are lower in front than behind. If the kyphosis is very considerable, the height of the vertebral bodies concerned is diminished. A single vertebra may also have melted away (Brigidi). The anterior surface of the vertebral bodies is very rough, which is not surprising, as the broad anterior longitudinal ligament is here attached. The upper and lower edges of the bodies often support small exostoses. The bodies are thick, somewhat porous, the longitudinal and transverse diameters increased. The processes are thick and rough, the spongy end of the spinal processes especially much thickened, which is well seen in our skiagraph, Fig. 10 (p. 54). The transverse foramen (vessel foramen) of the cervical vertebræ is widened, whereas the intervertebral foramina are narrowed, owing to increased size of the condyloid process and of the body.

The ribs are compact and considerably thickened and expanded. The expansion consists chiefly in this, that the lower edge which surrounds the intercostal artery is very greatly developed, also in the thickening of the intercostal canal. The roughnesses for the muscles are increased.

The sternum is greatly broadened and thickened. The

---

* M. Sternberg. An up to now undescribed canal in the sphenoid in man and many mammalia. (Archiv für Anatomie und Physiologie, Anatomische Abtheilung, 1890, S. 394.)

manubrium and xiphoid cartilage especially may be so much increased in breadth as to greatly exceed the length of the bone.

The cartilages of the ribs may be ossified to a considerable degree, and thereby the mass of the sternum and ribs increased. Their union with the bone may be swollen, which reminds one of the "rachitic beading."

The thorax, viewed as a whole, is spacious, and preserves a peculiar shape, partly from the spinal curvature and partly from the change in the increase of the sternum. It is laterally compressed, the longitudinal diameter increased, the sternum falls away obliquely towards the perpendicular anteriorly, from above downwards. The ensiform process especially greatly protrudes. Thus arises the double swelling (double bosse) of the thorax in acromegaly, which

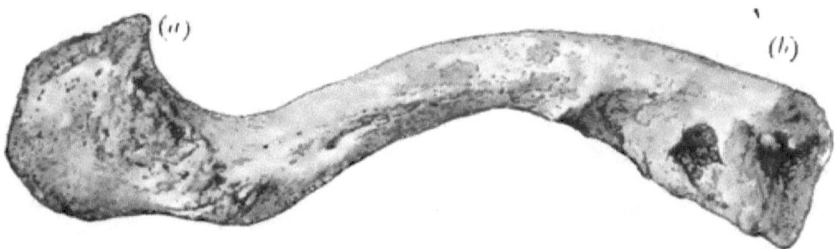

FIG. 9.—Right clavicle in a subject of acromegaly. 208·7 cm. high, under surface. (Anatomical Institute of Vienna.)

is very striking in well-marked cases (Brigidi, Fritsche-Klebs). Fig. 8 shows the form of the thorax in a subject of acromegaly during life.

The spine and acromion of the scapula, the coracoid process and the inferior angle are increased in size and roughness. The curve of the coracoid process is usually exaggerated. The rest of the scapula may be thinned.

The pelvis is heavy and large, the crest thick, rough, and pitted, so also the attachments for the other muscles and ligaments.

Of the long cylindrical bones, the clavicle is, as a rule, very characteristically altered. Fig. 9 shows in an especially instructive manner the type of the affection in the under surface of a clavicle in acromegaly. More minute analysis of the drawing shows that really morbid exostoses nowhere exist, but that the formation is solely brought about through exaggeration of the normal roughness. The acromial end is very broad and thick, and abundantly pitted: here the very strong coraco-clavicular ligament is attached. Its anterior portion, the so-called conoid ligament, has normally a tuberosity of bone at the point of attachment, in acromegaly this becomes a stout projection (*a*). The sternal end (*b*) also is extraordinarily thickened, and shows deep and wide hollows: here is attached the thick costo-clavicular ligament, and the stout ligamentous structures which bind the clavicle to the sternum, as well as both clavicles together. The very marked roughness in the shaft is the place of insertion of the subclavius muscle, the long furrow contains vessels and nerves, and ends in a distinctly widened nutrient foramen. As the strong ligamentous structures are attached at both ends of the bone, it is just here that the roughnesses are increased: the ends also are specially coarse and thick. As a result of this the S-shaped curve is, as a whole, exaggerated.

The true cylindrical bones of the extremities show like changes, developed in various degree. But, as a whole, the appearances of acromegaly are here less marked.

The humerus bears strong thickened borders for the muscles, the points of attachment of the ligaments of the joint round the head of the humerus are very rough, the tuberosities enlarged, so also the condyles (as they serve for attachments of muscles) of the lower end. Frequently a well developed supracondyloid process is present.

The radius and ulna show increase in size of the tuberosities, the edge of the sigmoid fossa of the ulna often bears osteophytic deposits.

In the femur, the head of the joint is surrounded by the exaggerated roughnesses of the attachment of the fibrous capsule of the joint: the trochanters, as places of attachment of numerous muscles, are large, very rough, and uneven. The linea obliqua is well developed. On the opposite side of the bone a stronger, rougher osseous crest is present immediately over the condyles, the place of attachment of both halves of the gastrocnemius muscle.

The tibia and fibula bear on their upper end very well marked roughnesses, the normal furrows for the tendons and muscles of the lower ends are sometimes more deeply hollowed out, in other cases, on the contrary, they are shallower as a result of osteophytic deposits.

The patella is thickened, the anterior surface, as attachment of the powerful tendon, very rough and warty, the upper and lower edges are also rough.

The study of the bones of the hand and feet, but especially of the hand which has been substantially advanced by means of the Röntgen rays, completes the anatomical examination.

Many of the attachments of the tendons and ligaments to the bones of the wrist and ankle are strengthened, therefore the bones which bear these are also somewhat thickened and larger. This is, however, not altogether very surprising. It predominates in the volar surface of the skeleton of the hand, and certainly the distal row of the carpus (trapezium, trapezoid, os magnum, and unciform) is increased in roughness, whilst the perforations for the vessels are everywhere increased. Of the tarsi, the os calcis especially supports a much exaggerated tuberosity.

The metacarpi and metatarsi are, as a whole, little altered. They are often somewhat thickened and flatter, and bear small exostoses on the palmar and plantar surfaces respectively (attachment of the interossei).

Changes in the phalanges are also not very pronounced. The epiphyses are frequently somewhat thickened (Holsti, Cepeda), and show small osteophytic formations: here and there on the diaphysis very tiny and flat ones are present. The whole shape of the phalanges is frequently to some extent more bulky. Marie has lately distinguished two forms of hand in acromegaly, a "Type en long," also called "Type géant," and a "Type massif." In the latter form, the bones are thick, the osteophytes distinct; in the first this is not the case, the bones are more slender, and the skeleton of the hand at the same time enlarged as a whole.

The condition of the terminal phalanges deserves some words. Numerous pointed roughnesses on the distal end are repeatedly described as being present in acromegaly. It must, however be emphasised that this is quite a normal result, which anyone can confirm in very many skeletons of hands of normal individuals. A visit to the bone room of any large dissecting room will confirm it. The Röntgen photographs of sound hands also clearly show it. In the numerous magnificent photographs which the Prussian Minister of War exhibited of different injuries to fingers, foreign bodies in the hand and the like, on the occasion of the 15th Congress for "innere Medicin" in Berlin, the most beautiful, abundantly studded prickly points on the terminal phalanges could be observed in very many hands. This form of the terminal phalanges has nothing to do with acromegaly.

If the changes in the skeleton are surveyed as a whole, it is seen that a number of these changes stand clearly related in genetic connection, as certain changes in the one bone necessarily evoke and give rise to changes in the other bone. If a certain abnormal increase in size takes place in any one bone, the mechanical relationships of the whole system which bears and supports that bone are altered. The alterations in the mechanical relationships (changes of size, weight, pressure, and direction) produce an alteration in the growth of the other bones. This change of growth leads again to new mechanical relationships, and so gradually the one bone adapts itself to another until a certain condition of equilibrium is arrived at. If, however, the increase of the one bone, which we have hypothetically regarded as primarily diseased, goes on increasing always in the same way, it is clear that the secondary changes in the remaining bones will also continue in a perfectly fixed manner.

Some such genetic relationship Langer and Klebs have already discussed. We place together as follows the conditions acknowledged at the present time, but especially emphasise that no hypothesis should be advanced as to which disease is the primary one.

The strong formation of the masticatory apparatus demands powerful points of compensation in the head. These come about either by thickening of the solid, or through dilatation of the hollow supports, or through distribution of the weight over a larger surface. To the first the hypertrophied zygomatic arch corresponds, to the second the dilatation of the air sinuses, and the increase of the skull to the third. All changes in the form of the skull thus stand in causal connection.

The monstrous skull requires a stronger apparatus from the trunk for suspension and support. The increased size of the vertebral bodies answers this requirement, as well as the strengthening of all places to which the muscular and fibrous attachments of the skull are affixed, also the increase of the roughnesses of the occiput and under surface of the skull, the swelling of the mastoid process, the increase in size of the spinal processes, sternum, and clavicles (sterno-cleido-mastoid muscle), and so forth from the upper opening of the chest to the pelvis. Thus the changes in the shape of the skull stand in genetic connection with the increase of its roughnesses and with all the bones of the trunk.

The alteration in shape and the increase in size of the head and its immediately surrounding parts displaces the centre of gravity of this section of the body forwards. The breast bone, by reconstruction, must accommodate itself to it. For these reasons the alterations in acromegaly of the skull, shape of thorax, and the kyphosis form a connected uniformity.*

The structure of the bones is very differently described in the literature on the subject. It seems that each author was inclined to declare as typical the result of his own case, in which frequently the observation was limited to a few or even only one bone. Systematic histological examination of the whole osseous system—certainly a very laborious task—has yet to be undertaken. If the reports existing up to the present are looked over in their whole extent, it is seen that very various results can occur in the bones in acromegaly. Not seldom different parts of one and the same

* A division into primary and secondary may indeed, if possible, be attempted in this place. As the kyphosis in a few published cases is trifling, in some cases absent, and has not led to a marked change ("benign form" of acromegaly, cf. Chapter v.), the opinion, therefore, of Duchesnau and Arnold, that it is a secondary change, is not to be dismissed. It might be a result of the removal of the centre of gravity in the skull and of the weakness and atrophy of the dorsal and cervical muscles, which occur with the advance of the disease. Whether a primary and secondary division can be distinguished in the changes of the vertebral column itself is very doubtful.

skeleton show an entirely different condition. One thing is clear in any case, that considerable changes in form of single bones are not to be explained by any simple methodical process, but only through co-operation of absorption, apposition, and interstitial increase.

There is invariably thickening of the periosteum, as also of the attachments of the tendons and aponeuroses. The periosteal bands of cellular tissue are increased, the arteries thickened and dilated. In many places there appear, as a result, layers of new formations on the bones. This occurs firstly, as has already been entered into and explained in the macroscopic description, especially in the position of the muscular and ligamentous attachments. This method of increased growth produces, in co-operation with the increase in size of the vessels, the rough, porous appearance of the bones. Secondly, the periosteal formation of new bone may also be very diffuse and appear as a sclerotic hypertrophy, as is found on the roof of the skull (Thomson), the diaphysis of the long bones (Femur, Brigidi), or the phalanges (Boltz).

A second series of changes arises from the marrow of the bones. They take place especially in those bones in which during growth the marrow remains preserved (Duchesnau*): skull, vertebræ, clavicle, metacarpi and metatarsi. The progress of absorption of old bone goes hand in hand with a slow new formation. The old and young bone are crowded together (Klebs, Duchesnau, Marie-Marinesco). Sometimes the process of absorption predominates. Thus in a case of Hutchinson's, the whole skeleton showed considerable osteoporosis, in a case of Broca's single parts of the pelvis, and especially the tarsi (the os calcis pitted under the finger). In general, in the bones in acromegaly, the medullary spaces between the osseous septa are enlarged, but these latter may themselves be hypertrophied. The whole medullary canal may be irregularly widened (Brigidi).

Since the myelogical and periosteal processes may be associated in various ways, manifold appearances may arise. At one time the compact tissue is much thickened at the

---

* The thesis of Duchesnau is fashioned under the guidance of Renaut, who has admittedly acquired very great merit concerning the histology of the bones.

expense of the cancellous part (Boltz), at another time the compact tissue is extraordinarily thin, the cancellous very vascular and greatly developed (Mossé and Daunic). Usually the process of absorption in the alveolar process of the under jaw appears to preponderate over the formation of new bone (Klebs, Duchesnau).

In the position of the cartilages also new osseous formation takes place (Klebs, Marie-Marinesco). The cartilage shows a large cartilaginous capsule, rich in cells, and is frequently thickened; the bone-forming vascular tracks penetrate into it. The young layer of bone, especially in the region of the periosteum, lies over the growing cartilage. These processes take place especially in the cartilages of the ribs (Klebs, Arnold). As a result of them, lengthening of the epiphysis may be brought about (Cepeda). Probably the augmented increase in length, which the long bones of the hand occasionally show (Holsti, "type géant" of hand of Marie) is connected with them.

Increase of cells and fibrous changes (Marie and Marinesco) are present in the cartilages of the nose.

The cartilages of the joints are, as just mentioned, in some cases thickened, in others, on the contrary, thinned, and uneven: the outer surface may be destroyed by fibrous tissue and be set with excrescences. The whole surface of the joint may be enlarged by a deposit of bone, or it may be compressed by small osteophytes on the edge, which can hinder the movements. All these are changes which may be spoken of as arthritis deformans.* These changes are not constant. Yet it is questionable whether they should be considered as accidental and not essential to acromegaly, as Arnold does, since strengthening of the muscular and ligamentous attachments, which is a typical acromegalic appearance, is also the rule in arthritis deformans (a characteristic of the disease). This points to a deeper connection.

Besides the changes in the structure of the bones, those of the skin are especially responsible for the surprising shape of the body in acromegaly. The cellular tissue of the skin and true skin are especially much thickened at the

---

* We have here to do with the well-known difficulties, which arise because the pathological anatomist and clinician denote by this name various conditions.

enlarged extremities of the body, in most cases also in the neck and trunk.

The epidermis is increased in thickness, frequently also the height and breadth of the papillæ is increased (Duchesnau, Marie-Marinesco). The cells of Meissner's touch corpuscles may also be increased. The cells of the rete Malpighii contain abundant pigment. The cutis is much thickened, often to double or treble the normal. Its bands of cellular tissue sclerosed. The sheaths of the nerves, vessels, and glands are thickened, their nuclei also may be increased. The sweat glands are hypertrophied, the sebaceous glands are often prominent (Arnold). The fat globules of the subcutaneous cellular tissue are enlarged, and closely enveloped by dense bands of cellular tissue. The small vessels at once attract notice owing to the thickness of their wall and dilatation. The thickening of the outer sheath of the cutaneous nerves extends up to the endoneurium, the nuclei of the sheaths of Schwann are increased, the fibres partly wanting in substance (Marie-Marinesco).

The other changes in the skin, such as those of the hair and nails, we describe, to avoid repetition, in the symptomatology (Chapter iv.).

The muscular system is, as a rule, lax and atrophied (Duchesnau, Holsti, Arnold, Claus and Van der Stricht, Comini, and others). Microscopically all possible forms of degeneration and atrophy of fibres are present, even in such muscles which, on dissection, show apparently a normal appearance. There is usually, in addition, an increase and sclerosis of the interstitial cellular tissue. Yet simple atrophy of the muscles without degeneration also occurs (Mossé and Daunic).

In individual internal organs, an uniform increase, an hypertrophy of the whole organ, "splanchnomegaly," is present in many cases. It is a condition which, except the true enlargement of the breast and congenital increases, *e.g.*, of the brain, is one of the greatest rarity, and stands quite alone in pathological anatomy. As it often occurs in acromegaly, it certainly belongs to the phenomena of this disease. It is present in the central nervous system, eyeball, gastro-intestinal canal, liver, and kidneys. By certain authors (Klebs, Dallemagne, Huchard) the increase of the heart, so frequently observed, is considered as belonging to it, by Dallemagne the equally frequent presence in acromegaly of increase in size of the spleen. Yet the enlargement of the two last-named organs, perhaps also that of the liver, may easily be conceived as a result of other changes. The great increase of the other organs must, on the contrary, be regarded as a peculiar and for the present inexplicable occurrence.

The vessels, especially the arteries, are, as a rule, dilated and thickened. The thickening affects all three coats. True atheromatous changes may exist, or be altogether absent. The changes in the vessels extend from the aorta and pulmonary artery up to the fine ramifications in the organs, as already described in connection with the skin. At one place thickening, at another dilatation predominates: this may vary in one and the same person in different vessels. Examination of the thickened vessels shows increase of the endothelium of the intima, decrease of the muscular and compensation by cellular tissue, and increase of the adventitia. According to Klebs, the dilatation is the primary, "the active phase of the process," and the cellular tissue hyperplasia of the intima, with the consequent narrowing of the vessels, a secondary occurrence. Much may be said for the opposite opinion, that the dilatation is the secondary process, a result of the atrophy of the muscular and elastic tissue, and of their replacement by new-formed cellular tissue. Lately Tichomiroff has especially laid stress on the signification of the changes in the vessels to explain the pathogeny of the disease.

The heart is, as a rule, enlarged—atrophy is described only by Henrot—especially dilatation and hypertrophy of the left ventricle. As in almost all cases disease of the vessels, just described, was present, the changes in the heart may be without difficulty conceived as a natural result. Defection of a valve through endocarditis or arterio-sclerosis is sometimes found as a complication. Verga, Sigurini and Caporiacco have seen congenital narrowness of the aorta.

The lymph and blood-forming organs are frequently hypertrophied.

The lymphatic glands are symmetrically enlarged, especially in the neck (first described by Henrot). Marie and Marinesco have found fibrous degeneration. Claus and Van der Stricht found absence of the individual lymph follicles, the whole tissue more symmetrical, numerous giant cells with fatty degeneration of the protoplasm, abundant amitotic division of the nuclei of the leucocytes, which also showed much fatty degeneration.

Waldeyer's segment of the pharyngeal tonsil, the mucous glands of the tongue (described by Brigidi), tonsils, pharynx, are almost always hypertrophied. In these cases also the enlargement may depend upon fibrous sclerosis.

A splenic tumour of very considerable size is usually found, normal condition of the spleen (Mossé and Daunic), or even diminution in size (Pineles) seldom.

In a number of cases remarkable congestive increase takes place in the abdominal organs, so that it is impossible to say which part belongs to the congestion, which to the primary enlargement. In other cases it is doubtless a condition of "independent" enlargement of the spleen. The enlarged Malpighian corpuscles project on section. Marie and Marinesco found microscopically thickening of the capsule and trabeculæ, increase of pigment in the lymphoid tissue, and venous endothelium. Claus and Van der Stricht noticed hypertrophy of the pulp and Malpighian corpuscles.

Finally, the thymus is frequently preserved at full size and shows the microscopical appearances met with in young children.* In other cases it is, as normally, reduced in size, even to the formation of scanty, occasionally calcined remnants in the adipose tissue of the anterior mediastinum.

The nervous system shows important changes.

The peripheral nerves are, as a rule, thickened. This depends, according to present views, on increase of bands of cellular tissue, as has been described above in connection with the small nerves of the skin. The cellular tissue is, at the same time, partly sclerosed, partly

* Mossé and Daunic have rightly given prominence to the fact, that it cannot be positively stated from anatomical results whether we have to do with a persistent organ or a rejuvenated one ("post-generation," Klebs).

hyaline or mucilaginous. The medullary sheaths are often injured (Arnold, Comini).

The spinal ganglia also, but chiefly the sympathetic, appear much enlarged (Henrot, Marie and Marinesco, Arnold, and others). This also depends on thickening of the bands of cellular tissue. The sheaths of the ganglionic cells may be enlarged, the cells themselves compressed and atrophied (Marie and Marinesco) or contain vacuoles (Arnold).

The nerve roots likewise show an increased amount of perineurium and may contain degenerated fibres. Duchesnau has observed constriction of the roots in the intervertebral foramina as a result of dense fibrous tissue, and looks on it as the cause of the degeneration, to which also he traces back the muscular atrophy. Arnold saw preponderance of the degeneration in the posterior roots, with normal width of the intervertebral foramina.

The arachnoid, in the cases of Henrot, Duchesnau, and Linsmayer, bore either strongly marked or many small plates of chalk—a condition to which we are accustomed, with Leyden, to deny any pathological significance.

The spinal cord has been found thickened by Linsmayer (Redlich); the diameters of the cervical ganglion 10·5 mm. and 15·5 mm. instead of 8·5 mm. and 13·5 mm.

Arnold found ascending degeneration of the posterior columns as a continuation of the degeneration of the posterior roots. Tamburini saw a slight degeneration of the collection of roots of Burdach's column in the cervical and dorsal parts of the cord. Dallemagne describes pseudo-systematic sclerosis as a consequence of arterio-sclerosis and thickening of the meninges. Finally, secondary affections of the spinal cord can arise in accession to changes of vascular origin in the brain centres (Arnold).

Fritsche and Klebs have found the medulla oblongata much enlarged. Dallemagne, in one of his cases, lays stress on a multiplication of cells under the ependyma of the fourth ventricle.

The brain may be, as a whole, enlarged (Fritsche-Klebs, Holsti). Just as in the enlargement of the spinal cord, the histological proportions remained normal, the enlargement must consequently be conceived as a true hypertrophy dependent on imperceptible small increase of single parts of the tissue.

The cranial nerves have also been found hypertrophied (Henrot, Fritsche-Klebs), especially the optic and oculomotor. Degeneration of the fibres may also occur. Dallemagne gives endo- and perineuritis of the optic nerve in one case, in which a trifling effect of pressure of the hypophysis existed.

Henrot found the pineal gland enlarged.

Important changes in the brain and cranial nerves may arise from disease of the hypophysis.* This peculiar organ has up to the last years been little considered; we therefore place together the morphological and physiological facts concerning it in an appendix to this chapter.

The hypophysis, but especially the anterior part, is always diseased in acromegaly. The diseased organ is nearly always enlarged. Microscopic examinations of twenty-eight cases have been up to now submitted.

The histological conditions met with in the hypophysis are to be received with a certain amount of reserve, owing to the consideration that the organ possesses a fairly complicated structure and our knowledge of its morphology is not thoroughly exhaustive. The interpretation of the reports is also rendered more difficult owing to the fact that the terminology of the pathological anatomy varies in different schools, so that we cannot attach, without further consideration, a similar meaning to designations which sound identical.

In some cases simple hypertrophy is described (Gauthier, Cepeda).

In four cases the diagnosis "Adenoma" has been made (Marie-Marinesco, Linsmayer, Tamburini, Boltz). The question concerns a new formation of tubular cells, which is usually found at the periphery of the organ. As a result, the posterior lobe completely disappears. In the inner part

---

* It seems incredible, but as a matter of fact is frequent, that the hypophysis should be confounded with the pineal gland (glandula pinealis). It is certainly in most cases a question of a clerical error. The mistake does not so infrequently occur in reports which bear the signature of well-known names—nomina sunt odiosa; it is, however, important to notice that in a circular lying before the writer, of a firm which produces "animal preparations," the name "pineal gland" is defined according to the Latin designation, "Hypophysis cerebri."

of the gland there occurs, in addition, necrosis of cells, which may lead to softening and condensation of the bands of fibrous tissue. In this group are, at all events, to be included the two cases of Fritsche-Klebs and Klebs, which the post mortem pathologist designated in one place as " simple hyperplasia," but in another as possessing the " character of a simple adenoma." In addition Holsti's case: enlargement with central softening, whereby " the texture of the organ was not so uniform as usual, in places also the cellular tissue stroma was somewhat increased in amount." Relative also to the first-named quite shortly described case of " Hypertrophy," the question must arise whether it really is not a case of true adenoma.

The case of Bonardi's perhaps represents the final stage of an adenoma consisting of sclerosed bands of tissue: the gland enlarged,* the fibrous tissue markedly hypertrophied, the follicles atrophied.

Dallemagne describes (Case iii.) hypertrophy with partial colloid degeneration.

Fratnich found extensive colloid degeneration with haemorrhage.

The colloid degeneration in Dallemagne's second case was restricted to the posterior lobe, which was also hypertrophied.

The " cystic tumours " of Boyce and Beadles and Dana (no microscopic examination) were also possibly cases of colloid degeneration.

It is very difficult to form a judgment on the sarcomata.

A number of authors report cases in which the tumour consisted of cells arranged in clusters, resembling lymphocytes, taking the place of the normal gland, so that the appearance resembled here and there a lymphatic gland (Brigidi, Claus and Van der Stricht, Comini, Sigurini, and Caporiacco, perhaps also Henrot's case belongs here). There may be associated besides, degenerative changes, softening or

---

* The author looks on the gland as not enlarged, but he gives by chance exact figures from which the contrary is elicited: weight, 2·975 (five times the normal); diameter, 18 mm. and 11 mm. We see how little we can rely upon the critical discernment of many authors. (In my article in the " Zeitschrift für klinische Medicin" I had been misled by this opinion, and classed the case with those of " not enlarged " glands.)

sclerosis of the cellular tissue. The explanation of the tumours is a very difficult matter. Claus and Van der Stricht would not altogether rank them with any of the known tumours, not even the lympho-sarcomata. Here should be included Arnold's case, unfortunately only shortly described, in which the author hesitates between the diagnosis of lymphadenoma and lympho-sarcoma. If we hold strictly to the want of a stroma as a characteristic of a sarcoma in the narrower sense, then the first-named cases are not sarcomata. Arnold says nothing on this point.

Roxburgh and Collis describe a case in which they cannot decide between " glioma " and " sarcoma."

The case of Mossé and Daunic also belongs here, which they describe as " Sarcome névroglique fuso-cellulaire fasciculaire." Here we have a true sarcoma.

The conditions met with by Wolf (hyaline degeneration of the vessels, so-called cylindroma), Caton and Paul (round-celled sarcoma), Strümpell, Dallemagne, Griffith, Pineles, Hansemann (large-celled sarcoma), Uhthoff, will be regarded as true sarcomata.

Bury describes his case as glioma.

The diseased hypophysis is almost always enlarged, only in a case of Linsmayer (softened adenoma within the gland) it was of normal size. Many have wished to construct in a methodical manner from the normal relationships the influence of the enlarged hypophysis on the neighbouring parts. But the tumour does not increase in concentric spherical layers, but presents in individual cases very various external appearances, which in a malignant new growth is not surprising.

Sometimes the tumour increases chiefly downwards, breaks into the sphenoidal sinuses, and destroys the whole bone, so as to rest immediately under the mucous membrane of the pharynx (Hansemann). The formations at the base of the skull are then scarcely compressed. Or the new growth penetrates laterally into a cavernous sinus (Pineles), where it may injure the sympathetic and abducens. In other cases the part of the organ surrounded by the tentorium cerebelli becomes at first increased in size, whereby the various structures which compose the hypophysis are replaced by the new growth. The dura mater becomes stretched, and thinner (Claus and Van der Stricht). The infundibulum and tuber cinereum are absorbed in the new growth, which grows upwards on the pedicle of the former to a certain extent. The canal of the infundibulum is dilated. The tumour now makes its bed in the excavated base of the brain. While the tumour lies in the region of the tuber cinereum the chiasma is pushed forwards. Anteriorly, in large tumours,* the frontal lobes may be compressed, laterally the gyrus uncinatus (Gauthier, Claus, and Van der Stricht), posteriorly the pedunculi cerebri with the oculo-motor nerves, as far as the pons (Cunningham). The cavity of the fourth ventricle may also be encroached upon, and the nucleus of the oculo-motor thereby damaged (Uhthoff). The changes in individual parts depend upon the configuration of the upper surface of the tumour. Frequently this is developed asymmetrically, projects, for example, on one side into the middle fossa of the skull, and draws in with it the one branch of the oculomotor nerve (Arnold). It may push forwards the tubercles and secondary nodules, which may here destroy the external part of the chiasma (Dallemagne). The chiasma is usually compressed into a kind of band, its breadth may amount to 1·5 cm., the thickness at the same time from 1—2 mm. The optic nerves also become compressed, very frequently asymmetrically (Fritsche-Klebs, Arnold, Dallemagne). The optic tracts become excessively wasted: in Roxburgh's and Collis' case the left had entirely disappeared.

Various degrees of degeneration are present in the compressed nerves.

Of the organs of the senses there is little reported. Klebs found the eyeball enlarged, Marie and Marinesco the papilla and retina atrophied. We have spoken above of the osseous part of the aqueductus vestibuli as well as of the degeneration of the cutaneous nerves.

Of the respiratory organs, the mucous membrane of the nose is frequently thickened, the vessels are dilated. The turbinated bones protrude into the pharynx.

The larynx and epiglottis may be enlarged in all dimen-

---

* To give an idea of the often considerable size of the tumour, the case of Mossé and Daunic may be quoted: Length, 6 cm.; breadth, 7 cm.; weight, 3½0 g.

sions. Their mucous membrane is thickened: it may become arched over the glottis. The condition resembles pachydermia laryngis (Marie and Marinesco, Mossé and Daunic). The cartilages also are larger and thicker, the cells of the cartilages abundant. Frequently there is ossification.

The lungs show frequently brown induration as a result of disease of the heart, and terminal broncho-pneumonia.

Of the digestive organs, the mucous membrane of the mouth is much thickened. The microscopical changes resemble those of the epidermis.

The tongue may be enormously broadened (7 cm. and more). The enlargement depends partly upon thickening of the mucous membrane, so that the papillæ become enormously long and broad, partly on the increase of the inter-muscular cellular tissue. The muscular tissue shows the most various forms of atrophy and degeneration.

The mucous membrane of the soft palate is also greatly thickened and, as already mentioned, all parts of the lymphatic glands of the throat are enlarged.

The œsophagus shows no abnormalities. In contradistinction, the stomach in Taruffi's and Cunningham's cases was of unprecedented size, in Brigidi's case very large. The two first patients suffered from polyphagia, so that a mechanical dilatation cannot be excluded. This, however, could hardly be the reason for the uniform dilatation of the whole small intestine, which Cunningham reports, and certainly the lengthening of the bowl to twice its size in the same case must be conceived as "splanchnomegaly." Carcinoma of the stomach has been seen by Dallemagne, ulcer by Boltz.

The liver is very frequently enlarged ("splanchnomegaly?") and shows congestion, as well as various other changes connected with chronic diseases.

Little attention has been paid to the pancreas. Hansemann found it in one case (diabetes), Dallemagne in two cases (one of them diabetes) had undergone fibrous induration, Pineles saw purulent pancreatitis with necrosis of the adipose tissue (diabetes). Nothing is exactly known of the salivary glands.

The kidneys have been found frequently enlarged. They very often show all kinds of serious changes and degenerations, as chronic nephritis, which, in a chronic disease, and especially connected with changes of the heart and vessels, is not exactly surprising. The enlargement may therefore provisionally, not with certainty, be conceived as true hypertrophy. There is nothing specially to be noticed as regards the urine.

Of the reproductive organs, as regards the external genitals, the penis, clitoris, and their prepuce, and the labia pudendi are often much enlarged. It is not known whether the changes are only in the skin or in the substance of the organs also. The skin of the scrotum is frequently thickened. On this point also histological observations are wanting to determine the condition of the smooth muscular fibres in the hypertrophy.

Hutchinson lays stress in his case on the man-like appearance of the female cadaver, and of the want of the pubis and breasts. There appears, however, to have been a cessation of development, as the internal genital organs were also not fully formed. The breasts moreover, in severe cases, quick in their progress, are firm (Pineles), in older women, atrophied, which is certainly an ordinary occurrence (Marie and Marinesco).

The uterus has been found in some cases very small, infantile (Lancereaux, Bury). In Hutchinson's above-mentioned case the uterus and tubes were very small, the fimbriæ rudimentary (aplasia). In other cases, associated also with long standing amenorrhœa, the uterus was normal or enlarged (Duchesnau, Claus and Van der Stricht, &c.).

The ovaries frequently show cystic degeneration, and not seldom other changes in addition. A detailed examination of the internal female reproductive organs, especially on account of the amenorrhœa, would be interesting and desirable.

The same applies to the impotence of the testicles, and the accessory male reproductive organs, regarding which hardly anything is reported. They have been described as atrophied (Mossé and Daunic), or moderately large, pale, and lax, or as normal.

Regarding the so-called blood glands, we have already described the hypophysis. The carotid and coccygeal glands have never yet been examined. The suprarenals are normal or slightly atrophied (Marie and Marinesco).

The thyroid is seldom found normal (Fritsche and Klebs, Roxburgh and Collis). Sometimes it is atrophied (Marie and Marinesco, Fratnich), more frequently enlarged. The enlargement depends upon a deposition of large colloid nodules (Arnold), or upon a more uniform increase of the colloid substance (Dallemagne) which may be combined with the first-named condition (Mossé and Daunic, Pineles). Cysts are recorded (Bury, Pineles). Frequently a fibrous condition of the interstitial tissue is described (Marie and Marinesco, Holsti, Duchesnau, Claus and Van der Stricht). Arnold finds hyaline degeneration of the tissue substance and vessels. The follicles are partly atrophied, sometimes in clusters (Marie and Marinesco, Claus and Van der Stricht). Certainly only little importance can be attached to all these changes. Possibly of rather more importance are the increase (although normally present) of isolated lymphoid tissue observed by Claus and Van der Stricht, and by Tamburini, the hyperplasia of single seemingly embryonal follicles by Marie and Marinesco, and the embryonal appearance of the whole thyroid by Comini. Duchesnau has seen carcinoma of the organ with secondary growths in the thorax.

Whether the mass of blood undergoes a change is not known. The extraordinary amount of blood in the veins is very surprising to many pathologists accustomed to hold post mortems, for instance, Cunningham, Klebs, Claus and Van der Stricht. The latter mention that they had never before dissected a body so rich in blood.

SUPPLEMENT.

Morphology* and Physiology of the Hypophysis.

Development.—The hypophysis is formed of three parts. The first part is produced from the oral diverticulum, the second from the anterior extremity of the intestine, the third from the thalamencephalon.

In a very early stage the anterior extremity of the head of the embryo, together with the forebrain, by which it is at first entirely occupied, is raised from the sac of the amnion. By this means there originates under the base of the forebrain a hollow, the "oral diverticulum," at first flat, later on deepened. It lies between the vesicle of the forebrain, the anterior extremity of the chorda dorsalis, and the anterior (upper) blind extremity of the intestinal canal, the so-called "pocket of Seessel."

In the place where the oral diverticulum adjoins the pocket of Seessel, no mesoblast is developed, so that that diverticulum is only separated from the lumen of the bowel by epi- and hypoblast. Both these layers are united here to the "pharyngeal membrane." The frontal swelling now grows ventrally, and simultaneously the oral diverticulum expands dorsally, so as to insert its dorsal summit between the anterior end of the chorda dorsalis and the brain. At the same time, from the summit of the pocket of Seessel, there grows upward dorsally from the pharyngeal membrane a solid epithelial bud, which presses back the anterior end of the chorda dorsalis and thus approaches the deepened oral diverticulum. In the region also of the pharyngeal membrane the oral diverticulum becomes deeper. By reason of this the pharyngeal membrane becomes thinned and finally gives way. The dorsal place of attachment is for some time longer perceptible as a transverse swelling.

The dorsal summit of the oral diverticulum now contracts

---

* The morphological descriptions are based upon preparations of the hypophysis from brains of executed criminals and from dissections of embryos, for which I have to thank Prof. Dr. J. Schaffer, Dr. H. Rabl, and Dr. J. Tandler.

so that it becomes a pocket-like diverticulum, "Rathke's diverticulum." The endodermal portion of the hypophysis, which the pocket of Seessel produces, becomes separated and closely attached to the anterior end of the chorda dorsalis and the adjoining part of Rathke's diverticulum. Towards the blind extremity of the diverticulum there now grows from the thalamencephalon a small protrusion, the foundation of the infundibulum. Whilst this occurs the endodermal portion of the hypophysis becomes reduced in size so as to appear as a cord-like appendage of the chorda dorsalis, and later on disappears with it.

The next step in the development is the constriction of Rathke's diverticulum from the primitive oral cavity. This occurs through the formation of the cartilaginous base of the skull. Firstly the aperture of the diverticulum in the oral cavity contracts to a small duct. Then this becomes obliterated, and there remains behind for some time a solid column of cells. Remnants of the communication are frequently yet present in the sphenoid bone of the newly born as the canalis craniopharyngeus medius (Landzert), which only disappears later on. The diverticulum has now become closed and solid, the longitudinal axis, in the first place, being directed towards the oral cavity. The axis then becomes bent into an anteriorly opened angle, while the part turned towards the oral cavity diverges forwards. The epithelium of the ventral part of the pouch grows into a solid process at the place where it unites with the obliterated duct. This process and the anterior wall of the hypophyseal cavity are now transformed into glandular-like tubes. Branches of both internal carotids penetrate them, and form a marked plexus in the hollow of the half-moon-shaped curved formation of the hypophysis. The epithelium grows in between the plexus of vessels. Thus the vessels with the adventitia are taken up into the inner part of the hypophysis. The hollow also is filled up with glandular tubes, and the tubes are cut off into isolated structures.

The hypophysis has now become a solid, kidney-shaped body. The anterior convex surface is directed towards the chiasma, the posterior (that turned above) concave surface surrounds the now much enlarged process of the infundibulum. Only in the posterior part are remnants of the original hypophyseal cavity preserved, generally two pairs of larger and some smaller hollow spaces, lying on either side of the median line. A longitudinal incision of the hypophysis shows, therefore, at this time three divisions: the so-called "anterior" (under) glandular part, the "middle" part with large cavities, and the "posterior" infundibular part.

The infundibulum, as mentioned above, is originally a small tip of the thalamencephalon, which is inserted between the diverticulum of the hypophysis and the middle trabeculæ cranii. It remains for some time a small conical process under the blind extremity of Rathke's diverticulum, and separated from it by scanty fibrous tissue supporting vessels. It is composed of round nucleated cells, like the embryonal nervous system generally.

Later on the process lengthens, presses down against the posterior wall of the hypophyseal cavity and invaginates it for a certain distance. It retains its central narrow duct, which is lined by radially arranged cylindrical cells. Round about lie the embryonal nerve cells. As the process becomes lengthened a finely granulated mass forms on these layers into which vessels from the surrounding pia mater grow. Simultaneously the process becomes thickened into a club-shape, its central duct obliterated. Only underneath remnants of the infundibular cavity survive in the form of some little hollow spaces. The original cells of the central nervous system vanish from the infundibular process until only a few clusters remain.

Thus the infundibulum in mammals is a species of anterior filum terminale (Burdach), whilst in fishes it remains a true part of the brain. In these latter, behind the infundibular process, there still exists a pouch of the thalamencephalon, the "saccus vasculosus" (Gottsche), remnants of which Retzius sees in man in the tuber cinereum.

Comparative anatomy and phylogeny.—The hypophysis in different animals cannot be compared without some explanation. The hypophysis consists originally of three parts: the epiblastic part, which is a remainder of the oral diverticulum of an old opening situated at the upper part of later-formed mouth ("Paläostoma"); the hypoblastic portion, which is developed from the præoral intestine (v. Kupffer, Saint-Rémy, Valenti), and the cerebral portion, namely the infundibulum and infundibular gland. In the amphibians (Rana, Salamandra) all three parts are preserved. In most mammals, including man, the Paläostoma is converted into a gland ("anterior lobe of hypophysis"). The hypoblastic portion has, on the contrary, disappeared in man, the infundibulum and infundibular gland are obliterated save for a few rudimentary cavities in the "posterior lobe of the hypophysis." In the larvæ of ascidians a communication exists between the most anterior segment of the gut and neural cavity, the canalis neurentericus anterior (v. Kupffer) on which the ciliated canal and a gland, the so-called "hypophysis," develop. This canal and the gland developed thereon are homologous with the infundibular process and gland of vertebrates. According to Andriezen, there yet exists in ammocoetes such a communication between gut and neural canal.

Anatomy.—The hypophysis (glandula pituitaria) is in full-grown men an oval body, flattened on the upper surface and of a greyish-red colour. The longitudinal diameter amounts to 6·0—10·5 mm., the frontal 10·0—14·5 mm., the vertical 5·0—9·75 mm. (Zander), the average weight is 0·6 g. (Schönemann, Boyce, and Beadles.) It consists of an anterior, larger bean-like lobe, and concave behind, therefore on horizontal section, kidney-shaped (anterior lobe, epithelial part, glandular portion, also called oro-hypophysis), and of a small posterior round lobe (infundibular part, nervous portion, also called neurohypophysis), which are united and enclosed by a common fibrous capsule. The anterior is greyish-red externally, internally more grey; the posterior is softer and light grey.

The infundibulum (funnel) is a cone towards the under surface, pointed, which arises from the base of the brain; under the chiasma it descends obliquely forward, and sinks with a somewhat thickened end into the hypophysis, particularly into the posterior lobe. It encloses in its upper part a short, funnel-shaped, gradually narrowing canal, the continuation of the third ventricle; this canal terminates before the depression in the hypophysis. As a rule the entrance of the infundibulum takes place in the middle of the notch on the posterior edge of the anterior lobe, but it may also happen that it enters into the centre of the upper surface of the hypophysis, and so ostensibly belongs exclusively to the anterior lobe. Sections show nevertheless, in such cases, that it only passes through the mass of the anterior lobe in order to reach the substance of the posterior lobe. Another variety exists in which no contact at all between infundibulum and anterior lobe of the hypophysis occurs, but the whole mass of the infundibulum, which is surrounded by the pia mater, passes over externally into that of the posterior section.

The arteries of the anterior lobe arise from the internal carotid, and are fine branches which spring directly from the trunk within the cavernous sinus. Very frequently also a small twig originates from the carotid during its passage through the dura mater in the fossa of the skull or shortly afterwards. The arteries of the posterior lobe pass down with the pia mater of the infundibulum. The veins collect into two little stems which fall into the circular sinus of Ridley.

Topography.—The hypophysis lies in the sella turcica of the sphenoid bone. It is divided from the fossa of the skull by the very tight diaphragma sellæ turcicæ, a part of the dura mater, so that only the pedicle of the infundibulum remains free, by which the hypophysis is connected with the tuber cinereum. Its larger part lies in the anterior angle of the chiasma, and does not normally reach beyond the posterior border of the chiasma. The chiasma lies not unfrequently asymmetrically, so that the intracranial portion of the optic nerves shows considerable variations in length.

Histology.—The anterior lobe consists of rows of cells, which unite in places with each other. It contains almost always two rows of cells of cylindrical shape. When fully developed they extend also upwards for a little distance upon the anterior surface of the infundibulum. Flesch was the first to distinguish two forms of cells. The one, "chromatophile cells," possess a round or polyhedral protoplasmic body, which is readily stained. The other, "mother cells" (Stieda), are smaller, have little protoplasm, indistinct cellular membrane, and do not take on stains. But there are to be found transitions between these two kinds of cells, and it is apparently only a question of different degrees of secretion (Saint-Rémy, Claus and Van der Stricht). Individual columns of cells are true tubes with a lumen, in which a homogeneous, sharply defined mass, readily taking up staining material, is present; it is described as colloid. Similar particles are present here and there in the interstitial fibrous tissue (lymph spaces?).

In the boundary between the anterior and posterior lobe the microscopical appearance changes. Here, firstly, are to be found a few small fissured cavities, the remains of the original hypophyseal cavity, which likewise contain a thin layer of "colloid" material. This is here much thinner, since not unfrequently blood is met with in the cavity, which evidently has got into it during section of the organ for the purpose of hardening. The lining membrane of the cavity consists of cylindrical cells, frequently more or less well preserved ciliated hairs are to be seen in single or numbers of the cells. In the acini also, and in the cavities described below, ciliated cells are present.

Besides the cavity of the hypophysis, the posterior part of the anterior lobe also contains a number of large acini, which possess a low cubical epithelium, and are completely filled with "colloid material." The mass often shows here variously formed wavy stratifications and vacuoles. This part calls to mind the structure of the thyroid, while the remainder of the anterior lobe more resembles the suprarenals. In many mammals the hypophyseal cavity is much widened and irregular. Its posterior wall forms in several species (*e.g.*, the dog) the so-called "epithelial border" (Lothringer, Retzius) of the posterior lobe, which at the lower boundary of the cavity, where it bends into the anterior wall, continues some distance further beyond the true cavity on the posterior wall. The cellular tissue framework of the anterior lobe contains numerous nuclei and very many and wide capillaries. Here and there, but more abundantly in the posterior part of the anterior lobe, the tissue cells contain a fine granular, yellowish-brown pigment. The tissue is delicate, only surrounding both principal veins, where numerous vessels meet, it is thicker and more fibrous, which must not be mistaken for pathological formations. It increases much with age.

The nerves of the anterior lobe—which were much discussed in older anatomical literature—arise from the carotid plexus of the sympathetic. Berkley has seen filaments with ramifying terminations in the glandular tubes. Rogowitsch describes masses of colloid in the vessels, Pisenta and Viola confirm this statement.

The posterior lobe has an abundant framework, composed partly of fine fibres, partly of spindle-shaped or branching cells with abundant yellowish-brown pigment. The pigment is in many places heaped together, and also contained in the meshes of the supporting tissue, as is found in old hæmorrhages. The framework is certainly neuroglia. It forms in places septa, in which lie cells, generally pigmented, partly polyhedral or roundish, and partly of a long or broad spindle shape. Some cysts are also present, partly containing colloid. The epithelium is ciliated in places. The cysts are explained partly as remnants of the infundibular cavity, partly as rudiments of an infundibular gland, partly as a dispersed portion of the hypophyseal cavity. Fine nodulated nerve fibres descend along the side of the infundibulum into the posterior lobe.

Retzius and Berkley have defined the structure clearly by the Golgi method.

The infundibulum contains a vast quantity of neuroglia and neuroglia-like cells of the most varied kind; on the contrary, few nerve cells (Berkley).

Physiological Chemistry.—Iodine is contained in the hypophysis in the same form (iodothyrin) as in the thyroid (Schnitzler and Ewald). The extract of the gland produces, according to Olliver and Schäfer, by intravenous injection, increase of the heart's action and raised blood pressure (while thyroid extract causes decrease). The use of dried pituitary gland evokes in man an increased secretion of phosphoric acid in the stools, which probably depends upon processes in the bones (A. Schiff).

Physiology.—Horsley, Gley, Marinesco, Vassale and Sacchi, Kreidl, Biedl, have performed destruction or extirpation of the hypophysis. According to Horsley, no symptoms, nervous or otherwise, occur. Gley partly destroyed the hypophysis in a rabbit, the spleen and thyroid were removed. The phenomena did not differ essentially from those met with after thyroidectomy. Vassale and Sacchi give as sequelæ: apathy, somnolence, feeble gait, dyspnœa, anorexia, lowering of temperature, emaciation, tonic and clonic muscular spasms, and fibrillary twitchings. A dog survived the operation one year.

Nowadays many admit a relationship of the hypophysis to the thyroid. As proofs are adduced: the histological resemblance of both organs, the enlargement of the hypophysis in myxœdema and cretinism (see Chapter vii.), in which conditions the thyroid is diseased, finally the fact that extirpation of the thyroid results in enlargement of the hypophysis. Rogowitsch, under Grützner's direction, was the first to see such changes in the hypophysis after thyroidectomy. He found vacuolisation and increase of protoplasm of the mother cells and of the ground substance. Stieda proved, by weighing, that the gland was hypertrophied, which was shown microscopically by abundant karyokinesis. In rabbits the principal increase is seen in the most anterior part of the anterior lobe. Gley and Hofmeister have found the same results. That at the same time it is not simply a question of a compensatory hypertrophy follows from the above-mentioned experiments of Olliver and Schäfer, according to which the extracts of both organs have a different physiological effect.

Relative to the function of the hypophysis, the idea is now again accepted, which originated somewhere about the middle of the century that the so-called "blood-vessel glands" withdraw some kind of material from the blood and return it transformed (Ecker).

IV. SYMPTOMATOLOGY.

We shall here complete the picture of the disease described in the second chapter by a more detailed consideration of the outward appearance of the body, and of the symptoms from the point of view of the individual organic systems.

EXTERNAL APPEARANCE OF THE BODY.

The contour of the sufferer from acromegaly depends essentially, on the one hand, upon the alterations in the osseous system, and on the other upon the changes in the skin and adjacent soft parts. According to their respective preponderance in the progress of the illness there arise in individual cases certain differences in the external appearance. Sometimes it is only a result of the gradual development of the disease, but sometimes it also depends upon various types.

A number of patients, about 20 per cent., show a striking "largeness of body," they are the so-called "giants" (Chapter vi.).

The increased size of the cranium is noticeable in many patients. Marie had originally assumed that a normal circumference of the skull was characteristic of acromegaly. Since then, however, numerous cases of considerable enlargement have been observed (see p. 19). The skull often grows rapidly. The patient of Pinel-Maisoneuve had to buy a larger hat every year. The sagittal suture is often felt as a thickened swelling. Other swellings are constantly formed, either lengthwise or crosswise, by the thickened skin, more especially at the occiput.

In the face, sometimes the alteration in the bones and sometimes the hypertrophy of the skin predominate. Both can now be distinguished by the Röntgen rays. Certain technical difficulties constantly arise in penetrating the thick-walled skull of a subject of acromegaly. Through the assistance of the firm of Reiniger, Gebbert, and Schall we have, however, succeeded in overcoming them. Fig. 10 (p. 54) shows the skiagraph, Fig. 11 (p. 55), the patient's own profile. In the skiagraph, the thick-walled skull, the widened frontal sinuses, the narrowed orbit, the prominent underjaw, the thickened spinal processes, &c., are clearly recognisable, and we can judge by comparison with Fig. 11 of the influence of the skeleton on the morbid appearance of the face.

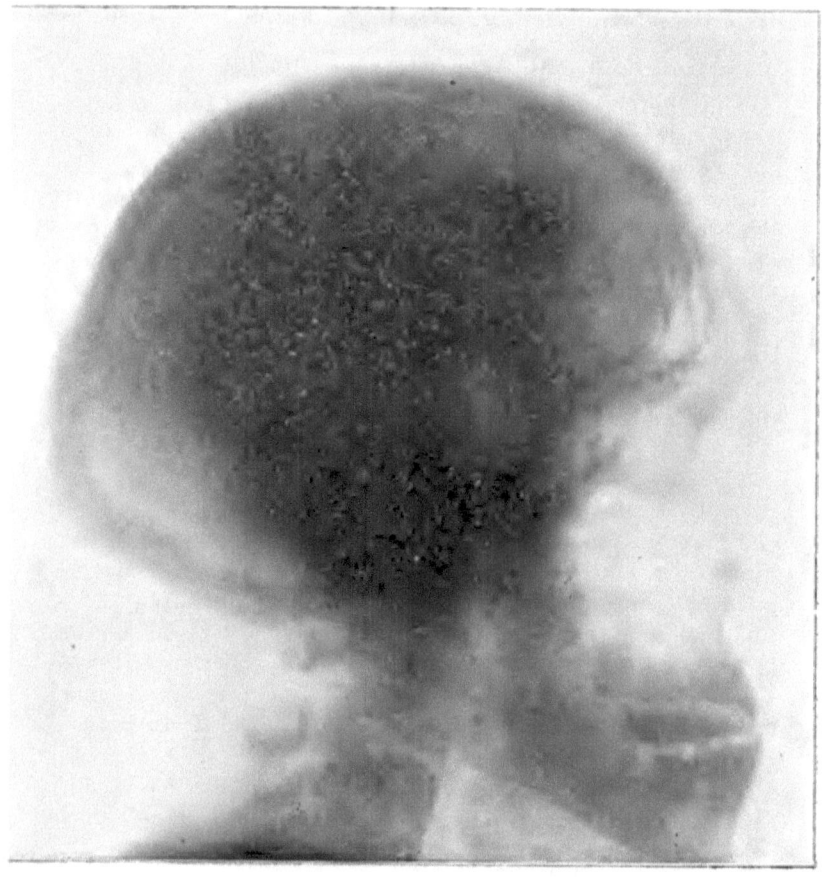

FIG. 10.—Picture of the head and cervical vertebræ of a man with acromegaly, 34 years of age, as seen by the Röntgen rays (of patient of Fig. 2).

If the bones of the face are chiefly affected, the enormously projecting zygomatic arch and process of the frontal bone, surrounding the temples like a wall, are most noticeable. The condition of the orbital region varies in different ways. In many cases the orbital curves are arched forwards, the skin of the lids and tarsus much thickened, the palpebral fissures narrowed, and the eyes lie deep in their sockets (Fig. 12, p. 56). Ptosis may, in addition, be present. In other cases severe exophthalmos exists, the thickened

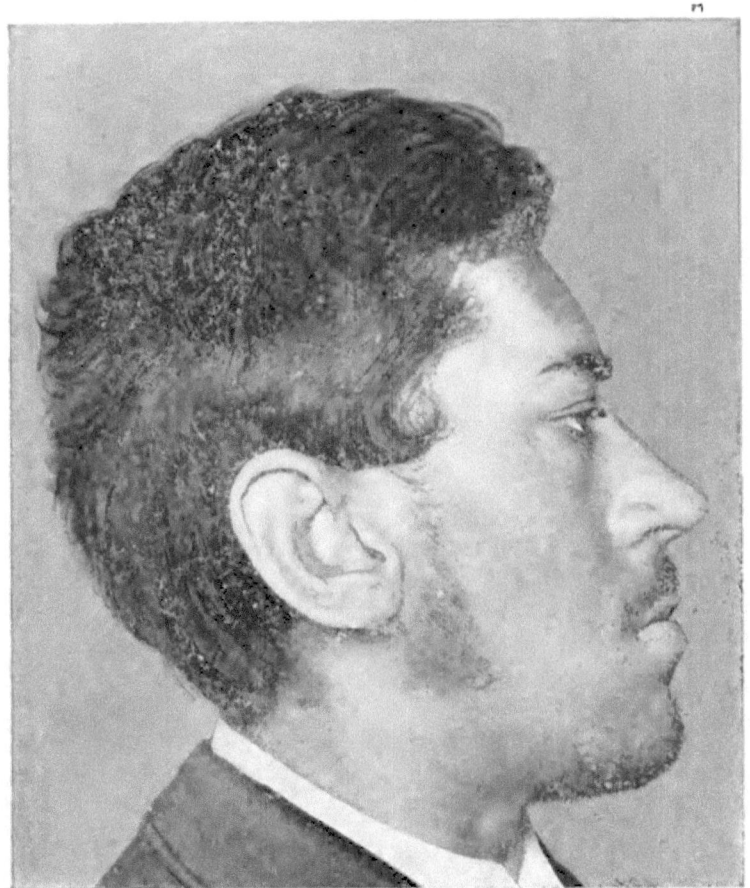

FIG. 11.—Profile of the patient of Fig. 10.

lids forming pocket-like swellings. The exophthalmos is occasionally more marked in one eye (Grocco), or entirely unilateral (Doebbelin, Sigurini, and Caporiacco). If the antrum of Highmore is dilated the cheeks project widely.

56 ACROMEGALY.

If this is not the case, they may even, by contrast with the puffy, pouting lips and the prominent malars, appear

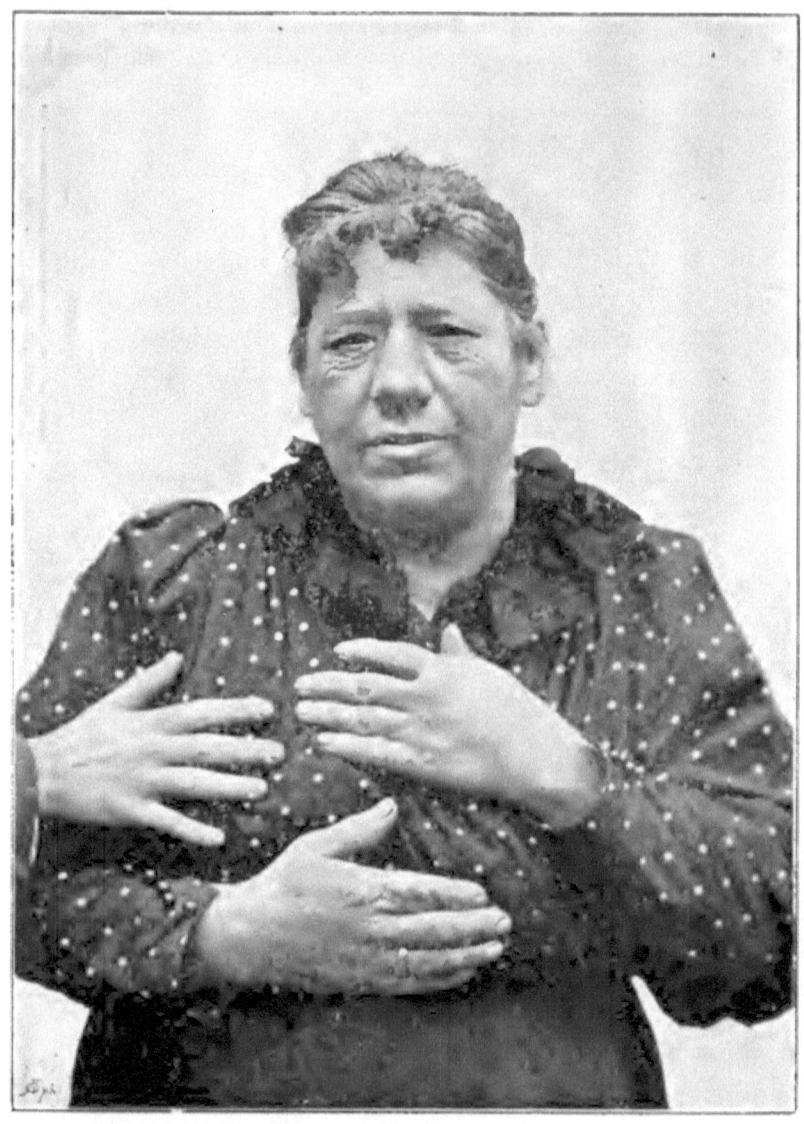

FIG. 12.—A woman 52 years of age, ill for 19 years with acromegaly. (Personal observation.)

shrunken (Duchesnau). The thickened upper lip is often raised to a surprising degree whilst speaking and eating. The tongue is often so large that it continually protrudes from the mouth. (Portrait of the Alsatian Giant by Langer; Henrot, Claus.)

Fig. 13.—Man 28 years of age with acromegaly. (Hofrath L. v. Schrötter's ward.)

The face, owing to the increase of the underjaw, is usually very considerably lengthened. There are cases, however, in which the lower jaw is not enlarged (Campbell (I), Hare, Mackie Whyte). Formerly I had classed these under the

Fig. 14.—Woman 59 years of age with acromegaly. Hofrath L. v. Schrötter's ward (Schwoner's case).

"formes frustes." Pierre Marie* has only lately observed such a case, in which the lower jaw had even become abnormally small in comparison with the upper, and has not hesitated to see in it a new type of acromegaly, "type carrée," in contradistinction to the customary "type ovoïde" of the face. To this class Marie also relegates the case of the giant "Mugnaio of Carrara," which is described by Tarufti. A more detailed communication from Marie is expected. The external part of the ear is often of giant size, with thickened cartilages, but in other cases it is unaltered.

The neck is in most cases thick and short, owing to the enlargement of the larynx, the thickening of the skin, and the cervico-dorsal kyphosis, often also to a goitre. Boltz (1) only has found the neck strikingly thin. Frequently enlarged glands can be felt. In Dreschfeld's patient huge swellings formed on either side of the sternocleido-mastoids, and appeared to extend as far as the cavity of the chest. In Henrot's patient the glands, especially in the parotid and submaxillary regions, were enlarged and hardened, which emphasised still more the disfigurement of the lower section of the face.

The shape of the thorax has been already described in the chapter on the pathological anatomy (p. 27 and Fig. 8). Sometimes the sternum is as strongly arched forwards as in aneurism of the aorta (Moritz).

In many cases the kyphosis is said to have originated after a trauma (Farge, Brissaud, and Meige). It is important to notice that the kyphosis and the deformity of the chest may, in certain circumstances, and also in pronounced cases, be absent (Schultze, Du Cazal, Dercum. Kalindero, Lichtheim, Roxburgh and Collis, Sears, Regnault).

The great increase in size of the hands chiefly depends on the soft parts. This fact was formerly not so clear, now it is easily discernible in the Röntgen photographs (Fig. 15).

Skiagraphs of the hand have been frequently taken and studied by Marinesco, Schultze, Broadbent, Gaston and Brouardel, Schlesinger. The soft parts press the metacarpal bones in particular away from each other into a fan shape. The osseous ends of the bones are often seen standing away

---

* Epistolary communication.

60   ACROMEGALY.

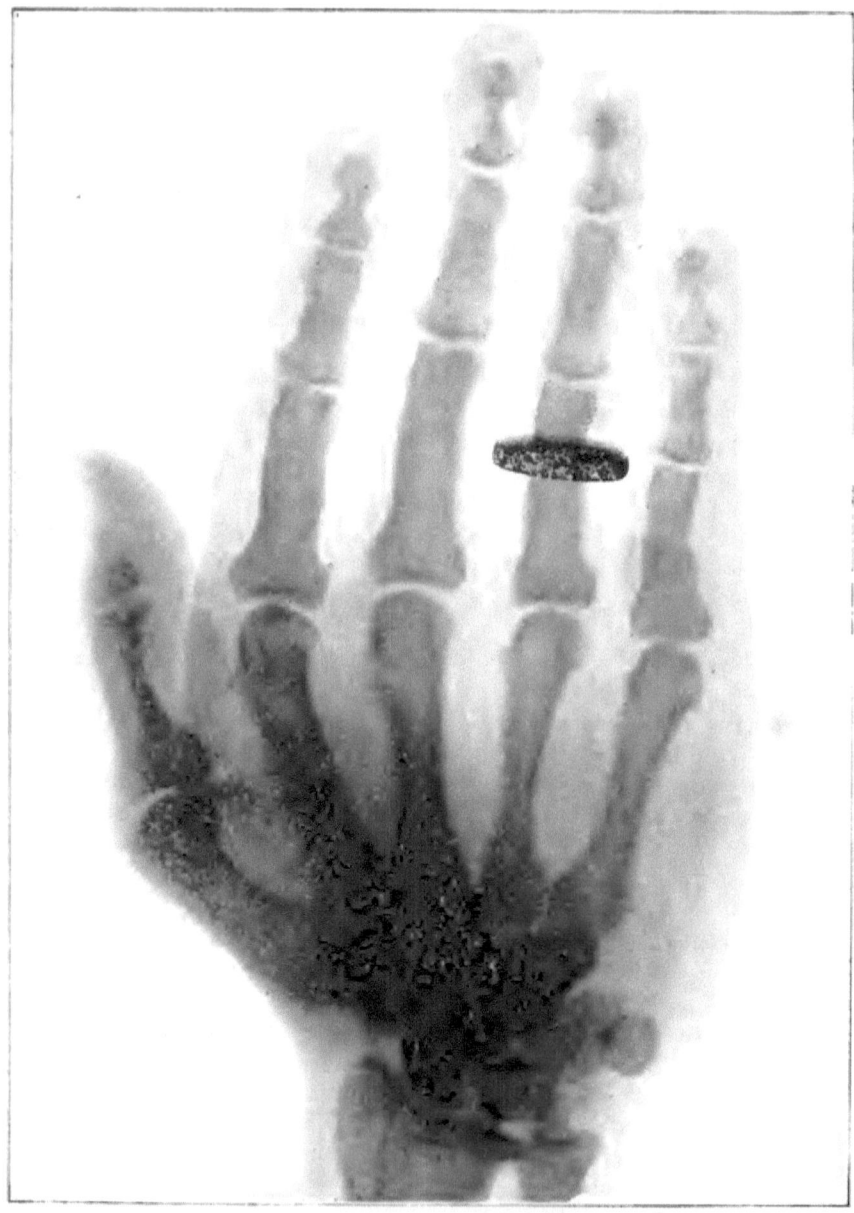

FIG. 15.—Skiagraph of the left hand of a subject of acromegaly (of patient of Fig. 2).

unusually far from each other (increase of the cartilaginous covering (?) Schlesinger).

It is important to notice, especially for a diagnosis in doubtful cases, that the hands are notwithstanding never deformed or disfigured, but merely enlarged. The substance of the soft parts is increased, and it is difficult to raise the skin of the dorsum into folds. The natural interphalangeal folds of the knuckles are especially well marked ("mains capitonnées," Péchadre), as are the lines in the hollow of the hand. The fingers are, as a whole, cylin-

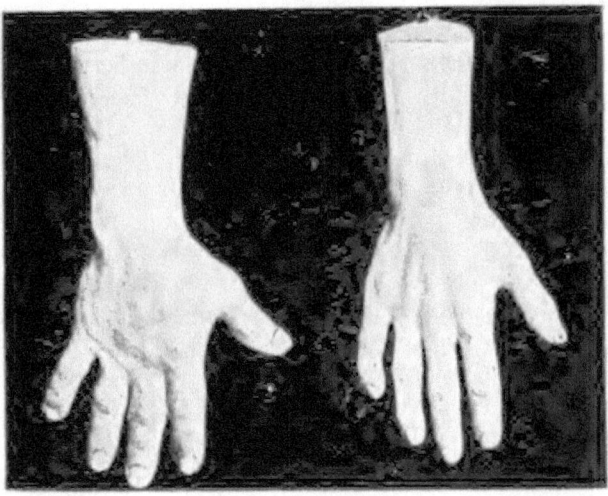

Fig. 16.—The two types of hand in acromegaly.

drical, and flattened from dorsum to palm. Since their circumference at the base and end is proportionately increased, the comparison to little sausages (Marie) is justifiable. The nails do not share in the enlargement, they rather appear small, often flat, and frequently show slight longitudinal cracks.

The bones of the hand are not affected to the same degree in all cases. Generally, as seen in the skiagraph (Fig. 15), the phalanges are somewhat coarser, with more marked lateral curves. Osteophytes, as already mentioned at p. 29, are not generally well marked. They may be even almost entirely absent; Boltz (2) found in his case, on post mortem examination, a tiny exostosis on only one single phalanx.

Our picture shows such a one very plainly on the metacarpal bone of the index finger.

In some cases the bones of the fingers show a decided increase of growth in length, through participation of the epiphysis, so that the hand becomes not only broadened but lengthened. It then appears as if the hand should belong to a much bigger individual than its actual owner.

It is possible also to distinguish with (6) Marie two types which represent extremes. The one type is more general: the broadened, massive, acromegalic hand, "main en battoir," "type en large"; the other represents an entirely enlarged giant hand, the "type en long," "type géant."

We give in Fig. 16 (p. 61) an illustration of both types, after a photograph kindly sent by P. Marie. The massive type is also well shown in Figs. 12 and 14.

Marinesco has examined both types by the Röntgen rays. In the massive type the hypertrophy of the soft parts is much more marked than in the giant type. The thickening of the diaphysis must, however, be also taken into account in some degree to explain the shape of this hand.

Great alterations in the digital joints are rare. Henrot and Gauthier saw nodulated thickenings.

The whole enlargement of the hands begins from the wrists; these are very slightly, and the forearms not at all affected by the morbid increase in size. The characteristic appearance of the extremity in acromegaly is due to the contrast between the giant hand and the disproportionately slender arm which bears it. In many cases this disproportion is increased by atrophy of the muscles.

The feet, like the hands, become substantially coarser and heavier with deepened wrinkles and enlarged folds. They are frequently flat. The enlargement terminates at the ankles.

Regarding the actual proportions and the amount of increase in size of the terminations of the extremities, the articles of dress, as gloves and shoes, and as the disease advances, rings and thimbles, often provide us with a fair amount of reliable information (*e.g.*, Verstraeten). The shoes are especially valuable in such lands as North America, where they are almost exclusively factory productions. Several times acromegaly has been recognised by this means in emigrants, who at home had their shoes made according to measure, but in America were unable to find any to fit in shops. We learn from statements that the increase in size is generally unequal, and often irregular. It has also been repeatedly noticed that the swelling at the commencement occurs intermittently, and by fits and starts (Fratnich), especially whilst menstruation decreases (Jorge). Diminution also has been reported as a result of treatment (Campbell, Fränkel). On the whole, however, our knowledge on this point is not entirely satisfactory. Although countless reports of minute single measurements of patients suffering from acromegaly are to hand, careful, year-long, continuous, numerical observations concerning the morbid increase in growth are still wanting.

The Skin.

The skin is usually thickened to the greatest extent in the enlarged extremities of the body. It may also be very dense in the neck. The hypertrophied skin is capable of being raised into thick folds, and makes the perception of the structures lying under it (*e.g.*, the thyroid) and the feeling of the pulse difficult. The skin of the palms of the hands and the soles of the feet is, on the contrary, often spongy and puffy; in the soles of the feet it swells over the sides when putting the foot to the ground. In the forearms and legs there is an impression as of the presence of too much skin.

Mollusca fibrosa of various size, especially on the face and eyelids, are frequent (Fritsche and Klebs, Marie, Souza-Leite, G. Brown, Paget, Surmont, Asmus, Osborne, Massolongo); abundant formation of warts has also been observed (Verstraeten, Erb-Arnold). Dallemagne saw very numerous xanthoma-like tumours.

The pigment of the skin may be increased so that the ἄκρα or the whole body becomes brownish or of an olive colour, almost like bronze, as in Addison's disease (Motais). Severe boils with glycosuria often appear to such an extent as to throw all the other troubles into the shade (Hansemann, Pineles).

The hair is generally unaltered. In some cases increase and thickening have been noticed. Dodgson observed a falling out of the hair. The beard is sometimes scanty (cf. Fig. 11), which perhaps is connected with the loss of the sexual functions. In women, on the contrary, the delicate small hairs of the face often develop into strong hairs resembling those met with in the beard in old people (Verstraeten).

Perspiration is in most cases morbidly increased. As a result, the epidermis may become softened and vesicles form (Erb). Berkley observed extraordinarily bad smelling perspiration in a negress, whose race, as is well known, possesses normally a peculiar secretion. There is, as in Basedow's disease, connected with the abundant perspiration, a marked feeling of heat. Both these are very troublesome to the invalid. The excessive perspiration sometimes decreases. The formation of sweat may, in the further course of the malady in the same patient, be entirely dried up (Ransome). The skin is seldom found permanently dry (Franke).

Spillmann and Haushalter found increase of the sebaceous secretion; in Franke's case, on the contrary, the hairs had during the illness lost their fatty material and lustre. It is important to notice that sometimes appearances of myxœdema are found in the skin. Comini saw them in the trunk, Sears on the face. We shall return to these appearances in Chapter vi.

The Circulation.

The disease of the vessels and heart met with on post mortem examination is in most cases prominent clinically.* The enlargement and affection of the heart may be, according to Huchard, accounted for in three ways. Firstly, by the splanchnomegaly, secondly by the arterial sclerosis, thirdly by the alteration in shape of the cavity of the chest. Very frequently the sufferers show signs of insufficient cardiac action. The colour of the face is more or less cyanotic, a certain amount of dyspnœa is always suffered from. The

* The disturbances of the circulation described in Fourrier's thesis are collected from some of these cases.

general feebleness of the body, which is seldom wanting as the disease advances, is partly of cardiac action. Fainting fits are frequent. Dilatation of the heart itself can be made out by percussion (Freund, Erb, Bury, Day, Wolf, Sternberg), the sounds are dull, systolic murmurs may be heard (Erb, Grocco, Gauthier), the heart's action is irregular (Schultze) or slowed (Fritsche, Spillmann, and Haushalter). Very often palpitation is complained of without objective signs. The disturbances of the circulation may be the most prominent condition in the disease. The patient becomes more and more dyspnœic, finally œdematous, at last confined to his bed, and sinks from cardiac failure (as for example in Linsmayer's case). The cardiac trouble naturally appears still earlier if the valves are diseased. Thus, in Brigidi's patient the aortic valves became incompetent as a result of shrinking, and the pulmonary valves as a result of perforation. Not unfrequently old disease of the cardiac valves complicates the condition (G. Brown, Holsti, Boyce and Beadles). Congenital stenosis of the aorta is spoken of at p. 35.

Varicose dilatations of the veins are frequent in the extremities as well as in the hæmorrhoidal veins.

Respiratory Organs, Thyroid, Sternal Dulness.

Swelling of the mucous membrane of the nose frequently exists during life (Packard).

The voice very often becomes unnaturally deep, hoarse, and rough, often at the same time very strong. The cause lies chiefly in the enlargement of the larynx and the changes in its mucous membrane. Disease and disturbances of innervation of the laryngeal muscles, which would be expected to occur, have not so far been proved. Marie explains the extraordinary powerfulness of the voice by resonance in the dilated air sinuses. The enlargement of the larynx may be often seen or felt externally.

The trachea is frequently covered by a large goitre. In some cases the appearance of a chronic inflammation precedes the disease for a long time. In Hàskovec's patient such a condition existed at puberty, and disappeared later. In the female patient of Mendel (twenty-five years of age) it appeared in the fifteenth year. In other cases the increase of the thyroid begins immediately before or simultaneously with the enlargement of the extremities (Godlee, Wolf, Lancereaux (2), Murray (2), Pineles, Hitschmann).

I made an observation regarding this matter on a woman thirty years of age, on October 22nd, 1896, in Hofrath Alibert's clinic in Vienna, from whom the greater part of a chronic inflammatory swelling had been removed on account of severe pressure symptoms. She had before suffered from pains in the hands, a dead feeling in the fingers at night, and pains in the loins. I found in January, 1897, distinct exophthalmos, surprisingly large, thick nose, enlargement of the tongue; the teeth bit exactly one upon the other, it was difficult for her now to bring the lower jaw behind the upper, the usual position having previously existed; the hands were very large and thick, the periods had not appeared for six weeks. Unfortunately neither I nor the physicians of the hospital were successful in getting hold of the patient again.

In Harris' patient the goitre appeared soon after the enlargement of the extremities and head.

In cases of the kind just discussed, the disease of the thyroid must certainly be considered as a symptom of acromegaly. It is worthy of notice that the patients, with the exception of Wolf's case, were of the female sex.

In other cases the gland is not enlarged, it may even not be felt owing to the thickening of the skin and the dense bands of tissue in the neck. But it must not on that account be diagnosed as atrophied. In Holsti's case, in which the gland was not palpable, post mortem examination revealed nevertheless an enlargement. The estimation of the size of a thyroid is even in a living subject fairly difficult.*

The thorax is more rigid owing to the anatomical changes, it is raised as a whole on deep inspiration, the normal respiration is chiefly or exclusively abdominal. The malformation of the thorax, in association with the changes in the heart is answerable for the shortness of breath of the patients.

Erb pointed out in many cases a cup-shaped dulness over the upper part of the breast-bone, which he considered due to a persistent thymus. Since Arnold, however, found, on post-mortem examination of these cases, only trifling remains

---

* Cf. also Ewald, Handbuch, Bd. xxii., S. 125.

of the thymus, and Mosler found the dulness appear for the first time during the progress of the disease, it must be explained by the thickening of the manubrium sterni and ribs.

It can easily be understood that with such rigidity of the thorax bronchial catarrhs are frequent. In addition, the expectoration indicates by a bloody or rusty colour the existence of congestion.

Organs of Digestion.

Among the most constant phenomena are the changes in the mucous membrane and lymphatic organs of the pharynx. The mucous membrane is often so thick as to hang into the mouth like a swollen mass at the boundary between the hard and soft palate (Naunyn). The enlarged tongue affects speaking and eating; the patients often bite into it.

Polyphagia and polydypsia are frequently observed, either together or alone. The patients often consume incredible quantities, to the wonder of their acquaintances. Such, for example, was the patient, whose skeleton was described by Taruffi, and who was a celebrated gourmandiser of Bologna.*
Alibert's patient drank eighteen bottles of water daily. Both symptoms sometimes disappear entirely after a few years duration (Valat).

Péchadre saw dyspeptic symptoms.

Diseases of the stomach as complications are mentioned at p. 42.

Obstinate constipation is a frequent and unpleasant symptom (Marie, Kojewnikoff, and others). In Verga's case the coprostasis remained for twenty-two days if artificial evacuation was not employed. The constipation often passes off again by itself (Dodgson).

Urine, Metabolism, Nutrition.

In the smaller number of cases, the quantity of urine is normal, but more frequently increased owing to the poly-

---

* Possibly the enormous appetite which Rabelais gives to his hero in "Gargantua and Pantagruel" was suggested by his observation of a giant with acromegaly; Rabelais was moreover a physician.

dypsia. The urine may, apart from the dilution, be at the same time perfectly normal: diabetes insipidus. Answering to the frequently observed changes in the kidneys, we sometimes find albuminuria and deposit of casts in the urinary sediment. Bouchard, in two of Marie's cases, is said to have found "Peptone": his method of testing is, however, very unreliable. In similar urine no "Peptone" could be found by Hofmeister's method (Souza-Leite). Jorge states that he found "Peptone" in the urine of one case, without mentioning the method employed. I must also express doubt regarding the similar statement of Duchesnau.

Bayer reports oxaluria.

The most important thing to be noticed is the frequent presence of sugar. The secretion of sugar is often only in traces (Kalindero), but often very considerable in amount, 500 grammes and more, even 600 grammes (Marinesco) per diem. It may remain for a long time and again entirely disappear, without special treatment (Rolleston). In some cases, the clinical appearance of severe diabetes may develop: excessive hunger and thirst, diabetic cataract (Pineles), extensive boils, separation of aceton and aceto-acetic acid. Death results from diabetic coma (Cunningham, Bury, Dallemagne, Hansemann, Pineles). The diabetes may be so prominent a symptom as to cause the presence of acromegaly to be overlooked (Hansemann).

While this severe form of glycosuria in acromegaly is already well known clinically, the same cannot be said of the milder forms. Thus, the dependence of the deposit of sugar on the food, the ultimate appearance of alimentary glycosuria, the possible fluctuations, &c., are as yet very insufficiently examined.

The cause for the separation of sugar is probably to be sought for in the changes in the pancreas, which have been established by Dallemagne, Hansemann, and Pineles. Dallemagne himself takes into consideration the changes of the ependyma of the fourth ventricle, in his case quite trifling, to explain the glycosuria, and does not consider the pancreas at all.

Formerly it was thought that the tumour of the hypophysis had a direct influence, since in the older cases of "tumours of the hypophysis" polyuria and glycosuria are repeatedly noted. But it is very probable, considering several of the reported symptoms, that in these cases acromegaly has been overlooked. The question can no longer be settled by the old material, new observations are necessary.

Ruttle and Duchesnau describe intermittent phosphaturia. In Duchesnau's case it was observed for many years. Renaut connects this appearance with the processes in the bones. According to present knowledge, this statement, although accompanied by exact calculations, is untenable, as a considerable portion of the phosphoric acid is normally separated with the stools, which were not examined.

We know little regarding the metabolic processes. According to a short communication by Magnus-Levy, an increase of oxidation should be present (respiratory experiments). Schiff, on the contrary, found that a patient weighing 82·40 kilogrammes maintained this weight with 33 "calories" per kilo., and in another case (combination with myxœdema?) he brought about with 30 "calories" a deposit of nitrogen. Probably the processes of metabolism depend on the various stages and types of the disease. The appearance of aceton, which Higier reports in a non-diabetic, points certainly to a lowered nutrition.

The general condition of the body is at the commencement of the illness usually good; the patients frequently increase much at the beginning in weight and circumference. A part of the enlargement of the soft parts depends doubtless on the hypertrophy of the small lobules of fat, which we have mentioned when discussing the pathological anatomy of the skin. The state of the nutrition often remains until the later stages, when the size of the body offers a sharp contrast to the general weakness (Unverricht). The dead body also in severe cases is not unfrequently well nourished (Claus and Van der Stricht). A true cachexia does not therefore belong to the essence of the disease. Certainly the disturbances of the digestive organs, the diabetes, and any complications often bring about a disproportion between the amount of nourishment absorbed and the calorific requirements, or even an increased wasting of the tissues of the body, and thus beget a cachectic condition for the rest of life.

Male Reproductive Organs.

The appearance of the external genitals is spoken of in the third chapter. It is often reported that sexual desire and power are extinguished (for instance, in Gauthier's patient at the age of 26). A patient stated to me that his sexual power was preserved, but the desire, in conjunction with the general apathy and dejection, had almost disappeared. In Silva's case (want of pubic hair and hair under the armpit, very small genitals) the condition may perhaps have been one of aplasia, analogous to Hutchinson's case in a woman mentioned at p. 43.

Female Genital Organs.

The hypertrophy of the clitoris and labia pudendi is mentioned at p. 43.

As regards the vagina no condition can be stated as constant. Verstraeten describes the vagina as thickened and dilated. The condition of the menstruation is important. In most cases it ceases with the appearance of the disease. Among seventy cases, of which I find in my excerpts minute records, the menopause appeared in the following years:—

Before the 20th year	... In 8 cases
Between the 21st and 30th years	... In 34 ,,
,, 31st ,, 40th ,, ...	... In 18 ,,
,, 41st ,, 50th ,, ...	... In 7 ,,
After the 50th year	... In 1 case.

The youngest case is reported by Surmont; the patient had only once menstruated, in her fourteenth year. Sears records the latest menopause in the fifty-third year. The patient of Lynn-Thomas (eighteen years old) showed a puerile condition of body, and had never menstruated.

The cessation of menstruation is usually one of the earliest manifestations of the disease. The periods seldom recur for any lengthened period when the disease is well developed.

Exceptions that have been reported:—

Naunyn	commencement of illness	19th year.	Menopause	30th year.
Roxburgh and Collis	,,	22nd ,,	,,	27th ,,
Becker	,,	27th ,,	,,	45th ,,
Guinon	,,	23th ,,	Continuance of menses at 39th yr.	
Schaposchnikow	ill a long time		Continuance of menses at 34th yr.	
Squance-Murray	commencement of illness	30th year.	Menopause	32nd year.
Wadsworth	,,	35th ,,	,,	39th ,,
Ransom	certain acromegaly in 41st year		,,	42nd ,,
Sears	certain acromegaly in 42nd year		,,	53rd ,,
Campbell	commencement of illness	43rd year.	,,	49th ,,
O'Connor	,,	45th ,,	,,	47th ,,

In many cases the periods cease all at once, and never return. Several times this happened during a period as a result of fright (Chalk, Pel, Spillmann, and Haushalter). Frequently the menses, failing to appear owing to impregnation, do not return after birth (Motais, Mosler, Sternberg, Roxburgh and Collis, Fazio, Naunyn), or after an abortion (Bignami). Twice has menstruation finally ceased during typhus fever (Grocco, Claus). In other cases nothing particular precedes the sudden cessation of the periods (Debierre, Hadden and Ballance, Péchadre). Often the menstruation ceases suddenly, which the patients impute to a cold or exertion; after thirteen to fifteen months they return once again, and then permanently disappear (Marie, Verstraeten, Reimar, Jorge). Finally, in many cases they are from one to two years irregular and scanty, and then permanently vanish (Freund, Pinel-Maisoneuve, Hare, Flemming, and others).

The gynæcological condition of the internal reproductive organs after the menopause has occurred is often positively described as "normal"—*e.g.*, Olechnowicz, Franke, Reimar; in other cases, on the contrary, atrophy is reported (Mosler, Pineles, and others). It is certainly, however, difficult to demonstrate slight changes in the reproductive organs by palpation, and examination by the sound may be deceptive as regards the cavity of the uterus, because the atrophied uterus may be soft and abnormally flexible.

It is of more importance in this connection that the uterus

on post-mortem examination, in cases associated with amenorrhœa, has repeatedly been found normal—*e.g.*, Duchesnau, Claus, and Van der Stricht. The cessation of the periods must certainly, therefore, be referred to the ovaries. At all events, in acromegaly not only menstruation but ovulation disappear; for among numerous cases it has never occurred that a patient suffering from amenorrhœa and acromegaly has conceived, while, as is well known, conception in women who do not menstruate owing to chlorosis or anæmia, or in suckling women before the appearance of the periods, frequently occurs.

The sexual appetite is said to be frequently extinguished. Gajkiewicz and Fazio have observed long-continued galactorrhœa. In Fazio's case it existed for four years, stimulated perhaps by protracted lactation. Schwoner describes cystosarcoma of the mamma.

Organs of the Senses.

The disturbances of the eyes have been thoroughly studied by Asmus, Mével, Hertel, Denti, Franke, Strzeminski, Uhthoff.

The condition of the lids, which participate in the hypertrophy of the soft parts, is mentioned in the description of the shape of the body (p. 56) and of the skin (p. 63).

Orsi and Gajkiewicz have observed hypertrophy of the lachrymal glands; Péchadre, Pick, and Mosler (2) increased secretion of tears.

The bulb of the eye may be enlarged (Fritsche and Klebs).

With reference to the refractory media, opacity of the lens is often described (Erb (1), Sternberg). This may be due to senium præcox or as a result of changes in the vessels. Pineles observed diabetic cataract in youth.

The subject of exophthalmos is not altogether explained (p. 56). In some cases it may depend upon the previously-mentioned enlargement of the eyeball. Often the narrowing of the orbit as a result of the swelling of the neighbouring air sinuses is to blame (Langer). Whether the increase of the fatty tissue of the orbit, which is cited as usual in morbus Basedowii, also plays a part here, or whether it rather, even when anatomically demonstrated (Lancereaux), only develops secondarily behind the eyeball which is driven forward by the bones, is not known. In certain cases the tumour of the hypophysis grows into the orbit and presses forward the eyeball. At any rate, the above causes can only explain the cases of exophthalmos, which form gradually, these certainly are the rule. But cases of acute exophthalmos do also occur (Motais). We must look to nervous processes to explain these ("Sympathetic irritation," Boltz), or hæmorrhages, similar to what occurs in Barlow's disease. The severity of the exophthalmos is liable to variations, it may also diminish.

Pains as supraorbital neuralgia, or pains in the bulb itself, are described (Marie, Campbell, Kalindero, &c.).

The movements of the eyes may show manifold disturbances.

Horizontal and rotary nystagmus occur (Tresilian, Boltz).

The projecting eyeball may show a general limitation of movement.

Paralyses and pareses of the muscles supplied by the oculomotor nerve are frequent; ptosis, paresis of the internal rectus, simple convergent paresis (Uhthoff), isolated paralysis of the inferior oblique (Hare), etc. It is important to notice that the disturbances may improve (Mosler, Schlesinger).

The paralysis of the oculomotor results from direct pressure of the hypophyseal tumour on the trunk in the region of the pedunculi cerebri, or on the oculomotor nucleus, during the growth of the tumour into the fourth ventricle (Uhthoff). More rarely the oculomotor is damaged during its progress through the fossa of the skull by the side of the hypophysis. The trunk of the nerve may, in addition, as mentioned at p. 38, be thickened. Under the presumption that in such cases degenerations of the nerve fibres are present, similar to those in the cutaneous nerves, the possibility of the disturbances of motion depending, in certain circumstances, also upon primary disease of the motor oculi must be admitted. Such a case has not as yet been authenticated.

Paralysis of the abducens has not as yet been seen, yet according to a discovery of Pineles (pressure of the tumour into the cavernous sinus) its appearance is to be expected. Paralysis of the trochlear has also not been observed, but it has probably been often overlooked, for it may certainly be surmised from the compression of the gyrus hippocampi.

The condition of the perception to light is important. In a number of cases, ophthalmoscopically and functionally, nothing abnormal was found (Appleyard, Bertrand, Claus, Erb (1), Farge, Guinon, Boltz, Hansemann, Linsmayer, Phillips, Siach, Snell, Sternberg, and others). Five such cases were examined post-mortem. In four of these (Claus and Van der Stricht, Erb, Boltz, Hansemann) a tumour of the hypophysis was found on post-mortem (p. 39 et seq.). The absence of disturbances of vision does not therefore entirely negative a tumour of the hypophysis. This may towards the end of life develop more quickly, or the damage to the optic tract may be trifling if the tumour grows deeply downwards into the sphenoidal sinuses (Hansemann), or if, owing to its softness, it exercises only trifling pressure (Boltz), or again, if the nervous substance adapts itself, as it may do, to a very great extent to a gradually increasing pressure.

The tumour of the hypophysis may, as follows from the pathological anatomy, damage the optic nerves, chiasma, or tract in various ways and to various degrees. Various kinds of disturbances of vision result from this, from just perceptible disturbances up to blindness.

Ophthalmoscopically either simple atrophy is found, or—more rarely—choked disc, with atrophy eventually succeeding (Marie and Souza-Leite, Pinel-Maisoneuve, Surmont, Stembo, Chauffard). The atrophy is not to be conceived as primary, but as resulting from the position of pressure of the tumour. Possibly it is also due to narrowing of the optic foramen pressing on the optic nerve, especially if the latter is thickened. Such a condition has not, however, yet been proved.

The same remarks mentioned under primary disease of the motoroculi, apply equally to the primary optic neuritis, which is often described among the disturbances of vision in acromegaly.* For Dallemagne's case, mentioned at p. 38, is not clear.

* In the literature the cases of Bury, Caton and Paul are brought forward as instances of thickening of the optic nerves and neuritis. In the original communications nothing is said on this matter. It is an incorrect quotation which has been handed down by one author to another.

The examination of the field of vision affords valuable information. It is possible to determine by it the region where the damage to the optic tract lies. Seldom is the disease of a tract so clearly indicated as in Dodgson's case; left unilateral homonymous hemianopsia with hemiopic pupillary reaction. Harris and Dulles report a like condition. Often the homonymous hemianopsia is only distinct for colours (Salbey-Strümpell). More frequently there is concentric limitation of the field of vision as result of lesion of the optic nerve. Finally also the classic symptom of tumour of the hypophysis, bitemporal hemianopsia, first pointed out by Schultz, has been found. It is seldom distinct, usually concealed by the two first-named forms of limitation of the field of vision, but by repeated and careful perimetric survey it usually shows itself at some stage of the disease, especially for colours (Church and Hessert), which is often decisive for the diagnosis of tumour of the hypophysis, and with it of acromegaly (Lynn-Thomas, Uhthoff).

The reaction of the pupil to light is frequently lowered or abolished, the contraction of the pupil to accommodation may at the same time be preserved (Pinel-Maisoneuve). In both forms of hemianopsia hemiopic pupillary reaction occurs.

The acuteness of vision, as a result of the co-operation of the retina, tracts, and cortex of the brain, is subject to considerable fluctuations, which the few observations which have been carefully carried on for a long time show. Thus Franke saw it sink, after a severe fright, in the right eye from $V = \frac{5}{36}$ to $V = \frac{4}{36}$, while the left remained unaltered, and the ophthalmoscope showed on both sides no changes. Later on the acuteness of vision again improved, so that it became $V = \frac{5}{36}$ still later $V = \frac{12}{36}$, with similar opththalmoscopic results and increased narrowness of the field of vision. Kojewnikoff observed considerable improvement, as did Schlesinger, in whose case it again disappeared after some years (Schwoner).

Often a sudden attack of blindness occurs, accompanied, as in Wolf's case, by severe headache (sudden increase of pressure in the skull?).

Hitschmann's observation of glaucoma for the present stands alone.

The hearing is often injured. Observations of "undoubted" cases, in which middle ear disease is excluded, do not exist. Osborne and Sternberg have seen contraction of the aqueductus vestibuli by exostoses, and also hyperostosis in the osseous portion, the meatus itself of a striking depth. Anatomical investigations confirm both these facts.

Anosmia and disturbances of taste are repeatedly described.

NERVOUS SYSTEM.

A portion of the cerebral phenomena belongs to the well-known symptoms of cranial tumour. To these belong above all the headache. It is sometimes permanent, but usually of varying severity, especially increased at night. Frequently it appears in paroxysms of especial violence, accompanied by dizziness, vomiting, unconsciousness. Such attacks, which are also described as "Migraine," may continue for several days (Erb, Mosler, Pel, and others). They often leave behind a deterioration, especially an increase of visual disturbances, as blindness (Chalk, Wolf), exophthalmos (Motais), or paralysis of the oculo-motor.

In certain cases such conditions are reported as of many weeks duration (Ruttle, Bruzzi).

Attacks of unconsciousness may also occur without headache.

To the symptoms of tumour belong further, giddiness, in some cases decrease of intelligence, the weakness of memory, and the almost regular presence in advanced cases of somnolence. Raymond and Souques also refer Jacksonian epilepsy observed by them in one case to a distant action of the tumour of the hypophysis.

Sleeplessness is a frequent complaint, especially in the earlier stages. It also appears in very advanced cases brought on by fearful headache, and alternates at other times with the typical somnolence. Thus the patient of Roxburgh and Collis for a long time fell asleep even whilst speaking, but in the last months of life could get no sleep.

A gloomy feeling of fear, despondency, præcordial anxiety are frequently reported. They frequently increase with the appearance of general weakness, which is partly of cardiac and partly of cranial origin.

The frame of mind is only in rare cases cheerful. It usually shows a surprising apathy, indifference, sluggishness, and despondency. This is not due to any consciousness of severe affliction, since this psychical condition often appears years before the development of the acromegalic shape of the body; being entirely unintelligible to the patient, it is usually interpreted by his friends as simply "idleness." Moyer's patient had become incapable of concentrating his attention on any regular occupation, ceased to care for his family, and was abandoned by his wife. A gentleman in the higher circles of society, examined by me, who had previously managed enterprises and mercantile businesses on a large scale, postponed every new project until it became impracticable, and could no longer decide in writing a letter, or looking through an account, &c. A patient of Murray's spent the whole day inactively in bed, when he was not absolutely obliged to work.

More rarely increased irritability, nervousness, and inclination to tears are reported (Erb (2), Bruns). Both conditions, moreover, may be combined as in Ransome's case.

Despondency and præcordial anxiety may occasion transitory conditions of excitement.

In the last stages, grievous confusion of ideas, delirium, destructive mania, are observed as in other general cranial diseases (e.g., case of Mossé).

Berkley, Boyce and Beadles, Pick, Tamburini, and Tanzi have reported peculiar mental conditions. Tschish's case was, perhaps, delirium tremens.

Among the sensory phenomena there occur pains of various kinds, and in all possible parts of the body.

Acroparasthesia forms one variety, the tingling in the hands and feet, often associated with a feeling of numbness, appearing chiefly at night. It shows the various types, which are described by these complex symptoms: the "vasomotor neurosis" of Nothnagel, the original "type" of acroparasthesia of Schultze and Laquer, or the "spasms of the vessels" of Nothnagel. It belongs to the earliest appearances of the disease, often showing itself in advance of the development of the enlargements (Sternberg), and is possibly the result of changes in the cutaneous nerves, but possibly also of the early cessation of the menses.

Pains in the loins, back, and abdomen may also occur with extraordinary severity.

The pains and parasthesiæ usually vanish later on by themselves, and rarely endure when acromegaly is fully developed. But in some cases very violent pains continue permanently, and are occasionally increased by movement (Adler). Sudden, shooting, lightning pains, as in tabes, also occur.

We have already mentioned the sensation of heat under the heading "skin." Some patients are much tormented thereby, as Rolleston's female patient, who could only wear very light clothing.

Pronounced disturbances of sensibility, such as diminution of the sense of touch, increase of the area of sensation, &c., are rare (Henrot, Erb, Strümpell, Bignami).

True paralyses do not occur except in the cranial nerves (p. 73). Here and there muscular atrophy is found in the region of individual nerve trunks affected with neuritis, which we shall touch upon later on.

The tendon reflexes are usually normal or increased. But considerable decrease (Bertrand) or absence of patellar reflex occurs (Tanzi, Nonne, Freund). In the female patient of Claus and Van der Stricht it was absent transiently. In Stembo's case the right patellar reflex was absent; in Mendel's patient, both were absent at the beginning, later on the left returned under treatment by pituitary extract.

The absence of tendon reflex in conjunction with the pains, disturbances of vision, and the local atrophies forms the picture of a kind of "pseudotabes acromegalica," although ataxia is always absent. Nonne has, in one such case, assumed an irregular disease of the posterior columns. A positive condition in the spinal cord, on which a diagnosis may be based, has been submitted by Arnold (p. 37); it was, however, just in this case that the patellar reflex was normal.

The epileptic appearances (Bourneville and Regnault, Marinesco, Panas) are certainly to be conceived as complications. So also the combination with hysteria (Guinon, Chauffard).

Muscular System, Motion, Speech.

In the beginning of the disease some patients are distinguished by especial strength, which may endure for a long time during the increase of the extremities (Marie and Souza-Leite, Herzog, Bourneville and Regnault, Solis-Cohen, Denti (I), Virchow-Möbius).

But as a rule by degrees great weakness develops. The patients are quickly tired after quite trifling exertions. The movements become slow and clumsy.

The speech also is very often surprisingly drawling and hesitating.

In the last stages, the weakness is so extreme that no movement is revealed by the dynamometer (Sears).

Atrophies of the muscles are frequent. Duchesnau saw a high degree of universal muscular atrophy, which, for a long time, was taken for progressive muscular atrophy. Atrophy of single groups of muscles, namely, in the hands, especially of the thenar and hypothenar muscles, the interossei (Mossé, Comini, Hagelstamm), the glutei (Holsti, Brissaud and Meige), and the calf (Holsti, Mossé) has been observed. The electrical reaction is usually normal: Comini saw reaction of degeneration, and found, on post mortem, neuritis of the radial nerve. Between these local atrophies and the general muscular weakness there are all possible gradations and transitions which are clearly made out on microscopical examination.

The Joints and Bones.

The frequent anatomical affections of the joints are manifested clinically either by painfulness and grating in the joints (Gubian) or by swelling. The knees are often swollen (Osborne, Middleton, Schultze, Hitschmann). Roswell Park describes genua vara and floating bodies in a cyst connected with the knee joint. The finger joints are seldom swollen (Henrot, Gauthier).

As regards the bones, it should be added that Thorne-Thorne observed an unusually marked affection of the long cylindrical bones, especially in the leg. The tibia and fibula were thickened and bent forwards and outwards.

The Blood.

Constant and unequivocal changes in the blood are not known. Leucocytosis (Marie and Marinesco, Hare, Kalindero), diminution of erythrocytes (Marie and Marinesco), decrease of the amount of hæmoglobin (Marie and Marinesco, Litthauer, Salbey), increase of erythrocytes (Salbey), also normal conditions (Mosler) are described. In an advanced case Marie and Marinesco found an increase of the nucleated blood corpuscles and of the eosinophilous cells, which is referred to the marrow of the bones.

V. DEVELOPMENT; COURSE; RESULTS; TYPES OF THE DISEASE; PROGNOSIS.

The age at which acromegaly commences is difficult to determine, since the first beginnings of the disease are very often altogether imperceptible. In women the patient's statement regarding the cessation of menstruation marks, in most cases, the point of time from which the commencement of the disease may be reckoned. Acromegaly becomes perceptible to many patients after an infectious disease, or trauma, which afford thus chronological assistance, although their etiological value may be small (see Chapter vii.).

I have placed together, from extracts of all kinds of cursory reports, 55 cases in men and 70 in women. The disease began:

Under 20 years	in 8 men	= 14·6 per cent.	10 women	= 14·3 per cent.
Between 21 and 30 years	„ 30 „	= 54·5 „	35 „	= 50·0 „
„ 31 „ 40 „	„ 14 „	= 25·4 „	18 „	= 25·7 „
After the 40th year	„ 3 „	= 5·5 „	7 „	= 10·0 „
Total	55 „	= 100·0 „	70 „	= 100·0 „

We see that the largest number of cases fall ill between twenty and forty years, about half between twenty and thirty. A smaller number are affected at puberty before the twentieth year. So far the proportion of numbers in both sexes is nearly equal. After the fortieth year, on the contrary, considerably more women are attacked than men; still later the commencement of acromegaly is also far more frequent in women than men.

The earliest trustworthy cases* reported date from the fourteenth to fifteenth year (Surmont, Lynn-Thomas, Uhthoff. We have mentioned Surmont's case at p. 70. In Lynn-Thomas' patient severe headache, confusion of ideas, and a condition of idiocy appeared in the fourteenth year. Soon after the hands enlarged; in the fifteenth year the power of vision became less (cf. also p. 70). Uhthoff's

* The cases which have been described in children are, taken as a whole, very doubtful. They will be mentioned separately in Chapter viii. (differential diagnosis).

patient was a boy, who was of unusual size ("giant"), but who showed between the fifteenth and sixteenth years positive signs of acromegaly (hemianopsia, diabetes).

Acromegaly, beginning later on in life, is not so rare as was formerly supposed, as the before-mentioned figures show.*

Acroparasthesia, pains in the limbs, loins and head, weariness and apathy, cessation of menstruation, belong to the early symptoms of the disease.

The course of the disease is not yet exhaustively studied. The many gaps in our knowledge are already referred to in Chapter iv.

The swelling of the extremities occurs at the beginning, often transiently, with increase of the pains (Holsti, Grocco, Fratnich). The individual symptoms appear in varied order, until by degrees the complete picture of the disease is developed.

In many cases the disease makes gradual and hardly perceptible progress. But frequently—and this has not formerly been sufficiently observed—an apoplectiform setting in of symptoms appears, which points towards deterioration, and this advances with well-marked cerebral appearances. The patients get sudden severe headache, vomiting, giddiness, often unconsciousness, take to their bed for one or several days, and after the disappearance of the acute symptoms suffer from paralysis of the oculo-motor, exopthalmos, or are even blind in one eye (cf. p. 75). Often then the appearance of the face and the size of the hands and feet quickly change.

At other times an acceleration in the progress of the disease occurs, especially after fright, or trauma (Gauthier, Franke, F. Meyer).

It is important to notice that not unfrequently very considerable remissions may occur—a point also which the observations of later years were the first to establish. They have been seen after the most varied remedies, often without them. We have already mentioned in the fourth chapter the disappearance of polyphagia and poly-

* The disease began in the 30th year and later in the cases of Packard, Campbell (1). Erb, Schwartz (men); Boltz (2), Hitschmann, Asmus, F. Meyer, O'Connor, Fazio, Harris, Ransom, Schwoner, Thomas, Sears, Spillmann and Haushalter, Campbell (2), Marinesco (2), Silcock (women).

dypsia, of the profuse perspiration, the amendment of the disturbances of vision, glycosuria, and of Westphal's symptom. The enlargement of the terminations of the extremities may also somewhat diminish (to be explained by the disappearance of fat). But of more importance to the patient is that with all these, so great an improvement may set in in the general condition that he may again, at least for a certain time, be quite capable of earning his living. Such a welcome change has, for example, occurred to the patient portrayed in Figs. 1, 2, 8, and 11.

Deuti (1), Schlesinger, and Kojewnikoff report like improvements. As regards the duration of such remissions little is known, at all events they may amount to a year or more.

Cessation of the disease also occurs for several years.

The troubles which bring the patient to a doctor may be extremely various. In the early stages they are parasthesiæ (Gubian, Packard, Sternberg), or pains in the loins, and the cessation of the menses, which excite the suspicion of disease of the reproductive organs (Salbey), later goitre (Godlee, and above p. 65), enlarged tonsils, the removal of which is sought for (Hadden and Ballance), muscular atrophy (Duchesnau), pains in the head (Marie), disturbances of vision (Motais, Pinel-Maisoneuve, Mosler, Wadsworth), shortness of breath (Schwartz), diabetes (Cunningham, Hansemann, Pineles), weakness and unfitness for work (Unverricht), and many others besides. The disease concerns, therefore, not only physicians and neurologists, but also the surgeon, gynæcologist, laryngologist, and not least of all the ophthalmologist.

In some cases, the sufferers from acromegaly are not sensible of any disorders, and come to the physician on account of accidental complications, as ulcer of the stomach (Boltz), carcinoma of the stomach (Dallemagne), bronchitis (Jorge), cystosarcoma of the mamma (Schwoner).

During the further course of the disease the weakness, as a rule, becomes more and more prominent; the patient becomes bedridden.

Two stages have many times been distinguished (Gauthier, Tamburini, and others); the first in which the hypertrophy, the second in which the weakness predominates. But those cases which have been carefully observed often show that just at the time when the weakness was greatest and the deterioration most rapid, the most marked enlargement of the parts ensued simultaneously with the diminution of strength, and this was especially perceptible in the last period of life. (We return to these cases presently.) Such a systematic division cannot therefore be made use of in the consideration of the disease.

Death may result in very different ways. In many cases it occurs fairly suddenly and unexpectedly, as is observed in tumours of the brain; or the common termination to any wasting disease occurs; bronchitis and broncho-pneumonia. Not a few die in diabetic coma; tuberculosis of the lungs, combined with the diabetes, may also bring about the end (Squance). In other cases disturbances of the circulation, and in mentally-diseased patients intestinal catarrh is often fatal (Tamburini), and in yet others complications are the cause of death.

We know nothing at present of a cure.

The duration of the disease was formerly usually declared to be between ten and twenty years. But if the considerable material of post mortems at present existing is examined, other practical and significant theoretical results are obtained.

With reference to the duration and course, it is possible to differentiate three types:—

The benign form, up to fifty years duration, and with trifling troubles.

The commonest form, chronic acromegaly, duration from eight to thirty years.

The acute, malignant form of from three to four years duration.

The benign form is best represented by Bonardi's case, whose patient died in the seventy-fourth year. To this type in addition belong the second case of Dallemagne (death in the seventieth year), and case two of Mossé.

The greater number of the cases of the disease are of the chronic variety.

The acute malignant form offers especial interest. To

this group belong six cases (Caton and Paul, Hansemann, Mossé and Daunic, Pineles, Uhthoff, Wolf). The clinical course in all these cases is alike, so that it is justifiable to class it as a special "type"; the disease develops very quickly; the abnormal growth, the enlargement of the terminations of the extremities succeed one another under the physician's eyes. In the space of a few weeks the changes of the features, as may be repeatedly gathered from the clinical histories, have astonished the observer. In the last period of life the increase proceeds still more. We have therefore every right to describe such cases as acute in comparison with the common forms. The most interesting point results from inquiry into the post mortem condition of this acute acromegaly; in all cases with acute progress—and only in these cases—a true sarcoma of the hypophysis is present.* We return to these etiologically important cases in the seventh chapter.

We have already spoken of (pp. 56, 61) Marie's types of hands and face, and the "formes frustes." As "formes frustes" Chauffard has lately accepted some cases with partially existing symptoms of acromegaly. It is a difficult thing to form such a diagnosis on an observation lasting for a short time, since we cannot at present know what symptoms, if any, will develop, and whether we have not simply to deal with a case of ordinary commencing acromegaly. Future observations will fill up these deficiencies.

The prognosis varies according to which of the three above stated forms the affected case belongs. We have, on that point, a guide in the patient's communications. The farther back the development of the disease can be traced, the more prospect is there of longer duration and milder progress.

Of the several symptoms, the pains in the limbs and trunk chiefly ameliorate, the acroparasthesia almost always; we may give the sufferers ground for hope on both these points. Since also considerable remissions occur in the other phenomena, we are besides entitled to express favourably, although with reservation as regards relapses.

---

* On the boundary line between this and the chronic form stands Bury's case (glioma).

The apoplectiform paralyses and the amaurosis almost always improve a little. The hope of a possible cessation of the disease progressing is not to be withheld from the sufferer. Complications naturally make the prognosis worse.

VI. RELATIONSHIP OF ACROMEGALY TO OTHER DISEASES AND CONDITIONS.

Cranium Progeneum.

L. Meyer has described those skulls as "Crania progenea," in which the row of teeth of the underjaw project over that of the upper. The masticatory surfaces of the lower incisors are turned backwards, those of the upper incisors forwards. Virchow, Zuckerkandl and Sternberg, in addition to Meyer, have made anatomical examination of such a skull. They have shown that "Cranium progeneum" is no special condition, but a collective name for a deformity, which may be of very various origin.

In the predominate number of cases it depends upon a decided pathological formation.

In many cases it is based on a hyperplasia of the upper jaw, which is congenital, or has been acquired in early youth through rickets or other diseases. The peculiarities of the teeth, especially the transverse furrow or rudimentary form, point to this. To this condition belongs the celebrated, enormously deformed skull of the "Pomeranian weaver" (Davis).

In other cases—and to these acromegaly belongs—the question, on the contrary, is one of hypertrophy of the lower jaw.

In certain cases, according to Virchow, ethnological causes have played a part (frequency in the Friseland race). Transmittance has also occurred in many generations. I have once seen it skip one generation; the grandfather and grandson possessed the same formation of jaw.

Clinically cranium progeneum is observed:—

1. In acromegaly.
2. In cretinism and cretinoid dwarfs.
3. In individuals who, in early childhood, have gone through severe small-pox (thin skin, atrophic facial bones, relatively more marked lower jaw).
4. In "degenerates": epilepsy, idiocy, weakness of mind, folie circulaire, chronic paranoia.
5. In apparently healthy individuals.

In the cases 3 and 4, the formation of the jaw is doubtless to be designated as a "sign of degeneration," and even in the apparently healthy—it is frequently to be seen, if looked for, in numbers of patients, and even in the street—there are frequently associated with it other signs of degeneration.

The relationship of acromegaly to cranium progeneum is, according to report, quite simple; the usual skull in acromegaly ("type ovoide" of Marie, cf. 56) belongs to the group of crania progenea. Besides this, there are various other forms of crania progenea, which, save the mere external characteristic of the under jaw overlapping the upper, have nothing at all in common with acromegaly.

The anatomical distinction between the various forms of cranium progeneum, especially of the acromegalic skull, is usually easily made on the one hand by means of the signs given in the second chapter, and on the other through the hyperplasia of the upper jaw. But in collections crania progenea are often found, with a large amount of osseous formation, which do not, indeed, possess all the characteristics of the acromegalic skull, but appear to resemble it in many respects, so that the diagnosis of the skull alone must remain in suspense. I have described two such skulls in my above-quoted work. Bourneville and Regnault have likewise brought forward a similar skull, in which they would see an "atypical partial acromegaly." It is indeed generally better to admit that a strict diagnosis of a macerated skull cannot always be made without a knowledge of the rest of the skeleton, and of the body, as on the ground of such an observation, the appearance of acromegaly becomes guess-work. I should, moreover, according to the description, assert without hesitation that the skull, described by Bourneville and Regnault, is the usual cranium progeneum of an epileptic.

Myxœdema and Cretinism.

Acromegaly on the one hand, and cretinism and myxœdema on the other, present a series of similar phenomena.

The tongue in cretins is very often enlarged to a considerable extent, the lips thick, puffy, and protruding, the nose thick and snubbed. The skin is thick, too plentiful as in acromegaly, and frequently forms, especially on the occiput, large swellings. The long cylindrical bones of cretins and cretinoid dwarfs often appear, owing to the deficiency in growth in length, very coarse and uniformly thick, which in many of them, as the clavicle, recall in a striking manner the type of acromegaly. Furthermore, as discussed in the former section, the skull of cretins and cretinoid dwarfs is, as in acromegaly, a cranium progeneum.

In many cases also an enlarged sella turcica is present in such skulls. In cretins and myxœdema, the hypophysis is frequently diseased and not seldom enlarged. Boyce and Beadles have collected the striking cases of Langhans, Nièpce, Dolega, Bourneville and Briçon, and have added two of their own observations.[*] Uthoff has proved clinically owing to the presence of bitemporal hemianopsia in one case tumour of the hypophysis.

It has often been the wish to consider the tumour of the hypophysis compensatory for the loss of the function of the thyroid. But there are also cretins in whom the hypophysis is very small (Schönemann), and de Coulon has found that the enlarged hypophysis of cretins is due to an increased amount of cellular tissue, the follicles are, if anything, atrophied.

However that may be, all the above named phenomena point to a certain connection between cretinism and acromegaly.

On the other hand, symptoms in acromegaly frequently exist which recall myxœdema. Indolence is common to both diseases, certainly it never reaches to so high a pitch in acromegaly as in myxœdema. The skin in acromegaly is, as a rule, utterly different to that of the myxœdematous; the former is moist, soft, capable of being raised into thick folds, often surprisingly thick, as in cretins; the latter is dry, squamous, difficult to separate from the layers under it. But in certain places, especially on the backs of the hands, the skin in acromegaly approaches, as

[*] Virchow, in addition, has described a cretinoid skull with enlarged sella turcica (Ges. Abh., S. 905).

regards consistency, to the myxœdematous skin. Again, in certain cases there is a decidedly true mixture with myxœdema. For instance, Comini found in his patient that the skin of the thorax was rough and scaly, Sears the skin of the face everywhere thickened and resembling a mask, Schiff the skin over the whole body scaly.

The relationship of acromegaly to the thyroid and to myxœdema have been often considered (Gauthier, Holsti, Graham, Lancereaux, Hâskovec, and others). A great number of theories have been adduced concerning the connection, but the fundamental question as to whether it is not purely a matter of mere external resemblance is still no nearer settlement. From the appearance of myxœdematous symptoms in acromegaly it is, however, justifiable to suspect that the cause and connecting link may be found in the frequent changes of the thyroid in the latter disease.

Morbus Basedowii.

Goitre, exophthalmos, disturbances of the heart, flushings, and perspiration are common to acromegaly and Basedow's disease. In both diseases hyperplasia of the glandular organs is present: "lymphatic constitution" (Sternberg). Magnus-Levy has also found an increase of oxidation in acromegaly. For these reasons a connection has been suspected for a long time, but first by Gauthier. This may exist perhaps only in the disease of the thyroid, but perhaps in the deeper and as yet unknown relationships of blood-forming glands to each other.

Both diseases have been found together in the cases of Lancereaux (2) and Murray (2).

Gigantism.

About twenty per cent. of acromegalians are over 177 cm. in height. It will be found by anyone who collects the cases described in the literature as "giants," and considers them strictly according to their pathological conditions, that about forty per cent. of all giants are also the subjects of acromegaly (Sternberg). This proportion suggests the inference of a closer connection. The question has been discussed abandantly (Klebs, Marie, Guinon, Tanzi, Dana, Bramwell, Hutchinson, Sternberg, Massalongo, Tamburini, Brissaud and Meige, Engel-Reimers, Chauffard).

Some have asserted the identity of both processes (especially Klebs, Massalongo, Brissaud and Meige.) Two arguments are chiefly advanced to support this theory.

1. In all carefully studied giants, according to Langer, an enlargement of the hypophysis is present.

2. All sufferers from acromegaly, in whom the disease has begun in youth, are of gigantic size. If the disease occurs in youth, there results at that time giant growth, later on acromegaly. Acromegaly is nothing else than "late giant growth" (Massalongo), gigantism is "acromegaly in youth" (Brissaud and Meige).

Both arguments are, as follows from the facts stated in Chapters i., ii., and iv., altogether untenable.

1. It is not true that in all giants an enlargement of the hypophysis exists; there are several forms of giants with very different anatomical characteristics. Langer has certainly not found in all giants an enlargement of the hypophysis, but only in "pathological" (acromegaly) cases, from which he expressly distinguishes the giants with "normal skull." The contrary assertion rests simply on a false citation of Klebs, which other authors have copied without comment (cf. p. 9).

2. There are cases of acromegaly which begin in youth, and which show no giant growth, but are only of medium size (p. 81). There are also cases of gigantism with which acromegaly only becomes associated later on in life (Uhthoff). It is necessary, in order to be clear regarding the relationship between these two conditions, to study, in the first place, apart from every theory, the several cases of "giants," and to arrange them clinically and anatomically.

The following groups can be distinguished on a survey of the material at present existing :—

I. Normal giants (no deformity, no diseases, reach old age).

As instances of normal giants, Langer, and in addition, Virchow's giant Winkelmeyer, 227·8 cm. in height.*

* Virchow quotes the case incorrectly in his work on acromegaly as 250·3 cm. high.

II. Pathological giants.

(a) Acromegalians. Form a very large portion of giants; the largest known skeleton, the "Irish giant," 259 cm. in height, is that of an acromegalian (Swanzy).

(b) Multiple tumour-like exostoses (leontiasis ossea and hyperostosis). Often show appearances of pressure in the brain and cranial nerves.

Buhl's case, 227 cm. in height.

Sirena's case, 240 cm. in height.*

Giant Mr. Wilkins, 245 cm. in height (Lamberg and Sternberg (2)).

(c) Hemihypertrophica facialis.

Dana's case, 226 cm. in height.

(d) Multiple curvatures of the bones, as scoliosis, bending of the humeri, genua valga; appearances resembling rickets.

Giantess Marianne Wehde (Bollinger), 255 cm. in height.

Berlin skeleton No. 3040 (Zitterland†), 220 cm. in height.

(e) Gigantism with hereditary syphilis.

Fuchs' case, 183 cm. in height.

(f) Premature development and rapid growth with tumour of the scrotum in childhood.

Sacchi's case, 143 cm. in height at the ninth year.

From this arrangement it is seen that the expression "Giant" is nothing more than a collective name for very various conditions, which have only in common with each other the more than moderate size of the body.

The relationship of acromegaly to gigantism is easily determined from the above remarks. Acromegaly is a well-defined disease, with perfectly sharply-marked characteristics. Gigantism is an anomaly of development, which in itself has nothing to do with disease, but may occur in connection with various illnesses, and certainly with universal dystrophies. Acromegaly is one of these illnesses. The number of persons who simultaneously suffer from acromegaly, and are of very large stature, is considerable, both in

---

* Hereditary syphilis accepted by the author is very doubtful.

† In my earlier work I have considered this case, judging from the description, to be one of acromegaly; but a consideration of the skeleton has convinced me that a special disease of the bones exists.

proportion to the number of acromegalians, as to the number of the other "giants."

Up to the present we have been dealing with bare facts. Now comes in the theory: the proportion of numbers, on the one hand, between acromegalian and non-acromegalian giants, and on the other between giant acromegalians and medium-sized acromegalians, suggests the idea whether a causative connection between that anomalous development and this disease does not exist.

For such a connection between gigantism and acromegaly there are, according to existing facts, two possibilities.

1. It is conceivable that acromegaly may occasion an increase in length of the bones, if it gives rise to an increase of bone at the epiphysis at the open cartilaginous sutures (Surmont, v. Recklinghausen). Such a process is proved by Marie, but only for some cases in the hands, in which the "type en long" is developed (pp. 29, 61), not for all the extremities or the whole body.

2. The fact that giants are almost twice as frequently acromegalians as acromegalians are giants, and the fact that in giants all sorts of extensive diseases of the organic systems occur (dystrophies, "Vegetationsstörungen," according to Kundrat*), permits of our adopting the view that giant growth predisposes to the appearance of universal dystrophies, and especially of acromegaly (Sternberg).

While only partial observations bear witness to the first theory, the second has lately obtained from Uhthoff's case very valuable support. There developed in a boy, who originally owing to his rapid growth, passed as the "giant boy," with the appearance of puberty, the signs of acromegaly. The value of this case is diminished, however, by the fact that it was not established on medical authority that the boy had not shown earlier any kind of acromegalic symptoms. Future observations on "gigantism in children," who are fairly frequently exhibited in shows, and on their ultimate destiny, will well fill in this deficiency.

Then, of course, the question of the kind of "disposition" will still remain a subject for future investigation.

* Kundrat, Ueber Vegetationsstörungen; Wiener Klin. Wochenschr., 1893, S. 505.

Diffuse Hyperostosis.

In the anatomical museum at Prague there is a skull which Toldt acquired for the museum, in which acromegaly and hyperostosis are associated. (Not to be confounded with the celebrated Prague skull described by Ilg and Gruber). It has the typical appearance of acromegaly, as well as at the same time an extraordinary thickening and condensation of the bones. The weight is enormous—1520 g. (Sternberg).

Acromegaly and general hyperostosis may also be combined in certain circumstances.

Diabetes.

The relationship between acromegaly and diabetes is not clear. Whether this latter is always a secondary appearance—"glycosuria"—and on what it depends (pancreas, medulla oblongata), or whether it, at least in certain cases, is to be conceived as "true diabetes," and as a co-ordinated disease, is not definitely known, although many opinions have been expressed regarding it (see the works quoted at p. 68).

VII. ETIOLOGY AND PATHOGENY.

Acromegaly has been observed in all countries, and in all races (Negress, Berkley; Indian, Dana). Both sexes are equally affected, which must be noted as contrary to the older opinions. Among the 210 cases on which this work is based, we find 104 were men, 106 women.

The age is discussed at p. 81.

Direct inheritance of the disease has been shown probable in two cases, by Bonardi and Schwoner. Hereditary defect with diseases of the nervous system has often been adduced; how far it really plays a part is not known. Occasionally the statement is found that the entire family consists of extraordinarily large persons—*e.g.*, Gajkiewicz.

Chronic poisoning with alcohol or lead (Chauffard) has not occurred, as far as can be gathered from the patient's statements, with undue frequency; the same applies to syphilis.

The commencement, in many cases, is connected by the patient with especially impressive events.

Bertrand's patient imputed her complaint to unusual excitement arising from an epidemic in her village, which lasted several months; after that her menses ceased. In Dulle's patient the trouble began during confinement in a Turkish prison.

The illness in the cases of Grocco, Claus and Holsti, began at the end of a typhus fever; in Lombroso's patient with a severe attack of bronchitis. How far infectious diseases may really be of etiological importance is illustrated by the case of Hadden and Ballance, where the patient traced back the illness to an attack of scarlet fever. Many months previously, however, the periods had ceased, and the patient had suffered from acroparasthesia.

Acromegaly began after severe fright in the female patients of Chalk, Spillmann and Haushalter, Pel, Naunyn, Schlesinger and Hansemann.

In Murray's case (1), poisoning by coal gas immediately preceded it.

Trauma is not seldom adduced. For instance, Marie (1): Fall on a snow heap; Farge: Blow on the body from a falling tree, after that a long bed of sickness; Gauthier: Fall on the occiput; Barclay and Symmers: Violent fall from a horse; Benson: Injury to the left leg; Marinesco: Fall from the second storey; Unverricht: Fall from a scaffold, and others. There is also a case which places the etiological value of trauma in a doubtful light; the patient of Sears traced her illness back to the fact that twelve years previously she had let fall a washing iron on to her left side whilst at work. She immediately suffered from severe bleeding from the uterus, and was excessively frightened. Shortly afterwards swelling of the hands was said to have begun. But the patient, by chance, had in her possession an old photograph which had been taken several months before the mishap, and which already showed marked changes in the face due to acromegaly.

In many cases, therefore, infectious disease, fright, or trauma may have been only the cause for attentively noticing the body, and drawing attention to a condition which had, so far, developed imperceptibly.

On the other hand, it is certain from the observation of Franke, cited at p. 75, that with already existing trouble a deterioration may be brought about by such influences. They may, therefore, be viewed as auxiliary causes.

Numerous theories have been advanced to explain the pathogeny of the disease; these are best grouped in the following manner:—

1. Nervous theory (Magendie, v. Recklinghausen, Panas). The disease, it is said, has its origin in the central nervous system. This hypothesis will scarcely be defended at the present time, especially since the case of Holschewnikoff-Recklinghausen has been recognised as syringomyelia.*

2. Theory of (atavistic) anomalous growth (Freund, Campbell). Acromegaly is no real disease, but an anomaly of growth. From the resemblance of the skull in acromegaly to that of animals, which had already struck older observers, as Brigidi and Cunningham, and from the general appear-

* Dallemagne appears to have a similar idea, as far as I can understand his deductions.

ance of the sufferer, a retrogression to the type of the anthropoid apes has been deduced. Freund also brings the sexual disturbances into causal connection with the alterations in growth—an old idea, which had already presented itself to Johannes Weyer (cf. p. 6). The reported cases of late menopause (p. 70) are not favourable to this view.

3. Thymus theory (Klebs). In the large thymus the plexuses of blood-vessels of the follicles are "a place for the formation of the endothelium of the vessels." These are washed away with the blood stream, and cause as "angioblasts" a "universal luxuriance of vessel germs," which leads to giant growth and acromegaly. Inasmuch as the persistence and enlargement of the thymus is not constant, the whole theory is untenable. The large thymus is probably only one part of the hyperplasia of the lymph organs (p. 36), the lymphatic constitution.

4. Hypophysis theory. Marie was the first (with Souza-Leite) to enunciate the hypothesis that acromegaly was a general dystrophy, which in some way or other was dependent on disease of the hypophysis, in the same way as myxœdema is connected with the thyroid. The theory rests, in the first place, on the invariable presence of disease in this gland. Since then it has been many times enlarged and modified, without, nevertheless, any substantially new facts being brought forward for proof. In almost every work on acromegaly a discussion is devoted to this theory.*

The fact disclosed on p. 85 is significant—viz., that in the acute developing cases of acromegaly a sarcoma of the hypophysis was always found, a new growth, of which we know in general that it takes a quick course, and progresses with a total annihilation of the structure of the affected organ. Notwithstanding the reserve we must maintain regarding the histological results met with in the hypophysis, the connection between the course of the disease and the post mortem

---

* Many have looked on the enlargement of the hypophysis as a partial phenomenon of acromegaly, either as enlargement of all "dependent parts" (Salbey), or as part of the hypertrophy of the extremities (Dreschfeld), or as part of the hypertrophy of the formation of the mouth, with which the hypophysis is connected during the process of development (Bury, Hutchinson, and others). But a heterologous new formation, a cyst, and such like, are not enlargements, but diminutions of the organ.

appearances is so striking that it adds no doubt an important support to that view which sees in the cessation of the normal function of the hypophysis the cause of acromegaly. Whatever may be imagined as to a closer connection, it is at present entirely left to conjectures, which are as numerously present in the literature as they are unproved. An especial difficulty, which is at present insurmountable, arises from the fact that there is no doubt that tumours of the hypophysis may exist without acromegaly. None of the older cases, for the reasons mentioned at p. 68, are applicable in this connection. But the later cases of Wolf, Boyce and Beadles, Packard, Handford, Waddell, Levy, &c., prove such an existence unanswerably.

Little is as yet known concerning the mutual relationships of individual symptoms. We have described at p. 30 this relationship as far as the skeleton is concerned. Macroglossia and increase of the jaw are to be considered as possibly co-ordinated to each other, inasmuch as one may occur without the other (Campbell, Dreschfeld, Flemming).

VIII. DIAGNOSIS AND DIFFERENTIAL DIAGNOSIS.

The diagnosis of fully developed acromegaly is not generally difficult for that physician who is accustomed to consider the patient as a whole. The unnatural appearance of the face and giant-like hands at once challenge a closer scrutiny. The alteration in the form of the body often also renders it possible to furnish the diagnosis at the first glance. Among the earliest features, the shape of the nose and lips, the tongue and soft palate, the symmetrical enlargement of the hands and feet without deformity, and no especial alteration of the complexion, are of importance; in addition there occur the condition of the bones of the skull, ultimately the kyphosis, the hollow and rough voice, the tired bearing, the slight cyanosis. It is very valuable for diagnostic purposes if a strict inspection of the eye shows a lesion of the optic tract or chiasma. Yet it must not be forgotten that disturbances of vision, as disturbances of the eyes generally, may be altogether wanting. If inquiry is made in addition after the appetite, subjective troubles and the menses, the whole picture of acromegaly will be quickly unfolded.

It is now still necessary to reflect on the differential diagnosis.

Unpleasant mistakes may occur, if the golden rule is omitted, in every examination of a patient, to review the whole individual at least in a hasty manner. Since, as a rule, the patients know nothing, or say nothing, of the changes in shape of their body, it may happen that acromegaly is completely overlooked. This may naturally more easily happen if the disease has not yet reached its full development.

The differential diagnosis must be founded on rather a broader basis than is customary in the literature on the subject, in which usually only those diseases originally considered by Marie are quoted. The perusal of the abundant clinical descriptions shows that many a case was considered as acromegaly which is not acromegaly; and many cases of acromegaly have been diagnosed for a longer or shorter time even until post mortem examination as other diseases.

Two possibilities are to be borne in mind in the differential diagnosis:—

1. Single symptoms, particularly on the side of the internal organs, may force their way so much to the front that they appear as independent diseases, and the disease as a whole is overlooked.

2. The changes in the external shape of the body may give rise to mistakes.

Of the independent diseases, which, by reason of partial appearances of acromegaly, may be confounded with it, we must consider: tumour of the brain, Basedow's disease, diabetes, progressive muscular atrophy, disease of the reproductive organs, acroparasthesia, rheumatism, traumatic neuroses, and feigned diseases.

Cranial tumour, owing to headache, apoplectiform attacks, disturbances of the eyes, often early directs the patient's attention to himself. If the disease can now be localised by means of homonymous hemianopsia, with hemiopic pupillary reaction in the middle fossa of the skull, or even through bitemporal hemianopsia in the region of the chiasma, then the possibility of acromegaly should not be forgotten. Exophthalmos, amenorrhœa, glycosuria, polyuria* (which, according to the older descriptions, were said to be symptoms of hypophyseal tumour—cf. p. 68) immediately suggest this possibility. The idea is supplied with proof in the changes of the shape of the body. But it is to be remembered that a tumour of the hypophysis may exist without acromegaly, and that it may be combined with one of the conditions similar to acromegaly to be described hereafter (as cranium progeneum or syringomyelia), and therefore the minute details must be carefully considered.

Acromegaly, especially at the commencement, has been repeatedly mistaken for Basedow's disease (Lancereaux, Wolf). Exophthalmos, goitre, palpitation of the heart, abnormal

---

* All these symptoms are present in the case of H. P. Potter and G. M. Atkinson (Brit. Med. Jour., 1884, I., p. 57), which is on that account highly suggestive of acromegaly.

perspiration, flushings, sleeplessness, are frequent in acromegaly. It is important for the differential diagnosis that the frequency of the pulse in acromegaly is not substantially increased, at all events not to the same extent as in Basedow's disease, that tremor is seldom present in acromegaly and that exophthalmos in acromegaly is frequently associated with disturbances of vision, in Basedow's disease hardly ever. These considerations would also, in the earlier stages, even if the abnormal growth does not strike one at first sight, make the adoption of the case as one of Basedow's disease doubtful, and draw the attention to the possibility of acromegaly. Perhaps many cases of so-called "atypical Basedow's disease" and "symptomatic Basedow's disease with goitre," belong to acromegaly.

Diabetes in acromegaly may, owing to its severe progress, so much overrule the picture of the disease that the acromegaly may be overlooked (Hansemann). Here there is no differential diagnostic indication. To avoid mistakes nothing remains except to keep before one's mind the fact that severe diabetes, and also that form which we, since Lancereaux, are accustomed to refer to the pancreas as "diabète maigre," may be a local phenomenon of acromegaly, and therefore in every such case to be suspicious of this disease.

In some cases atrophy of the muscles is so prominently marked that it may mislead and cause one to adopt the diagnosis of a "progressive muscular atrophy," or one of the diseases clinically resembling it, as anterior chronic poliomyelitis, amyotrophic lateral sclerosis, pachymeningitis cervicalis hypertrophica, &c. (Duchesnau). On this point also strict observation of the whole subject will guide us in the right direction, but especially the contrast between the enlargement of the hands and the atrophy of the muscles of the hand and arm.

The conditions of the reproductive organs may, in certain circumstances, entirely attract the attention. The absence of the menses, the pains in the abdomen, back, and legs, may lead to the acceptance of the diagnosis of disease of the uterine appendages (neoplasm, gonorrhœal disease, extra-uterine pregnancy, &c.), especially if an enlargement of the appendages happens to be felt. This occurred, in fact, in Salbey's case. The patient had, on account of pain in the abdomen and loins and of amenorrhœa, gone to a gynæcological hospital. A tumour of the appendages was plainly diagnosed, and the ovaries which were "enlarged" removed. Several months later the appearance of acromegaly was confirmed by physicians.

Acroparasthesia in acromegaly in the earlier stages may occasion a mistake with the harmless independent acroparasthesia, especially as this latter readily occurs at the climacteric, and the former likewise coincides frequently with the morbid cessation of the periods. If both occur somewhere between thirty and forty, the hasty diagnosis of premature decay must therefore be guarded against; a presentiment of the other early symptoms of acromegaly should be entertained, and at least a prognosis should be given somewhat cautiously if the diagnosis is not possible at the commencement of the illness.

The pains in the extremities and back have been often, as we learn from the patients' statements, covered by the popular name of "rheumatism," and treated with all sorts of baths, salicylate compounds, &c. In the earlier stages of the disease it is conceivable that no other diagnosis may be possible; later on, with a certain degree of detailed investigation, it ought certainly not to occur.

Whereas acromegaly is frequently ushered in by traumata, the numerous nervous symptoms of the disease have also given occasion for confusion with traumatic neurosis and feigned diseases (Unverricht). Pareses, muscular atrophies, reflex changes, parasthesiæ, headache, vertigo, fainting fits, anxiety, sleeplessness, palpitation of the heart, perspiration, impotence, polyuria, and restriction of the field of vision may, in a patient suffering from acromegaly, readily give rise to the diagnosis of a traumatic neurosis occurring after an accident; the contrast between the size of the body and the weakness, and the countless troubles, may make a transitory suspicion of feigned disease excusable. But in both these cases a thorough examination of the body is so plainly called for that acromegaly can only be overlooked if the physician is ignorant of its very existence.

No differential diagnosis can guard against an accidental complication (*e.g.*, cancer of the stomach in Dallemagne's third case), causing acromegaly to be overlooked until death.

The diseases and conditions, in which the external shape of the body bears a resemblance to acromegaly, are numerous. Amongst them a number of very rare and imperfectly known affections are present. It is frequently easy to say that some one case of disease is not acromegaly, but very difficult or impossible to determine its true nature. We divide, for the purpose of consideration, the cases into three groups, according as to whether changes of the whole body, or chiefly the head or extremities, predominate.

Myxœdema, firstly, shows changes of the whole body. The face is large, turgid, roundish, the skin everywhere thickened. The hands and feet increased in circumference; the tongue is also broader. The patients are sluggish and sleepy. More minute observation shows at once that the change is limited only to the soft parts, that the bones are not at all affected, that the skin feels tough and inelastic, the epidermis rough and scaly. The mental functions are not disturbed to such an extent in acromegaly as in myxœdema. Only if a tumour of the hypophysis occasions severe pressure symptoms is this the case; but then also the other signs of cranial tumour stand out much more clearly than has ever been observed in the moderately enlarged hypophysis of myxœdema. Finally, in myxœdema metabolic processes are decidedly reduced, in acromegaly normal or increased. It must certainly not be forgotten that both diseases may be associated together (p. 89). Confusions with myxœdema have been very frequent, as the history of acromegaly shows.

The appearance of the adult cretin and cretinoid dwarf is so characteristic that confusion with any other disease is impossible. But it is otherwise in children. The puffy lips and nose, the macroglossia, the cranium progeneum, the hypertrophied skin over the roof of the skull and on the extremities, the short, thick, coarse, cylindrical bones, and the disturbance of the power of vision, may make the distinction between cretinism and acromegaly difficult in a child. The disturbances of the intelligence and muscular energy are decisive. Since all these were found combined in the case described by Moncorvo as "acromegaly" in a fourteenth month microcephalus child, this is without doubt a case of sporadic cretinism.

The osteitis deformans of Paget is one of the diseases similar to osteomalacia, perhaps connected with it (v. Recklinghausen), which causes considerable curvature of the extremities, enormous increase of the skull, and curvature of the vertebral column. Pains usher in and accompany the disease. Similarity to acromegaly is seen in the enlargement of the skull, the kyphosis, and the thickening of the cylindrical bones. The increase of the soft parts present in acromegaly is, however, wanting; the bones of the face are scarcely or not at all affected, the tibiæ are often enormously curved, which never occurs in acromegaly, and what is very important, the changes in acromegaly are symmetrical, in osteitis deformans, on the other hand, frequently very irregularly distributed. Thomson has discussed the anatomical distinction between both diseases.

Arthritis deformans may occasion exuberance of bone, thickening of the hands and feet, and later on kyphosis. Inasmuch as the overgrowth of bone in this disease also occurs in the region of the muscular and ligamentous attachments, the macerated skeleton bears some resemblance to the acromegalic. Thomson has laid stress on this point. The changes, however, preponderate in the joints; changes in the skin and soft parts, the exophthalmos, and most of the general appearances of acromegaly are wanting.

Gigantism, after the explanations on p. 90, requires no special differential diagnostic discussion. The normal giants have nothing in common with acromegaly, neither have the giants with multiple curvatures of the bones, with hemihypertrophica facialis, hereditary syphilis, &c.; acromegalic giants who suffer from real acromegaly differ in no way from the ordinary acromegalic cases; only giants with leontiasis ossea require some words, which we will devote to them when we describe this disease (p. 106).

A very strange form of pachydermia sometimes arises in the extremities and skin of the face after local asphyxia. In winter the hands and feet are cold, of marble-like blue, less sensitive than the normal, and awkward. By degrees, increasing year by year, a thickening of the cellular tissue develops, and with it an appearance similar to myxœdema, yet without the general phenomena. Kaposi often showed such a case to visitors to his ward, in the person of a well-known attendant Wg., who, originally a patient, has been under observation there for many years. The disease has doubtless, owing to the thickening of the extremities and the changes in the features—the skin of the face also taking part in the process—a certain resemblance to acromegaly. Yet changes in the bones, disturbances of the eyes, cessation of the menses and the collective general appearances are entirely wanting, while the colour of the skin and the increase of the disturbance in winter are very characteristic. An entirely analogous case has been published by M. Hoffmann as "acromegaly."

Similar general pachydermata develop often after erysipelas, in places also which are not attacked by the original inflammation. The cases are mostly confounded with myxœdema; confusion with acromegaly should also be guarded against.

Sometimes general hyperostosis spreads over several parts of the skeleton, usually, however, it is confined to the head. Two forms are distinguished: the diffuse symmetrical thickening, and the tumour-like hyperostosis, "leontiasis ossea" according to Virchow.

The diffuse hyperostosis was only studied in earlier times anatomically in the rare and remarkable skulls in museums.[*] Now, however, we possess several clinically observed cases (the latest by Allen Starr, Putnam and Prince), so that we are able to thoroughly examine all the phenomena of the disease. Usually in youth, seldom in adults, there commences a remarkable enlargement of all the bones of the skull. In many cases the rest of the skeleton is also involved by curvature of extremities, kyphosis or scoliosis, but usually only the enlargement of the head is noticeable ("megalocephaly," "ophthalmomegaly"). The essential features of the disease are due to the disease of the skull:

[*] The cases of Malpighi, Jadelot, Bojanus, Ilg-Gruber, Kilian, Otto, Vrolik, Albers, Huschke, Gaddi, Daniels.

exophthalmos, blindness, deafness, facial paresis of both sides, troubles of mastication, deglutition, respiration, headache, sleepiness, imbecility, epileptic convulsions, paralysis of the extremities, death.

A consideration of the described symptoms shows no doubt, that with regard to the changes in the bones, the exophthalmos, blindness and deafness, &c., the disease can bear a resemblance to acromegaly. In the diagnosis, especially in young patients, they should be taken into consideration.

This form of hyperostosis may be combined with acromegaly (p. 94), and would then be discernible, especially by bulbar symptoms.

The tumour-like hyperostoses are present in the skull, as "leontiasis ossea," and also in the whole osseous system. The latter is especially the case in "giants" (p. 92). If the disease is only developed in the skull (mostly in the bones of the jaw), then, of course, all hypertrophy of the extremities is wanting. Moreover, the formation of tumours is a characteristic distinct from acromegaly. If the disease is extensive and combined with giant growth, a confusion with acromegaly becomes more easy, as occurred, in fact, in the case of the "giant" Mr. Wilkins (Lamberg). In this case it was to be observed that the colossal hands and feet were in proportion to the excessive size of the body, and a minute consideration showed the existence of tumours of the bones on the one hand, and the absence of the changes of the bones and soft parts associated with acromegaly on the other.

The illness of the brothers Hagner (pp. 7, 11), studied by Erb and Arnold, is best included in this place. Knowing as one does at the present time the changes of the skeleton in acromegaly, it is only necessary to cast a glance on the beautiful illustrations by Arnold of the bones of this case to say with certainty that these bones, studded irregularly with large, warty, stalactiform-like exostoses, do not belong to acromegaly. I do not like to rank them either with the "ostéoarthropathie hypertrophiante" of Marie; inasmuch as the disease began independently in youth without any previous affection of the respiratory, urinary, or other organs, and not only affected the bones, but also the skin and nerves. It is best provisionally to conceive it as a special disease, which preferably should be placed at the side of the before-mentioned diffuse tumour-like exostotic formations. The distinction from acromegaly rests, besides the changes in the bones, on the familiar appearance, the diffuse enlargement of all the extremities, the absence of changes in the soft parts of the face and mucous membrane of the mouth, and the absence of disease of the hypophysis, &c.

As far as the head is concerned, the various forms of cranium progeneum (p. 87) may give rise to confusion with acromegaly. It is important to notice that in this form of skull—the cretinoid excepted—only the under lip hangs down loosely; the upper lip, on the contrary, is not enlarged, nor does it appear reverted and puffy. In addition, there is no enlargement of the nose and tongue. The skeleton of the face of that cranium progeneum which is unassociated with acromegaly is chiefly thin and frail, especially the hard palate, which is little developed, pressed together laterally, narrow and soft. The teeth show a transverse furrow or rudimentary form. Characteristic signs of rickets or of past severe small-pox are not unfrequently to be seen: often we learn by inquiry that the same formation of jaw has been present for more than one generation. The diagnosis may be difficult if an enlargement—*e.g.*, a congenital partial macrosomia—is added to the malformation of the jaw. Most careful observation is then necessary. The case of Gordinier, published under the name of acromegaly, ought certainly to be interpreted as a simple cranium progeneum.

Often in the lymphatic constitution, the soft parts of the face offer an appearance resembling acromegaly: thickening of the nose, swollen lips, and thickened eyelids. If the condition is combined with rickets, as is so frequently the case, the hands are thick and coarse, and kypho-scoliosis may exist. But the resemblance is so superficial that a careful consideration must directly destroy the delusion.

The diseases of the extremities which come under consideration as far as differential diagnosis is concerned are various.

The conditions, collected under the name of partial gigantism or hypertrophy of single sections of the body, are of importance. There is no doubt that very various conditions are to be found under these names. Since, according to the plan of our hand-book, this department, which tradition ascribes to surgery, is treated of in no other place, we must go into it here somewhat more minutely, especially since some very incorrect statements regarding it have become current in the literature of acromegaly.

The frequently-employed name "gigantism" is scarcely applicable, as it is not a question of lengthening, and this expression causes the mind to connect ordinary giant growth with the idea of those other conditions, a connection which only exists in words and not in fact. It might be desirable to apply this term (identical with "gigantosomia") only to the lengthening of the whole body, and in our cases to speak of "partial enlargement" ("partial macrosomia"). A distinction has also to be made between "true" and "false" partial macrosomia. The first depends upon a symmetrical enlargement of bones and soft parts; in the other the enlargement is deceptive, owing to the development of swelling of the soft parts, especially of the adipose tissue. But there is between both these forms all possible transitions, since lipomata, dilatation of the veins and lymphatics, and thickening of the skin resembling elephantiasis are very commonly present in the affected parts or in their neighbourhood.

As to the causes and conditions of the development, or its relation to the central nervous and other systems, hardly anything is known. The anatomical investigations are also very insufficient: Hornstein's case is perhaps the best examined.

Provisionally, it is only possible to arrange the cases according to mere external characteristics, with the consciousness that possibly all sorts of heterogeneous conditions are being classified together.

According to the topographical distribution, it is possible to distinguish enlargement of an extremity or single digits (macrocheiria, macropoda, macrodactyl), unilateral or transverse enlargements. There is no hard and fast line between these forms; the enlargement of an arm is frequently associated with great increase of a breast (Hahn, Wagner); often in so-called unilateral enlargements only the extremities participate, the trunk is quite slightly or not at all changed. The hemihypertrophica facialis must be mentioned here.

According to the present relationships three groups can be distinguished: the congenital, the congenital and progressive, and the acquired partial macrosomia.

In the congenital form Adams was probably the first to describe the condition of affairs; the tissues of the affected part of the body have already shown an increased development before birth, and retain it during extra-uterine life, so that this part of the body during growth increases *pari passu* with the rest of the organism, and the malproportion of the bulk of the body is maintained.

There is a transition from this form to the congenital and progressive enlargement. The morbid increase is often, during the first years of life, less striking; later on it occurs more quickly or continues for a very long time after growth of the body has ceased. But those cases especially deserve the name "congenital and progressive" macrosomia, in which after birth, and in the first years of life, only a small part, as a finger, shows enlargement; later on the rest of the member, hand, lower and upper arm, are hypertrophied as a result of the formation of lipomata and teleangiectasis. Such cases are described by Friedberg, Busch, Wulff, Fischer.

The acquired forms have seldom been mentioned. The assertion is very often made that the partial macrosomia is always congenital. We place together further on the knowledge we at present possess.

The motor function of the limb is only disturbed, when the changes of the bones, or the formation of tumour, give rise to mechanical hindrances. The condition of the sensibility has been very carefully examined in a case by Goldscheider. In some very few congenital cases severe disturbances of sensibility have been found, as total anæsthesia (Higginbotham), reduction of the sense of touch and pain, abolition of the feeling of cold (Fischer). It is very questionable whether these cases are of the same value as the others. Possibly the enlargement is not congenital, notwithstanding the patient's statement, but produced by syringomyelia.

The distinction of congenital partial enlargement from

acromegaly demands, then, only some consideration, when the enlargement affects several parts of the body, and shows a certain symmetry. The fact is first of all to be established that the changes in form are congenital, or have descended from the earliest years. It is then important that they are strictly partial, very frequently affecting only single toes, fingers, &c., but never symmetrically all four extremities in their whole extent. Again, the enlarged parts have often monstrous shapes, partly owing to the enormous increase in length, partly to curvatures (which are caused mechanically post partum), partly to a tumour-like development of the adipose tissue. In addition, the skin often shows diffuse teleangiectasis or circumscribed vascular nævi. Lipomata are frequently present in the affected parts or near them. Prickly exostoses or enchondromata are not unfrequently present on the bones. Finally, other congenital malformations often simultaneously exist, either in the enlarged limb or in others, such as syndactyl, multiple formations in the skin, aplasia of a single section of the skeleton, removal of digits or digital joints, formation of fissures, rotation of the whole extremity, implantation of parts of one fœtus on another (fœtus in fœtu), chorioretinitis areolaris, &c. Naturally the other appearances of acromegaly are absent. There are not a few such cases published in the literature as "acromegaly," in which the diagnosis of a congenital or congenital and progressive hypertrophy may, from the description or illustrations, be safely made. Such cases are: Cénas (fourteen-year-old boy, combined with cranium progeneum), Kanthack, Beaver Rake (ten-year-old boy), Burchardt (eleven-year-old girl, described as "unilateral acromegaly"). In Jacobson's case the child was brought to the hospital under the diagnosis "acromegaly."

The acquired partial enlargements are, as already stated, almost unknown. The subject is one on which little is known; probably this symptom appears in very different diseases.

Several observations have been reported of unilateral hypertrophy; thus an old case by Barilli.

An enlargement of the right half of the body occurred in a woman after confinement between twenty and thirty years of age, which increased still more after a blow on the right leg. The soft parts of the right side were thickened as in elephantiasis, the hair, eyelashes, and teeth fell out. The right arm was an inch longer than the left, the fingers twice as thick. Hypertrophy of the soft parts in the right leg still greater. Death at the forty-seventh year.

Post mortem: The right half of the skull broader than the left, the right half of the jaws increased. The brain on the right side 185, on the left 170 mm. long, on the right 90, on the left 70 mm. broad. The right side of the thorax wider, the ribs thicker, the vessels on the right side dilated and more filled, the subcutaneous tissue on the right side firm.

I had the opportunity of seeing such a case.

On October 2nd, 1896, there came to me into my waiting room a woman, H. of F. in Bohemia, aged 33, sent by Primarius J. Schnitzer. She had had five normal labours. Menses regular. For some years she had often suffered from giddiness and pains in her left arm and shoulder. The left arm ever since became thicker and diminished in strength. The woman looked healthy and strong. The left half of the neck gives the impression of being thickened, the left breast much enlarged, the nipple more prominent. The left arm is considerably larger in circumference, the skin thick, more markedly furrowed than the right, of normal colour. Little distinction in the hands. Size:—

Neck, left half, 17 cm.; right half, 16 cm.
Largest circumference of upper arm, left. 37 cm.; right, 33 cm.
,, ,, forearm, left. 29 cm.; right, 26·5 cm.

No difference in length. Legs quite equal. Slight touches on the left arm badly localised, perception to heat equal on left and right sides, slight hyperalgesia on left arm. Grasp of left hand somewhat weaker than the right, no ataxia. Cranial nerves, bulb of eyes, all other extremities, chest and abdominal organs, also urine, normal.

Schlesinger's observation perhaps also belongs here, which he describes as " partial macrosomia with bulbar symptoms."

A man in his eighteenth year, dyspnoeic and hoarse, six months later enlargement of the right hand. At nineteen years of age patient shows an uniformal increase in size of right hand, unilateral paralysis of the crico-arytenoidei postici, paresis of left half of palate, increased patellar reflexes, kypho-scoliosis. The author thinks there is sclerosis or formation of a tumour in the region of the medulla or cervical part of the cord.

Perhaps here also should be included P. Wagner's case of enlargement of the left arm after a trauma (child), also

Eastes' case of enlargement of the right leg after trauma (child), and finally Mosler's analogous communication.

Lastly also, the very rare cases of acquired unilateral hypertrophy of the face (Lewin's collected cases) belong here.

Acquired partial hypertrophy may, it is conceivable, be more easily confused with acromegaly than the congenital form. In the matter of diagnosis, attention will have to be paid to the asymmetrical appearance of the enlargement and the want of the other typical characteristics of acromegaly. As far as a decision is possible from a short report, the case Ascher represented as "commencing acromegaly" (enlargement of the right thumb and index finger and the left half of the face, pain in the brachial plexus on pressure) appears to belong to this group of diseases.

Much which has been said on the obscure disease of acquired partial macrosomia should apparently be more rightly placed under the heading of neurotic hypertrophy, which is clinically better known, although not nearly sufficiently explained pathogenetically.

In the first place, the enlargement of the extremities in syringomyelia is extremely important; it has been repeatedly confused with acromegaly. We now know, through the works of Lonazel, Karg, Bernhardt, Charcot and Brissaud, Hoffmann, H. Fischer, Marie, Chantemesse, Schlesinger, and others, that thickening of the hands and feet occurs in syringomyelia. The characteristic signs, according to the summarised arrangement of Schlesinger, are: The hands and feet are deformed in syringomyelia, curved, contracted, often single fingers are surprisingly thickened, sometimes only single phalanges enlarged. Muscular atrophies are, in most cases, very striking, seldom entirely concealed by changes in the skin. The skin is often, especially in the palms, enormously thickened; callosities and deep rhagades are present. Very often scars as a result of whitlows. The changes in the skin are not present equally over the whole body. The nails are often only rudimentary, like claws. Some single bones may be thickened to a surprising extent, others affected in a less degree. In addition, not unfrequently changes in the joints occur. The enlargement often only occurs in an upper extremity or unilaterally. Besides, we have the familiar disturbances of sensation in syringomyelia, which are common characteristics of both diseases. The following must be mentioned as mistakes in the literature: The cases of Holschewnikoff (published as "acromegaly"), Bier (also described as "acromegaly," but in a later communication from the same hospital correctly indicated by H. Fischer as syringomyelia), and Peterson (described as "combination of acromegaly with syringomyelia").

There are besides yet many forms of disease to which the term neurotic hypertrophy may aptly be applied.

One of these is the case of lengthening of the fingers and toes described by P. Wagner.

A woman, formerly healthy, was taken ill in her thirty-eigth year, after an abortion, with pains in the hands. She felt as if paralysed, apathetic, and a considerable lengthening of the fingers and toes occurred. The skin and soft parts of these sections of the body became thin and atrophied.

P. Wagner has discussed the difference from acromegaly. Possibly to this disease belongs Sarbo's case published as acromegaly (enormous lengthening of the fingers), which has already been several times (*e.g.*, by Pershing) separated from acromegaly. Perhaps also Rendu's case should be inserted here (very long fingers), which he conceived as "forme fruste" of acromegaly.

The case described by Gasne and Souques as "hypertrophy of the hands and feet in an hysterical person" appears to be a special form of disease, if it is not one of commencing acromegaly.

Neurotic hypertrophy is also present in those complex symptoms which are described after Weir Mitchell as erythromelalgia. Here also considerable enlargement of the hands and feet occurs. Of importance for a differential diagnosis are the vasomotor disturbances in this syndrome, the absence of participation of the bones of the extremities, which may easily be discovered by the Röntgen rays (Marinesco), in addition disturbances of sensibility, in many cases symptoms of such a kind as point to underlying disease of the central nervous system, and lastly want of the changes in the head associated with acromegaly. There are also cases which occupy an intermediate position between the pachydermia mentioned at p. 104 and erythromelalgia, and which, like these latter diseases, require stricter investigation and classification, e.g., the case of G. Meyer.

Doubtless confusion with acromegaly has been occasioned by the "ostéoarthropathie hypertrophiante" of Marie or "secondary ostitis hyperplastica" (Arnold) cf. p. 11. The disease is now clinically well known. The essential differences from acromegaly are: the hands in osteoarthropathy are quite deformed, paw-like, true "caricatures." This is due to the considerable swelling of the terminal joints of the fingers (like a drum-stick); the metacarpal region is little, the wrists considerably enlarged. The nails in acromegaly are rather small, in secondary ostitis, on the contrary, large and broad, markedly convex, similar in shape to a "watch glass" or "parrot's beak," often cracked. The long bones of the forearm are much thickened at the joints. The face shows no changes in the soft parts, no lengthening of the lower jaw. There is, as a rule, a primary disease demonstrable: tuberculosis, bronchiectasis, empyema, cystitis and pyelonephritis, dysentery, sarcoma or carcinoma of the lungs, sarcoma of the parotid. In certain circumstances a connection between this disease and neurotic hypertrophy exists (Möbius, Teleky). Of the cases which have been published as "acromegaly," but which most probably belong to this disease, must be named, besides those mentioned at p. 11, the observations of Waldo, Gerhardt, Redmond, Renner, Gessler, Field.

There are still a number of cases remaining which are certainly accompanied by an enlargement of the extremities, but at the same time almost always with a deformity of such a kind that the distinction from acromegaly can offer no difficulties. We will enumerate them shortly.

Under the name of adiposis dolorosa Dercum has described an exuberance of growth of the adipose tissue of the true skin, which develops with pain symmetrically on the trunk and extremities, the latter becoming enormously enlarged. The great enlargement of the shoulder, upper arm, and gluteal region is characteristic.

Hersmann describes a disease as "progressive enlargement of hands," which consists in the formation of lumpy and knotty tumours in the regions of the tendons and in the subcutaneous tissue of the back of the hands, which causes a claw-like enlargement of the hands.

Claw-like, shapeless hands often also arise from chronic inflammation of the tendinous sheaths on the palmar surfaces.

In very rare cases multiple enchondromata are developed at the time of growth, symmetrically in both hands and feet, which make thick, shapeless, strangely curved and deformed appendages of the fingers and toes. The case of Annandale's, copied by all surgical manuals, is familiar: Whittaker gives splendid illustrations of a lately observed case.

Claw-like hands as a result of swelling of the soft parts occur in elephantiasis neuromatodes (creeping neuroma).

Elephantiasis, in the narrower sense, cannot certainly be mistaken for acromegaly; it is as a rule limited to the legs, and leads to so tremendous a disfigurement that its recognition causes no difficulty.

The same applies to the various forms of secondary elephantiasis (pseudo-elephantiasis) arising from local abscess formations (abscess of the skin, syphilis, caries, &c.).

Mistake also with œdema in pregnancy has occurred (Jorge).

It is desirable to look over once more in a systematic survey the conditions and diseases, which come into consideration, in the differential diagnosis of acromegaly. They are as follows:—

A. Diseases which, through partial appearances, may be mistaken for acromegaly.
 1. Tumour of the brain.
 2. Morbus Basedowii.
 3. Diabetes.
 4. Myopathies.
 5. Diseases of the reproductive organs.
 6. Acroparasthesia.
 7. Rheumatism.
 8. Traumatic neurosis and simulation of such.

B. Diseases and conditions, with changes in the external shape of the body, resembling acromegaly.
 I. Anomalies of growth.
  1. Gigantism.
  2. Congenital partial macrosomia.
  3. Congenital and progressive partial macrosomia.

II. General disturbances of growth (dystrophies).
   1. Myxœdema.
   2. Cretinism.
   3. Morbus Basedowii.
   4. Lymphatic constitution with rickets.
III. Diseases of the nervous system.
   1. Syringomyelia.
   2. Erythromelalgia.
   3. Various "neurotic hypertrophies."
   4. Acquired unilateral macrosomia.
IV. Diseases of the bones and joints.
   1. Diffuse hyperostosis (megalocephaly).
   2. Multiple tumour-like hyperostosis (leontiasis ossea).
   3. Osteitis deformans Paget.
   4. Arthritis deformans.
   5. Cranium progeneum.
   6. Secondary hyperplastic ostitis (hypertrophic osteo-arthropathy).
   7. Multiple symmetrical enchondromata.
V. Diseases of the sheaths of tendons.
   1. "Progressive enlargement of hands," Hersmann.
   2. Chronic inflammation of the palmar sheaths of tendons.
VI. Diseases of the skin.
   1. Peculiar form of pachydermia after continued reduction of vascular tonus.
   2. Adiposis dolorosa Dercum.
   3. Elephantiasis neuromatodes.
   4. Elephantiasis Arabum.
   5. Elephantiasis after chronic inflammations.
   6. Œdema.

IX.—TREATMENT.

In the treatment of acromegaly care has, above all, to be taken to hinder as much as possible the decay of strength which threatens those attacked. The physician who satisfies himself of this most important indication already does much for the patient.

The style of living and the nutrition must therefore be carefully regulated; in bulimia suitable choice of food should be attended to. Glycosuria may disappear by timely withdrawal of carbohydrates (Marie), at the same time attention must, of course, be paid to the calorific requirements. Sometimes the symptoms of diabetes require the continued attention of the physician, as far as the food is concerned. Constipation should be removed in suitable cases by an ample supply of vegetable food, which may have the most favourable effect on the general state of health.

Since the pathogeny of the disease is not established, we are unacquainted with any prophylactic measures, or effectual etiological treatment. If one works on the assumption that the disease of the hypophysis is the cause of the trouble, then the bold idea of Horsley is justifiable, to extirpate the tumour of the hypophysis as any other new growth. Caton and Paul have attempted it with an unfortunate result.

Schultze has, on account of the relationship of the hypophysis to the thyroid, and the fact that goitre has diminished in size from the use of iodine, given iodide of potash to his patients, but without any obvious result. However, Kojewnikoff has seen improvement from its employment (and various revulsives). So also Kovács' patient, illustrated in Fig. 2 in this book, became again capable of work after the use of potassium iodide, the eye symptoms diminished, the pains in the head vanished.

Possibly mercury has a direct influence on many non-syphilitic tumours of the hypophysis; at least the considerable remission of the eye symptoms, which Schlesinger obtained in a case by means of inunction, speaks for such an assumption.

It would be right to prescribe iodide of potash or sodium in 2-3 g. doses per diem, and at least make one trial with a series of from twenty to thirty accurate inunctions or subcutaneous injections of corrosive sublimate.

Very much is at present talked about the treatment with pituitary and thyroid preparations. Some have seen improvement (Thyroid—Putnam, Parsons, Bramwell, Comini, Mossé, Solis Cohen, Sears, Bruns; Hypophysis—Franke, Fränkel, Mendel, Dodgson; Pituitary and Thyroid—Dinkel). Others have found no sort of effect (Thyroid—Osler; Pituitary—Marinesco and Rolleston). Others, again, report bad effects from thyroid (Benson, Franke, Hagelstamm). When we consider that remissions in acromegaly are very frequent, the reports of improvement will be regarded somewhat sceptically. On the other hand, it is to be remembered that the use of thyroid extract may accelerate the decline of strength, and cause permanent glycosuria. As a matter of fact several impartial observers report noticeable increase of muscular weakness, notwithstanding that the patient seemed to himself to be improving—*e.g.*, Bruns. I have seen the same in one case, and must therefore recommend, in the employment of this by no means harmless remedy, the greatest prudence and most careful attention. By no means ought it to be prescribed to a subject of acromegaly on the first consultation. The more harmless pituitary tabloids should rather be prescribed.

Denti and Campbell have seen favourable results from arsenic.

The symptomatic treatment is of importance. First may come in the question of palliative treatment by trephining, if the symptoms due to the cranial tumour demand it. Lynn-Thomas has in his case obtained a brilliant result by the removal of a parallelogram from the roof of the skull.

The pain in the head may be very beneficially influenced by the modern anti-neuralgics (antipyrin, antifebrin, exalgine, phenacetin, &c., &c.), as in cranial tumours generally. Certainly reckless doses, even to cyanosis, are often necessary, but, with regard to the cardiac changes, dangerous. The parasthesiæ of the arms and legs are improved by faradisation. It is necessary to pay careful attention to the removal of constipation. Attempt may be made to control the very troublesome perspiration by agaricin, atropin, or tellurates.

The comfort and hope obtained from systematic massage, hydrotherapy, electricity, and climato-therapeutics, which make many a chronic invalid bear up, ought not to be withheld from the patient.

BIBLIOGRAPHY.

LITERATURE OF ACROMEGALY.*

Adler, J.: Some Remarks on Acromegalia, New York County Med. Association, 1888, Oct. 15. The Med. News, 1888, Vol. LVIII., p. 492.
— Ein Fall von Akromegalie, New Yorker Med. Monatsschr., Mai, 1889.
Alibert: Précis théorique et pratique des maladies de la peau. Paris 1822, III., p. 317.
Appleyard: A Case of Acromegaly, Lancet. 1892. I., p. 746.
Arnold, J.: (1) Akromegalie, Pachyakrie oder Ostitis? Ein anatomischer Bericht über den Fall Haguer I., Ziegler's Beiträge zur pathologischen Anatomie und zur allgemeinen Pathologie, X., 1891, S. 1.
— (2) Weitere Beiträge zur Akromegaliefrage, Virchow's Archiv für pathologische Anatomie, etc., CXXXV., S. 1.
Asmus, E.: Ein neuer Fall von Akromegalie mit temporaler Hemianopsie; Graefe's Archiv für Ophthalmologie, 1893, Bd. XXXIX., 2, S. 229.
Balzer: Présentation d'un cas d'acromégalie, Bull. et mém. de la Soc. méd. des Hôpit. de Paris, 1892. p. 237.
Barclay, J., and Wm. St. C. Symmers: A Case of Acromegaly, The Brit. Med. Journ., 1892. II., p. 1227.
Bard: Un cas d'acromégalie, Lyon médical, 1892.
Barrs, A. G.: A Case of Acromegaly, Lancet, 1892, I., p. 683.
Bassi: Acromegalia cefalica, R. Accademia Lucitrese, 1896.
Bayer, A.: Tagblatt der 66 Versammlung deutscher Naturforscher und Aerzte, Wien, 1894, S. 309.
Becker: Wanderversammlung der Südwestdeutschen Neurologen und Irrenärzte, 2 Juni, 1894; Neurologisches Centralbl., 1894, S. 505.
Benson, A. H.: A Case of Acromegaly with Ocular Complications, The Brit. Med. Journ., 1895, II., p. 949.
Berkley, H. J.: A Case of Acromegaly in a Negress, Johns Hopkins Hosp. Bull., 1891, 16.
Bertrand, L. E.: Observation d'acromégalie, Revue de médecine, 1895, II., p. 118.
Bettencourt-Rodriquez: Un caso d'acromegalia, Journ. Soc. méd. de Lisbonne, 1890.
Bignami, A.: Un osservazione di acromegalia, Boll. della Società Lancisiana degli ospedali di Roma, Anno X., Fasc. III., p 259.
Bollinger, O.: Aerztl. Verein, München, 8 Februar, 1893; Münch. med. Wochenschr., 1893, S. 391.
Boltz, R.: (1) Ein Fall von Akromegalie mit bitemporaler Hemianopsie, Deutsche med. Wochenschr., 1892, S. 635.
— (2) Ein Fall von Akromegalie mit Sectionsbefund, Jahrbuch der Hamburgischen Staatskrankenanstalten, III., Hamburg und Leipzig. 1894, S. 250.
Bonardi, E.: Un caso di Acromegalia, Archivio ital. di clinica medica (Rivista clinica), 1893, XXXII., p. 353.
Booth, A.: New York Neurol. Society, Journ. of Nerv. and Mental Disease, 1893, p. 587.

* The doubtful cases are included under other headings, with the exception of some historical ones, which are worthy of notice.

Bourneville and F. Regnault : Acromégalie, Bull. de la Soc. anatomique de Paris, 1896, p. 537.
Boyce, R., and C. F. Beadles : A Farther Contribution to the Study of the Pathology of the Hypophysis Cerebi, The Journ. of Pathology and Bacteriology, I., 1893, p. 359.
Bramwell, B. : Acromegaly in a Giantess. The Brit. Med. Journ., 1894, I., p. 21.
— Acromegaly, Atlas of the Clinic. Medicine. Edinburgh. 1892. II., p. 104.
Brigidi : Studii anatomo-patologici sopra un uomo divenuto stranamente deforme, Società Medico-fisica fiorentina. Aug., 1877.
Brissaud, E. : Un cas d'acromégalie. Revue Neurologique. 1893, I. p. 55.
Brissaud, E., and H. Meige : Gigantisme et acromégalie, Journ. de Médecine et de Chirurgie, 1895, p 49.
Broadbent, W. H. : A Case of Acromegaly, The Lancet. 1896. I., p. 846.
Broca, A. : Un squelette d'acromégalie, Archives générales de médecine. 1888, p. 656.
Brown, F. Gordon : Acromegaly. The Brit. Med. Journ., 1892. I., p. 862.
Brown, S. : Acromegaly, Chicago Clinic. Review. 1893-94, p. 575.
Brown Séquard, E. : Soc. de Biol., 1893. 29 Mai ; La Progrès méd., I., 1893.
Bruns, L. : Ein Fall von Akromegalie und seine Behandlung mit Schilddrüsenextract, Neurol. Centralbl., 1895, S. 1173.
— Schilddrüsentherapie, Encyklopädische. Jahrbücher, VI., Wien und Leipzig, 1896.
Bruzzi : Un caso di acromegalia. Gaz. degli ospedali, Milano. 1892. p. 866.
Bullard, E. L. : Acromegaly. The Med. and Surg. Reporter, 1895, April 27. (Referred to in The Journ. of Nerv. and Ment. Disease, Vol XX., p. 743).
Bury : Acromegaly, Manchester Patholog. Society, 1891, May 13 : The Brit. Med. Journ., 1891, I., p. 1179.
Buzzer : Ein Fall von Akromegalie, Aerztliche Rundschau, München, 1892. S. 500.
Campbell, H. : (1) Two Cases of Acromegaly, Transact. of the Clin. Society, London, 1890, p. 257.
— (2) Clinic. Society of London, 1894, Nov. 9. The Brit. Med. Journ., 1894 II., p 1110.
— (3) Acromegaly. North-West London Clinic. Society. 1894, Dec. 12. The Brit. Med. Journ., 1895, I., p. 81.
— (4) Clinic. Society of London, 1896, April 24, The Brit. Med. Journ., 1896, I, p. 1091.
Carr-White : Acromegaly, Edinburgh Med. Journ., 1889.
Caton. R., and F. T. Paul : Notes on a Case of Acromegaly Treated by Operation, The Brit. Med. Journ., 1893, II., p. 1421.
Cepeda, G. : Rev. Balear. de Cienc. med. Palma de Mallorca. 1892, VIII., 7. (Referred to by Collins.)
Chalk, W. O. : Partial Dislocation of the Lower Jaw from Enlarged Tongue, Transact. of the Patholog. Society, London, 1857, p. 305.
Chauffard : Acromégalie fruste avec macroglossie, Soc. méd. des Hôpit., 12 Juillet, 1895 ; La Semaine médicale, 1895, p. 305.
Chéron, P. : De l'acromégalie, L'Union médicale, 1891, I., p. 25.
Church, A., and W. Hessert : Acromegaly, with the Clinical Report of a Case. Medical Record, 1893, Vol. XLIII., p. 545.
Claus, A. ; Un cas d'acromégalie, Annal. et Bull. de la Soc. de Médecine de Gand, 1890. p. 281.
Claus, A., and O. Van der Stricht : Contribut. à l'étude anatomique et clinique de l'acromégalie, ibid., 1893, p. 71.
Collins. J. : (1) Acromegaly, Journ. of Nerv. and Ment. Disease. 1892. p. 917. and 1893, p. 48 and p. 129.
— (2) American Neurol. Association, 1892, June ; ibid., 1892, p. 739.

Comini, E.: Contributo allo studio clinico ed anatomo-patologico dell'acromegalia, Archivio per le scienze mediche, XX., 1895, p. 435.
Crego, F. S.: Med. Society of the State of New York, 1894, Feb. 7, Medical Record, 1894, Vol. XLV., p. 215.
Cunningham, D. J.: A large Sub-Arachnoidal Cyst involving the greater part of the Parietal Lobe of the Brain, The Journ. of Anatomy and Physiology, Vol. XIII., 1879, p. 503.
Dallemagne: Trois cas d'acromégalie avec autopsie, Archives de Médecine expérimentale et d'anatomie pathol., VII., 1895, p. 589.
Dana, Ch.: (1) On Acromegaly and Gigantism, with Unilateral Facial Hypertrophy, Journ. of Nerv. and Ment. Disease, 1893, p. 725.
— (2) Anatomical Report on the Brain of a Bolivian Indian, with a Study of Cortical Thickness, ibid., 1894. p. 141.
Day, F. L.: A Case of Acromegalia, The Boston Med. and Surg. Journ., 1893, I., p. 391.
Debierre: Un cas d'acromégalie avec symptomes tabétiques et hémianopsie, Revue générale d'ophthalmologie, Paris, 1891.
Denti, F.: (1) Breve commun. di un caso d'acromegalia con emianiopsia tempor. bilat., Atti della Soc. med. lomb., Milano, 1891, 41.
— (2) L'acromegalia nei sui rapporti coll'organo di viso, Annali d'ottalm, XXV., 1896, fasc. 6.
Dercum, F. X.: Two Cases of Acromegaly with Remarks on the Pathology of the Affection. The American Journ. of Med. Sciences, 1893, Vol. CV., p. 263.
Dethlefsen: Akromegali, Med. aarssk. Kjöbenhavn, 1892.
Dinke, H. H.: Acromegaly, Medical Record, 1896.
Dodgson, R. W.: Harveian Society of London, 1896, March 5, The Lancet, 1896, I., p. 772.
Doebbelin, C.; Pseudo-Acromegalie and Acromegalie, Dissertation, Königsberg, 1895.
Dreschfeld, J.: A Case of Acromegaly. The Brit. Med. Journ., 1894, I., p. 4.
Du Catal: Acromégalie. Le Progrès médical, 1891, II., pp. 295 and 585.
Duchesneau, G.: Contribution à l'étude anatomique et clinique de l'acromégalie et en particulier d'une forme amyotrophique de cette maladie, Thèse de Lyon, 1891.
Dulles, Ch. W.: A Case of Acromegaly, The Med. News, 1892, Vol. LXI., p. 515.
Dyson: A Case of Acromegaly, Quarterl. Med. Journ., Sheffield, 1893, II., p. 109.
Ellinwood: San Francisco West Lancet. 1893, p. 159 (Referred to by Souza-Leite).
Erb, W.: (1) Ueber Akromegalie (krankhaften Riesenwuchs), Deutsches Archiv für klin. Medicin, Bd. XLII., S. 295.
— (2) Ueber Akromegalie, Tageblatt der 62 Versammlung deutscher Naturforscher und Aerzte, Heidelberg, 1890, S. 395.
— (3) Naturhistorisch-medicinischer Verein in Heildelberg, 5 Juni, 1894; Münchner med. Wochenschr., 1894, S. 514.
Eulenberg, A.: Akromegalie, Realencyklopädie der gesammten Heilkunde, Herausgegeben von Eulenberg, I., Wien und Leipzig. 1894, S. 333.
Farge: Observation d'acromégalie, Le Progrès médical, 1889, II., p. 1.
Fazio, F.: Sopra un caso di acromegalia, La Riforma Medica, 1896, II., p. 399.
Flemming, P.: A Case of Acromegaly, Transact. of the Clin. Soc., London, 1890, Vol. XXII., p. 253.
Fournier, J. B. C.: Acromégalie et troubles cardio-vasculaires, Thèse de Paris, 1896.
Fraenkel, A.: Verein für innere Medicin in Berlin, 5 April, 1897, Münchner med. Wochenschr., 1897, S. 401.
Franke: Ein Fall von Akromegalie mit temporaler Hemianopsie, Klin. Monatsblätter für Augenheilkunde, XXXIV., 1896, S. 259.

Franke: Aerztlicher Verein zu Hamburg, 5 November, 1895. Therapeutische Monatshefte, 1396. S. 35.
Fratnich: Ein Fall von Akromegalie, Allgemeine Wiener med. Zeitung, 1892, S. 405.
— Weitere Mittheilungen über einen Fall von Akromegalie, Allgemeine Wiener med. Zeitung, 1893, S. 451.
Freund. W. A.: Ueber Akromegalie. Volkmann's Sammlung klin. Vorträge, 1889, Nr. 329.
Friedreich: Hyperostose des gesammten Skelettes, Virchow's Archiv, XLIII., 1868, S. 83.
Fritsche and E. Klebs: Ein Beitrag zur Pathologie des Riesenwuchses, Klinische und pathologisch-anatomische Untersuchungen. Leipzig. 1884.
Gajkiewicz: Drugi przypadek akromegali. Gaz. lekarsk., Warszawe, 1893, II., p. 786.
Gaston and Brouardel: Un cas d'acromégalie vu à travers par les rayons de Röntgen. La Presse médicale, 1896. Nr. 61.
Gause, A.: Ein Fall von Akromegalie, Deutsche med. Wochenschr., 1892, S. 891.
Gauthier. G.: Un cas d'acromégalie, Le Progrès médical, 1890. I., p. 400.
— Un cas d'acromégalie, autopsie, Le Progrès médical, 1892, I., p. 4.
Godlee: A Case of Acromegaly, Transact. of the Clin. Soc. London, 1883.
Goldsmith. G. P.: Bedford Med. Society, 1896, March 26, The Lancet, 1896, I., p. 993.
Gorjatscheff: Chirurgitscheska lepopisj, Moskau, 1892.
Graham, E.: Two Cases of Acromegaly, The Med. News, 1890, II., p. 390.
Griffiths Hill: Brit. Med. Association, 1895, The Brit. Med. Journ., 1395, II., p. 950.
Grocco: Di un caso d'acromegalia. Riv. General. ital. Pisa. 1891, p. 17.
Gubian: Bull. du dispensaire de Lyon, 1891, Nr. 16.
Guinon, G.: L'acromégalie, Gaz. des Hôpit., 1889. p. 1161.
— Un cas d'acromégalie à début récent, Nouvelle Iconographie de la Salpêtrière, III., 1890, p. 160.
Gulliver: Transact. of the Pathol. Soc. of London. Vol. XXXVII., p. 511.
Hadden, W. B., and Ch. Ballance: A Case of Hypertrophy of the Subcutaneous Tissues of the Face, Hands, and Feet, Transact. of the Clin. Soc. of London. Vol. XVIII., 1885.
— A Case of Acromegaly, ibid., Vol. XXI., 1888.
Hagelstamm, J.: Ett Fall af Acromegali, Finska läkaresällskapets handlingar, Bd. XXXVIII., Juli, 1896, p. 623.
Hansemann, D.: Ueber Akromegalie. Berliner klin. Wochenschr., 1897, S. 417.
Hare, H. A.: A Case of Acromegaly, Journ. of Nerv. and Ment. Disease, 1892, p. 250.
— A Case of Acromegaly, The Med. News, 1892, Vol. LX., p. 237.
Harris, H. F.: A Case of Acromegaly, The Med. News. 1892, Vol. LXI., p. 520.
Haskovec, L.: Note sur l'acromégalie, maladie de P. Marie, Revue de Médecine, 1893, p. 237.
— Ein Fall von Akromegalie, Wiener klin. Rundschau, 1895, S. 257.
Henrot, H.: Notes de Clinique médicale, Reims, 1877.
— Notes de Clinique médicale, des lésions anatomiques et de la nature du myxœdème, Reims, 1882.
Hertel, E.: Beziehungen der Akromegalie zu Augenerkrankungen, Graefe's Archiv für Ophthalmologie, Bd. XLI., 1895. I., S. 187.
Herzog, B.: Neurologische casuistische Mittheilungen, II., Ein Fall von Akromegalie, Deutsche med. Wochenschr., 1894, S. 316.
Higier: Tagblatt der 66 Versammlung deutscher Naturforscher und Aerzte. Wien, 1894, S. 309.

Hitschmann, R.: Akromegalie mit eigenthümlichem Augenbefunde, Wiener med. Club, 1897, 16 Juni. Wiener klin. Wochenschr., 1897. S. 659.
Holsti, H.: Ein Fall von Akromegalie, Zeitschr. für klin. Medicin, XX., S. 298.
Huchard, H.: Anatomie pathologique, lésions et troubles cardio-vasculaires de l'acromégalie, Journ. des Praticiens, 1395, II., p. 249.
Hutchinson: Three Cases of Acromegaly, Archives of Surgery, London, IV., 1890, p. 296.
Hutchinson-Woods: A Case of Acromegaly in a giantess, The American Journ. of Med. Sciences, Vol. CX., 1895, II., p. 190.
Jorge, R.: Contributions à l'étude de l'acromégalie, Archivio di psichitria, scienze penali ed antropologia criminale, 1894, Vol. XV., p. 412.
Kaliudero, N.: Sur l'acromégalie, La Roumanie médicale, 1894, p. 65.
Keen, W. W.: Excision of the Supraorbital, Supratrochlear, Auriculo-temporal, Auricularis magnus, Occipitalis Major and Minor Nerves in a Case of Acromegaly. Internat. Clinics, Philadelphia, 1893, p. 191.
Kerr: Bradford Medico-Chirurgical Society, The Lancet, 1893, II., p. 1256.
Klebs, E.: Die allgemeine Pathologie, II., Störungen des Baues und der Zusammensetzung, Jena, 1897. S. 559.
Kleikamp: Ein Fall von Akromegalie, Dissertation, Greifswald, 1893.
Kojewnikoff: Sluch acromegal. Med. Obszr., Moskau, 1893.
Lancereaux: Traité d'anatomie pathologique, Tom. III., 1. Paris, 1838, p. 29.
— Des trophonévroses des extrémités ou acrotrophonévroses, La Semaine médicale, 1895, p. 61.
Langer, C.: Wachsthum des menschlichen Skelettes mit Bezug auf den Riesen, Denkschriften der Kaiserl. Akademie der Wissenschaften in Wien, Mathemat-naturw. Classe, Bd. XXXI., 1872. S. 1.
Lavielle: Un Nouveaux cas d'acromégalie, Journ. de Médecine de Bordeaux, 1894, p. 1.
Lévi, L.: De l'acromégalie. Archives générales de Médecine, 1893, II., p. 579.
Lichtheim: Verein für wissenschaftliche Heilkunde in Königsberg, 6 Februar, 1893, Deutsche med. Wochenschr., 1893. S. 876.
Linsmayer, L.: Ein Fall von Akromegalie, Wiener klin. Wochenschr., 1894, S. 294.
Litthauer, M.: Ein Fall von Akromegalie, Deutsche med. Wochenschr., 1891, S. 1232.
Little: Brit. Med. Association, 1895. The Brit. Med. Journ., 1895, II., p. 950.
Lombroso, C.: Caso singulare di macrosomia, Giorn ital. delle malattie venere, 1868.
— The same translated by Fraenkel, Merkwürdiger Fall von Allgemeiner Hypertrophie (Macrosomie) oder scheinbarer Elephantiasis, Virchow's Archiv, XLVI., S. 253.
Long: Lehigh Valley Mag., 1891, No. 3. (Referred to in The American Journ. of Med. Sciences, 1892, Vol. CIII., p. 323).
Lovegrove: Nottingham Medico-Chirurg. Society, 1891, November 18, The Lancet. 1892, I., p. 91.
Luzet: De l'acromégalie, Archives générales de Méd., 1891, I.
Mackie Whyte, J.: A Case of Acromegaly. The Lancet, 1893, I., p. 642.
Magendie, M.: Leçons sur les fonctions et les maladies du système nerveux, Paris, 1839, p. 34.
Magnus-Levy: Verein für innere Medicin zu Berlin, 5 April, 1897, Münchner med. Wochenschr., 1897, S. 400.
Marie, P.: (1) Sur deux cas d'acromégalie, hypertrophie singulière non congénitale des extrémités supérieures, inférieures et céphalique, Revue de Médecine, 1885, p. 293.
— (2) L'acromégalie, Nouvelle Iconographie de la Salp'trière, I., 1888, and II., 1889.

Marie, P : (3) L'acromégalie, Etude clinique, Le Progrès médical, 1889.
— (4) Acromegaly, Brain, XII., p. 59.
— (5) De l'ostéo-arthropathie hypertrophiante pneumique, Revue de Médecine, 1890. p. 1.
— (6) Sur deux types de déformation des mains dans l'acromégalie, Bull. et mémoires de la Soc. des Hôpit. de Paris. 1896, 1 Mai.
— (7) Leçons de clinique médicale. Paris, 1895, p. 51.
Marie, P., et G. Marinesco : Sur l'anatomie pathologique de l'acromégalie, Archives de Médecine expérimentale et d'anatomie pathologique, 1891, p. 539.
Marina. A. : Osteo arthropathia ipertrofica pneumica parziale ed acromegalia. Riforma Medica, Napoli, 1893, Nr. 63.
Marinesco, G. : (1) Un cas d'acromégalie avec hémianopsie bitemporale et diabète sucré, C. R. de la Soc. de Biologie, 1895. p. 176.
— (2) Trois cas d'acromégalie traités par des tablettes de corps pituitaire, Soc. médicale des Hôpitaux, La Semaine médicale. 1895, p. 484.
— (3) Étude des mains d'acromégaliques au moyen des rayons de Röntgen, C. R. de la Soc. de Biologie, 1895, p. 615.
Massalongo : Sull' acromegalia. Riforma medica, Napoli, 1891, VIII., p. 74.
Mendel, E.: Ein Fall von Akromegalie, Berliner klin. Wochenschr., 1895, S. 1120.
Mével, P. : Contribution à l'étude des troubles oculaires dans l'acromégalie, Thèse de Paris, 1894.
Meyer : Congrès français d'ophthalmologie, 1891, Le Progrès méd., 1891, p. 413.
— Brit. Med. Association, 1895, The Brit. Med. Journ., 1895, II., p. 949.
Meyer, F. : Ein Fall von Akromegalie, Kieler Dissertation, Hamburg, 1894.
Middleton, G. S. : A Marked Case of Acromegaly with Joint Affections, Glasgow Journ., 1894, June 6.
Minkowski, O. : Ueber einen Fall von Akromegalie, Berliner klin. Wochenschr., 1887, S. 371.
Möbius : Berichte der medicinischen Gesellschaft zu Leipzig, Schmidt's Jahrb., CCXXXV., 1892, S. 22.
Moritz : Tagblatt der 66 Versammlung deutscher Naturforscher und Aerzte, Wien, 1894, S. 309.
Mosler : Ueber die Sogenannte Acromegalie (Pachyacrie), Festschr., Radolf Virchow gewidmet zur Vollendung seines 70 Lebensjahres, Bd. II., Berlin 1891, S. 101.
— Demonstration eines Falles von Akromegalie, Deutsche med. Wochenschr., 1891, S. 793.
Mossé, A. : Note sur deux cas d'acromégalie, C. R. de la Soc. de Biologie, 1895, p. 686.
Mossé, A., et Daunic : Lésions anatomiques dans un cas d'acromégalie, Bull. de la Soc. anatomique, Paris, 1895. p. 633.
Motais : Un cas remarquable d'exophthalmos, Annales d'oculistique, 1885.
— Congrès français d'ophthalmologie, 1891, Le Progrès méd., 1891, p. 413.
Moyer, H. N. : A Case of Acromegaly, Internat. Med. Magazine, 1894, Vol. III., p. 34.
Murray, G. R.: (1) Clinical Remarks on Cases of Acromegaly and Osteoarthropathy, The Brit. Med. Journ., 1895, I., p. 296.
— (2) Acromegaly with Goitre and Exophthalmic Goitre, Edinburgh Med. Journ., 1897, I., p. 170.
Naunyn : Akromegalie, Unterelsässischer Aerzteverein in Strassburg, 28 April, 1894, Vereinsbeilage der Deutschen med. Wochenschr., 1896, S. 87.
Noël : Sur l'accroissement considérable des os dans une personne adulte. Journal de méd., 1779, p. 225 (Translated in Sammlung Auserlesener Abhandlungen für praktische Aerzte, XV., S. 541.

Nonne: Akromegalie mit Symptomen einer nicht systematisch-tabischen Hinterstrangsaffection, Aerztlicher Verein in Hamburg, 5 Februar, 1895, Deutsche med. Wochenschrift, Vereinsbeilage. 1896, S. 14.

Occhiuzzi: Dell'acromegalia, Incurab., Napoli, 1892.

O'Connor, J. T.: New Americ. Journ. Homœop., New York, 1888, p. 345. (Referred to by Collins.)

Olechnosicz, W.: Gaz. lekarska, 1894, Nr. 5.

Orsi, F.: Caso di acromegalia, Gaz. med. lomb., Milano, 1892, 21.

Osborne, O. T.: A Case of Acromegalia, The Amer. Journ. of Med. Sciences, 1892. Vol. CIII., p. 627.

Osler, W.: Principles and Practice of Medicine, 1895, p. 1047.

Packard, F. A.: A Case of Acromegaly, and Illustrations of two allied conditions, Amer. Journ. of Med. Sciences, 1892, Vol. CIII., p. 657.

Paget, St.: Clinic. Soc. of London, The Lancet, 1891, I., p. 253.

Panas: Brit. Med. Association, 1895, The Brit. Med. Journ., 1895, II., p. 950.

Park-Roswell: A Case of Acromegaly, Presenting also Floating Bodies in a Cyst connecting with the Knee Joint, Internat. Medical Magazine, Vol. IV., July, 1895, p. 431.

Parsons, R. L.: Report of a Case of Acromegaly, New York Neurol. Soc., The Journ. of Nerv. and Ment. Disease, 1894, p. 120.

— Report of a Case of Acromegaly, ibid., p. 717.

Pécha Ire; Un cas d'acromégalie, Revue de méd., 1890, p. 175.

Pel, P. R.: Ein Fall von Akromegalie in Folge von Schreck, Berliner klin. Wochenschr., 1891, S. 53.

Pershing, H. T.: A Case of Acromegaly, with Remarks on the Pathology of the Disease, The Journ. of Nerv. and Ment. Disease, 1894, p. 693.

Philipps, Sidney: A Case of Acromegaly, Med. Soc. of London, The Lancet, 1892, I., p. 473.

Pick, A.: Ueber das Zusammenvorkommen von Akromegalie und Geistesstörung, Prager med. Wochenschr., 1896, S. 521.

Pineles, F.: Wiener Med. Club. 12 Juni, 1895, Neurol. Centralbl., 1895, S. 702.

— Ueber die Beziehungen der Akromegalie zum Diabetes Mellitus. Jahrbuch der Wiener k. k. Krankenanstalten, Jahrgang, 1895, Wien, 1897.

Pinel-Maisonneuve: Acromégalie, Soc. Méd. des Hôpit., 20 Mars, 1891, L'Union médicale, 1891, I., p. 457.

Putnam: Cases of Myxœdema and Acromegalia Treated with Benefit by Sheep's Thyroids. The American Journ. of Med. Sciences, 1893, p. 125.

Rampoldi, V.: Caso di acromegalia, Gaz. med. lomb., Milano, 1894, p. 101.

Ransom, W. B.: Notes of Two Cases of Acromegaly, The Brit. Med. Journ., 1895, I., p. 1259.

Rauzier: De l'acromégalie, Montpellier médical, 1893, II. Suppl., p. 623.

Raymond, F., and A. Sonques: Epilepsie partielle dans l'acromégalie, Congrès français des médecins alienistes et neurologistes, 3 août, 1896.

Recklinghausen, F. v.: Ueber die Akromegalie, Virchow's Archiv, CXIX., S. 30.

Regnault, F.: Sur un squelette d'acromégalie trouvé au musée de Clamart, Bull. de la Soc. Anatomique de Paris, 1896, p. 862.

Reimar, M.: Ein Fall von Amenorrhoe bei Akromegalie, Dissertation, Halle a. S., 1893.

Renaut's Ansichten in der Thèse von Duchesnau, p. 155 ff.

Rieder: Aerztl. Verein, München, 8 Feb., 1893, Münchener med. Wochenschr., 1893, S. 391.

Riegel: Akromegalie, Med. Gesellschaft zu Giessen, 24 Jan., 1893, Deutsche med. Wochenschr., 1883, S. 776.

Rolleston, H. D.: Case of Acromegaly, The Brit. Med. Journ., 1890, II., p. 957.

Rolleston, H. D.: A Case of Acromegaly treated by Pituitary Extract. Remarks, The Lancet, 1896, I., p. 1137.
Roxburgh, R. and A. J. Collis: Notes on a Case of Acromegaly, The Brit. Med. Journ., 1896, II., p. 63.
Ruttle, R.: A Case of Acromegaly, The Brit. Med. Journ., 1891 I., p. 697.
Sacchi: L'acromegalia, Rivista veneta di scienze med., Nov., 1889.
Salbey, M.: Ein Fall von sogenannter Akromegalie mit Diabetes mellitus. Dissertation. Erlangen. 1889.
Saucerotte: Mélanges de Chirurgie. I.. Paris, 1801.
Schapnikow: Med. Oboszr., Moskau, 1889.
Schiff, A.: Hypophysis und Thyreoidea in ihrer Einwirkung auf den Menschlichen Stoffwechsel. Wiener klin. Wochenschr., 1897, S. 277.
Schlesinger, H.: (1) 66, Versammlung deutscher Naturforscher und Aerzte, 1894, Neurol. Centralbl., 1894, S. 741. (In the "Tagblatt," epitomised).
— (2) Wiener Med. Club, 23 Jänner, 1895. Wiener Med. Presse, 1895, S. 186.
— (3) Zur Kenntniss der Akromegalie und der Akromegalieähnlichen Zustände (partielle Makrosomie), Wiener klin. Wochenschr., 1897, p. 445.
Schultze, F.: Ueber Akromegalie. Deutsche med. Wochenschr., 1889, S. 981.
— Die Hand der Akromegalischen in der Beleuchtung durch die Röntgenstrahlen, Niederrheinische Gesellschaft für Natur- und Heilkunde in Bonn. 10 Februar, 1896; Vereinsbeilage der Deutschen med. Wochenschr., 1896, S. 151.
Schwarz, J.: Ein Fall von Trophoneurose, Mittheilungen des Vereines der Aerzte in Niederösterreich, 1882, S. 55.
Schwartz: Petersburger med. Wochenschr., 1890, S. 315.
Schwoner, J.: Ueber hereditäre Akromegalie. Zeitschr. f. klin. Med., XXXII. Suppl., S. 202.
Sears, G. G.: A Case of Acromegaly Treated with Thyroid Extract. The Boston Med. and Surgical Journ., 1896, Vol. CXXXV., p. 16.
Siach, Allan S.: A Case of Acromegaly. The Lancet, 1893, II., p. 339.
Sigurini, G., and A. Caporiaceo: Un caso di Acromegalia, La Riforma Medica, 1895, II., p. 376.
Silcock: A Case of Acromegaly, Transact. of the Clin. Soc., London. 1890, p. 256.
— Acromegaly, Brit. Med. Association, The Brit. Med. Journ., 1890, I., p. 19.
Silva: Caso di Acromegalia con atrophia dei testicoli. Societá Medico-Chirurgica di Pavia, La Riforma Medica, 1895, II., p. 532.
Snell: Brit. Med. Association, 1895, The Brit. Med. Journ., 1895, II., p. 950.
Solis-Cohen S.: A Case of Acromegaly, The Med. News, 1892, p. 518.
— Philadelphia County Med. Society, The Med. News, 1894, Vol. LXIV.
Sollier: Sur une affection singulière du système nerveux characterisée essentiellement par de l'hypertrophie des extrémités des membres, des phénomènes paralytiques et des troubles variés de la sensibilité. France médicale, 1889, No. 68-69.
Somers, G. B.: A Case of Acromegaly, Occidental Med. Times, 1891. October, p. 537. (Referred to by Collins).
Souques, A.: "Acromégalie" in: Traité de Médecine par Charcot-Bouchard-Brissaud. Paris, 1894, VI, p. 965.
Souques: Macceus, Polichinelle et l'acromégalie, Nouvelle Iconographie de la Salpêtrière, IX., 1896, p. 375.
Souza-Leite, J. D.: De l'acromégalie. Maladie de P. Marie, Thèse de Paris, 1890.
Spillmann, H., and P. Hanshalter: Un cas d'acromégalie, Revue de méd., 1891, p. 775.
Squance, Coke T.: Notes on a Post-Mortem Examination of a Case of Acromegaly, The Brit. Med. Journ., 1893, II, p. 903.
Stembo, L.: Akromegalie und Akromikrie, St. Petersburger med. Wochenschrift, 1891, S. 397.

Sternberg, M.: Beiträge zur Kenntniss der Akromegalie, Zeitschr. für klin. Medicin, 1894, XXVII., S. 85.
Strümpell. A.: Münchner med. Wochenschr.. 1839, S. 571.
— Wanderversammlung der südwestdeutschen Neurologen und Irrenärzte, 1894, Neurol. Centralbl., 1894, S. 503.
Strzeminski: Troubles oculaires dans l'acromégalie, Archives d'ophthalmologie, Février, 1897.
Surmont. H.: Acromégalie à début précoce, Nouvelle Iconographie de la Salpêtrière, III., 1890, p. 147.
Tamburini, A.: Contributo alla patogenesi della acromegalia, Rivista sperimentale di freniatria, XX., p. 559.
— Congresso internazionale di Roma, La Riforma Medica. 1894, II., p. 392.
— Beitrag zur Pathogenese der Akromegalie. Centralbl. für Nervenheilkunde und Psychiatrie, 1394, S. 625.
Tanzi. E.: Dne casi di acromegalia, Archivio Italiano di Clinica Medica (Rivista Clinica), XXX., 1891, p. 533.
Taruffi. C.: Scheletro con prosopoectasia e tredici vertebre dorsali, Memorie della Reale Accad. delle Scienze dell'Instituto di Bologna. Ser. III., t X., 1879, p. 63.
Thayer, W. S.: Hypertrophic Pulmonary Osteoarthropathy and Acromegaly, New York Med. Journal. 1896, January 11.
Thomas: Note sur un cas d'acromégalie, Revue méd. de la Suisse Romande, 20 Juin, 1893, No. 6.
Thomas, Lynn J.: A Case of Acromegaly with Wernicke's Differential Symptom, The Brit. Med. Journ., 1895, I., p. 1193.
— Satisfactory Palliative Treatment of a Case of Acromegaly, The Brit. Med. Journ., 1896, II., p 909.
Thomson, H. A.: Acromegaly with description of a skeleton, The Journal of Anatomy and Physiology, XXIV., 1890, p. 475.
Thorne, Thorne L.: Harveian Society of London, 1896, March 5, The Lancet, 1896, I., p. 771.
Tichomiroff: Étude anatomo-pathologique d'un cas d'acromégalie, Revue Neurologique, 1893, p. 310.
Tresilian: A Case of Myxœdema, The Brit. Med. Journ., 1888, I., pp. 642 and 886.
Tschisch, V.: Ein Fall von Akromegalie, Wissenschaftliche Verhandlungen der Dorpater Medicinischen Facultät, St. Petersburger med. Wochenschrift, 1891, S. 443.
Uhthoff, W.: Ein Beitrag zu den Sehstörungen bei Zwergwuchs und Riesenwuchs. resp. Akromegalie, Berliner klin. Wochenschr., 1897, S. 461.
Unverricht: Akromegalie und Trauma. Münchner med. Wochenschr., 1895, S. 302.
Valat: Une acromégalique. Gaz. des Hôpit., 1893, p 1209.
Verga. A: Caso singolare di prosopectasia, Rendiconti del Reale Instito di Lombardo. Milano, 1864, III.
Verstraeten, C.: L'acromégalie, Revue de Médecine, 1839, p. 377.
Virchow, R.: Ein Fall und ein Skelett von Akromegalie, Berliner klin. Wochenschr., 1839, S. 81.
— Veränderungen des Skelettes durch Akromegalie, Berliner med. Gesellschaft, 4 December, 1895: Berliner klin. Wochenschr., 1895, S. 1102.
Wadsworth: A Case of Myxœdema with Atrophy of the Optic Nerves, Boston Med. and Surgic. Journ., 1835, Jan. 1.
Wieri. Joannis: Medicarum observationum rararum liber unus, Basileae per Joannem Oporinum, MDLXVII.
Wilks: Transact. of the Clinical Society of London, 1838, April 13.
Wolf, K.: Ein Beitrag zur pathologischen Anatomie der Hypophysis. Ziegler's Beiträge zur pathologischen Anatomie und zur allgemeinen Pathologie, XIII., S. 629.

DEVELOPMENT AND ANATOMY OF THE HYPOPHYSIS.

Andriezen, L.: The Morphology, Origin and Evolution of Function of the Pituitary Body and its Relation to the Central Nervous System, The Brit. Med. Journ.. 1894, I., p. 54.

Balfour: Handbuch der vergleichenden Embryologie, II., Jena, 1881, S. 339.

Berkley, H. J.: The finer Anatomy of the Infundibular Region of the Cerebrum, including the Pituitary Gland, Brain, Vol. XVII.. p. 515.

Boyce, R., and Beadles, C. F.: A Further Contribution to the Study of the Pathology of the Hypophysis Cerebri, The Journ. of Pathology and Bacteriology. I.. 1893, p. 359.

Bickford, E. E.: The Hypophysis of Calamoichthys calabaricus (Smith), Anatomischer Anzeiger, 1895, S. 465.

Burdach, C. F.: Vom Baue und Leben des Gehirns, Leipzig, 1819-1826, II., S. 107, and III , S. 169.

Chiarugi, G.: Di un organo epiteliali situato al dinanzi della ipofisi in embrioni di Torpedo oceellata, Rendic. d. R. Accad. Med. Fis. Fiorentina, 1895.

Claus, A., and O. Van der Stricht: Contribution à l'étude anatomique et clinique d'acromégalie, Annales et Bulletin de la Soc. de Méd. de Gand, 1893, p. 71.

Davidoff, M. v.: Ueber den Canalis neurentericus anterior bei den Ascidien, Anatomischer Anzeiger, 1893, S. 301.

Dohrn, A.: Studien zur Urgeschichte des Wirbelkörpers. Mittheilungen der Zoologischen Station zu Neapel, III., S 252.

Dostojewski: Ueber den Bau des Vorderlappens des Hirnanhanges, Archiv für mikroskopische Anatomie, Bd. XXVI., S. 592.

Edinger, G : Untersuchungen über die vergleichende Anatomie des Gehirnes, 2. Des Zwischenhirn, 1. Theil. Das Zwischenhirn der Selachier und der Amphibien. Abhandlungen der Senckenberg'schen naturf. Gesellschaft, 1892.

Flesch. M.: Tageblatt der 57 Versammlung deutscher Naturforscher und Aerzte zu Magdeburg, 1884, S. 195.

Gaupp, E : Die Anlage der Hypophysis bei Sauriern, Archiv für mikroskopische Anatomie, Bd. XLII., S. 569.

Goette: Entwicklungsgeschichte der Unke, Leipzig, 1875, S. 288 and 314.

Gottsche, C. M.: Vergleichen de Anatomie des Gehirns der Grätenfische, Joh. Müller's Archiv für Anatomie und Physiologie, 1835, S. 433.

His, W.: Zur allgemeinen Morphologie des Gehirns, Archiv für Anatomie und Physiologie Anatomische Abthlg., 1892, S. 346.

Julien, M. Ch.: Étude sur l'hypophyse des Ascidies et sur les organes qui l'avoisinent, Bulletins de l'Académie roy. de Belgique, 1881. p. 895.

Kölliker: Entwicklungsgeschichte des Menschen und der höheren, Thiere, 2, Aufl., S. 529.

Krause, W.: Allgemeine und mikroskopische Anatomie, Hanover, 1876, S. 437.

Kraushaar, R.: Entwicklung der Hypophysis und Epiphysis bei Nagethieren, Zeitschr. für wissenschaftliche Zoologie, Bd. XLI., 1885, S. 79.

Kupffer, C. v.: Die Deutung des Hirnanhanges, Sitzungsberichte der Gesellschaft für Morphologie und Physiologie in München, 1894, S. 59.

Landzert, Th.: Ueber den Canalis cranio-pharyngeus am Schädel des Neugeborenen, Petersburger med. Zeitschr., XIV., 1868, S. 133.

Langen, Th.: De hypophysi cerebri disquisitiones microscopicae. Dissertatio, Bonn, 1864.

Lothringer, S.: Untersuchungen an der Hypophyse einiger Säugethiere und des Menschen, Archiv für mikroskopische Anatomie, Bd. XXVIII., S. 257.

Luschka, H.: Der Hirnanhang und die Steissdrüse des Menschen, Berlin, 1860.

Manasse, P.: Ueber die Beziehungen der Nebennieren zu den Venen und dem venösen Kreislauf, Virchow's Archiv für patholog. Anatomie, &c., Bd. CXXXV., S. 263.

Mihalkovics, V. v.: Wirbelseite und Hirnanhang, Archiv für mikroskop. Anatomie, Bd. XI., S. 389.

Müller, W.: Ueber den Bau der Chorda dorsalis und des Processus infundibuli cerebri, Jenaische Zeitschr. für Naturwissenschaft. Bd. VI., 1871, S. 354.

Peremeschko: Ueber den Bau des Hirnanhanges, Virchow's Archiv für patholog. Anatomie, etc., Bd. XXXVIII., S. 329.

Pisenti. G., and G. Viola: Beitrag zur normalen und pathologischen Histologie der Hypophysis und bezüglich der Verhältnisse zwischen Hirnanhang und Schilddrüse, Centralbl. für die med. Wissenschaften, 1890, S. 450.

Rathke, H.: Ueber die Entstehung der Glandula pituitaria, Muller's Archiv für Anatomie, Physiologie, etc., 1838, S. 482.

Retzius, G.: Die Neuroglia des Gehirns beim Menschen und bei Säugethieren, III., Die Neuroglia der Neuro-Hypophyse der Säugethiere, Biolog. Untersuchungen, Bd. VI., 1894, S. 21.

— Ueber ein dem Saccus vasculosus entsprechendes Gebilde im Gehirn des Menschen und anderer Säugethiere, Biolog. Untersuchungen, Bd. VII., 1895, S. 1.

— Ueber die Hypophysis von Myxine, ibid., S. 19.

Rogowitsch, N.: Die Veränderungen der Hypophyse nach Entfernung der Schilddrüse, Zeigler's Beiträge zur patholog. Anatomie u. z. allg. Pathol., Bd. IV., 1889. S. 453.

Romiti, G.: Sopra il canale cranio-faringeo nell'uomo e sopra la tasca ipofisaria o tasca di Rathke. Atti della Società Toscana di Scienze Naturali, Vol. VII., fasc. 1.

Saint-Rémy. G.: Contribution à l'histologie de l'hypophyse, Archives de Biologie, T. XII., 1892, p. 425.

— Sur la signification morphologique de la poche de Seessel, C. R. de la Soc. de Biologie, Paris, 1895, p. 755.

Schönemann, A.: Hypophysis und Thyreoidea, Virchow's Archiv für Patholog. Anatomie, etc., Bd. CXXIX., S. 310.

Schultze, O.: Grundriss der Entwicklungsgeschichte des Menschen und der Säugethiere, Leipzig, 1897.

Valenti, G.: Sulla origine e sul significato dell'ipofisi, Atti Accad. Med. Chir. Perugia, 1894, Vol. VII., fasc. 4.

— Sullo sviluppo dell'ipofisi, Anatom. Anzeiger, 1895, S. 538.

Van Beneden and Julin: Le système nerveux des Ascidies adultes et ses rapports avec celui des larves modèles, Bull. de l'Académie roy. de Belgique, 1884.

Virchow, R.: Untersuchungen über die Entwicklung des Schädelgrundes, Berlin, 1857.

Zander: Ueber die Lage und die Dimensionen des Chiasma opticum und ihre Bedeutung für die Diagnose der Hypophysistumoren, Verein für wissenschaftliche Heilkunde in Königsberg, Deutsche med. Wochenschr., 1897; Vereinsbeilage, S. 13.

PHYSIOLOGY OF THE HYPOPHYSIS.

Biedl: Sitzung der Gesellsch. der Aerzte in Wien, 19 Februar, 1897; Wiener klin. Wochenschr., 1897, S. 196.

Ecker, A.: Handwörterbuch der Physiologie, IV., Braunschweig, 1854, S. 107, et seq.

Fliess, W.: Die Beziehungen zwischen Nase und weiblichen Geschlechtsorganen, Leipzig und Wien, 1897, S. 239.

Gley, M.: Recherches sur la fonction de la glande thyroide, Archives de Physiologie norm. et pathol., 1892, p. 311.
Hofmeister: Zur Physiologie der Schilddrüse Fortschritt der Medicin, 1892, S. 81.
Horsley, V.: Abstract of Brown Lectures, III., Functional Nervous Disorders due to Loss of Thyroid Gland and Pituitary Body, The Lancet. 1886, I., p. 5.
Kreidl, A.: Sitzung der Gesellsch. der Aerzte in Wien, 19 Februar, 1897, Wiener klin. Wochenschr., 1897. S. 193.
Marinesco, G.: De la destruction de la glande pituitaire, C. R. de la. Soc. de Biol., 1892, p. 509.
Olliver, G., and E. A. Schäfer: On the Physiological Action of Extracts of Pituitary Body and certain other Glandular Organs, The Journ. of Physiology, Vol. XVIII., 1895, p. 277.
Rogowitsch, N.: Die Veränderungen der Hypophyse nach Entfernung der Schilddrüse, Ziegler's Beiträge zur pathol. Anatomie und zur allgemeinen Pathologie, IV., 1889, S. 453.
Schiff, A.: Hypophysis und Thyreoidea in ihrer Einwirkung auf den menschlichen Stoffwechsel, Wiener klin. Wochenschr., 1897, S. 277.
Schnitzler, J., and K. Ewald: Ueber das Vorkommen des Thyreojodins im menschlichen Körper. I., Jod in der Hypophyse, Wiener klin. Wochenschr., 1897, S. 657.
Stieda, H.: Ueber das Verhalten der Hypophyse des Kaninchens nach Entfernung der Schilddrüse, Ziegler's Beiträge zur pathol. Anatomie und zur allgemeinen Pathologie, VII., 1890, S. 535.
Vassale, G., and E. Sacchi: Sulla distruzione della ghiandola pituitaria, Rivista sperimentale di freniatria e di medicina legale, XVIII., 1892.
—Ulteriore esperienze sulla ghiandola pituitaria, ibid., XX., 1894, p. 83.

CRANIUM PROGENEUM.

Carabelli, G., v. Lunkaszprie: Anatomie des Mundes, Wien, 1842.
Davis, J. B.: On Synostotic Crania among Aboriginal Races of Man, Natuurkundige Verhandelingen van de hollandsche Maatschappij der Wetenschappen te Haarlem, Bd. XXI., 1864, p. 85.
Gordinier, H. C.: Two Cases of Acromegaly, The Med. News, 1895, II., Vol. LXVII, p. 262.
Iszlai, J.: Illustrirte Skizzen zu Carabelli's, "Mordax prossus" und dessen Verhältniss zur sogenannten Prognathia ethnologica und Meyer's Crania progenaea, Transactions of the Internat. Med. Congress, VII. Session, London, 1881. Vol. III., p. 555.
Meyer, L.: Ueber Crania progenaea, Archiv für Psychiatrie und Nervenkrankheiten, I., S. 96.
—Grammatikalische Berichtigung zu den Crania progenaea, ibid., S. 336.
Sternberg, M.: Beiträge zur Kenntniss der Akromegalie, Zeitschr. für klin. Med., Bd. XXVII., S. 120.
Sternfeld, A.: Ueber Bissarten und Bissanomalien, München, 1888.
—"Anomalien der Zähne" in J. Scheff, Handbuch der Zahnheilkunde, I, Wien, 1891, S. 439.
Thon, O.: Von den verschiedenen Abweichungen in der Bildung der menschlichen Kiefer und Zähne, Inaugural-Dissertation, Würzburg, 1841.
Virchow, R.: Die Camburger Dolichocephalen. Correspondenzbl. der deutschen Gesellschaft für Anthropologie, Ethnologie und Urgeschichte, Jahrgang, 1876, München, 1876, S. 77.
Zuckerkandl, E.: Zur Morphologie des Gesichtsschädels, Stuttgart, 1877, S. 91.

ACROMEGALY, MYXŒDEMA, AND CRETINISM.

Boyce, R., and C. F. Beadles: Enlargement of the Hypophysis Cerebri in Myxœdema, with Remarks upon Hypertrophy of the Hypophysis Associated with changes in the Thyroid Body, The Journ of Pathology and Bacteriology, Vol. I., p 223.

— A Further Contribution to the Study of the Pathology of the Hypophysis Cerebri, ibid., p. 359.

Coulon, W. de: Ueber Thyreoidea und Hypophysis der Cretinen, sowie über Thyreoidealreste bei Struma nodosa, Virchow's Archiv f. Patholog Anat., &c., CXLVII., S. 13.

Ewald, C. A.: Erkrankungen der Schilddrüse. Myxödem und Cretinismus. Dieses Handb., Bd. XXIII

Moncorvo: Sur un cas d'acromégalie chez une enfant de 14 mois, compliqué de microcéphalie, Annales de la Policlinique de Rio de Janeiro und Revue mensuelle de maladies d'enfants, 1892, Dec.

—Ein Fall von Acromegalie compliciert mit Mikrocephalie bei einem Kinde von 14 Monaten, Allgemeine Wiener med. Zeitung. Wien. 1895, S. 14.

Schönemann, A.: Hypophysis und Thyreoidea, Virchow's Archiv, CXXIX., S. 310.

Virchow, R.: Ueber den Cretinismus, namentlich in Franken und über pathologische Schädelformen, Gesammelte Abhandlungen zur wissenschaftlichen Medicin, Frankfurt a. M., 1856, S. 891.

—Ueber die Verbreitung des Cretinismus in Unterfranken, ibid., S. 939.

—Zur Entwicklungsgeschichte der Cretinen und der Schädeldifformitäten, ibid., S. 969.

GIGANTISM.

Bollinger, O.: Ueber Zwerg- und Riesenwuchs, Sammlung gemeinverständlicher Vorträge, herausgegeben von R. Virchow und Fr. v. Holtzendorff, Heft 455, Berlin, 1885.

Brissaud, E.: Gigantisme et acromégalie, Soc. méd. des Hôpit., 8 mai, 1896. La Semaine médicale, 1896, p 196.

Brissaud, E., and H. Meige: Gigantisme et acromégalie, Journ. de Medecine et de Chirurgie, T. LXVI., 1895, p. 49.

Buhl, v., Mittheilungen aus dem pathologischen Institute zu München, Stuttgart, 1878, S. 301.

Dana, Ch.: On Acromegaly and Gigantism with Unilateral Facial Hypertrophy, The Journ. of Nerv. and Ment. Disease, 1893, p. 725.

Engel-Reimers, J.: Die athletische Körperform, Jahrbücher der Hamburgischen Staatskrankenanstalten, III., Jahrg., 1891–1892. Hamburg und Leipzig, 1894.

Fuchs, Th.: Hereditäre Lues und Riesenwuchs, Wiener klin. Wochenschr., 1895, S. 668.

Lamberg: Demonstration in der Gesellschaft der Aerzte in Wien, 24 April, 1896, Wiener klin. Wochenschr., 1896, S. 359.

Langer, C.: Wachsthum des menschlichen Skelettes mit Bezug auf den Riesen, Denkschriften der kaiserl. Akademie der Wissenschaften in Wien, Mathemat.-naturw. Classe. Bd. XXXI., 1872, S. 1.

Massolongo, R.: Hyperfunction der Hypophyse, Resenwuchs und Akromegalie, Centralbl. für Nervenheilkunde und Psychiatrie, 1895, S. 281.

Sacchi, E.: Di un caso di gigantismo infantile, Pedomacrosomia, con tumore del testicolo, Rivista sperimentale di freniatria e di medicina legale, XXI., 1895, p. 149.

Sirena, S.: Osservazioni anatomo-patologiche sul cadavre di un gigante, Contributo alla macrosomia e sifilide ereditaria tardiva, La Riforma medica, 1894, II., p. 783.

Sternberg, M.: (1) Beiträge zur Kenntniss der Akromegalie, II., Akromegalie und Riesenwuchs, Zeitschr. für klin. Med., Bd. XXVII., S. 104.
—(2) Sitzung der Gesellschaft der Aerzte in Wien. 24 April, 1896. Wiener klin. Wochenschr., 1896, S. 359.
Swanzy: Brit. Med. Association, 1895, The Brit. Med. Journ., 1895, II., p. 950.
Taruffi, C.: Della macrosomia. Annali universali di medicina, Vol. CCXLVII., CCXLIX., 1879.
—Intorno alla macrosomia, Memorie della Reale Accademia delle Scienze dell'Istituto di Bologna. 29 gennaio. 1888, Ser. IV., Tom. VIII.
Virchow, R.: Riese Winkelmeyer aus Oberösterreich. Zeitschr. für Ethnologie, 1885, S. 469.
Zitterland: De duorom sceletorum praegrandium rationibus, Dissertatio. Berolini, MDCCCXV.

TUMOUR OF THE HYPOPHYSIS WITHOUT ACROMEGALY.

Beadles, C.: Malignant Disease Involving the Hypophysis Cerebi, Pathological Society of London. The Brit. Med. Journ., 1894, II., p. 1430.
Boyce, R., and C. Beadles: A Further Contribution to the Study of the Pathology of the Hypophysis Cerebi, The Journ. of Pathology and Bacteriology, I., p. 359.
Handford: Large Tumour of the Pituitary Body. Increased Knee-jerks, no Acromegaly, no Glycosuria, Brain, 1892.
Levy, A.: Ein Beitrag zur Casuistik der Hypophysentumoren, Heidelberger Dissertation, Berlin. 1890.
Packard, F. A.: A Case of Acromegaly and Illustrations of Two Allied Conditions, Americ. Journ. of Med. Sciences, 1892.
Waddell, W.: Some Clinical Notes on a Case of Tumour of the Pituitary Body, The Lancet, 1893, I., p. 921.
Wilks: Tumour of Pituitary without Acromegaly, Brain, 1892.
Wolf, K.: Ein Beitrag zur pathologischen Anatomie der Hypophysis, Ziegler's Beiträge zur pathologischen Anatomie, Bd. XIII., S. 629.

Older Literature has been collected by W. Rath, Ein Beitrag zur Casuistik der Hypophysis-Tumoren Dissertation, Göttingen, 1888. Besides, there are numerous special works on the Pathological Anatomy of Tumours of the Hypophysis.

PACHYDERMIA OF THE FACE AND EXTREMITIES.

Hoffmann, M.: Bemerkungen zu einem Falle von Akromegalie, Deutsche med. Wochenschrift, 1895, S. 383.
Kaposi, M.: Wiener Dermatologische Gesellschaft, 25 November, 1896, Wiener klin. Wochenschr., 1896, S. 1199.

DIFFUSE HYPEROSTOSIS.

Albers, J. F.: Jenaische Annalen, 1851, II., S. 1.
Baumgarten, F.: La Léontiasis ossea (hyperostose des os de la tête), Thèse de Paris, 1892.
Bojanu: Ueber den ungewöhnlich verdickten Menschenschädel der Darmstädter Sammlung, Froriep's Notizen. XV., 1826, Nr 317.
Daniëls, C. E.: Un cas de Léontiasis ossea (Cranioselerosis), Natuurkundige Verhandelingen van de Hollandsche Maatschapij der Wetenschappen, 3 Verz., Deel IV., 3 Stuk, Haarlem, 1883.
Gaddi, P.: Iperostosi scrofolosa cefalo vertebrale e cefalo-sclerosi rachitica, Modena, 1863.

Gruber, W.: Monographie nes merkwürdigen osteo-sclerotischen Kopfes des anatomisch-physiologischen Museums in Prag. (Abhandlungen der königlich böhmischen Gesellschaft der Wissenschaften, Bd. V.) Beiträge zur Anatomie, Physiologie und Chirurgie. II., Abth., Prag, 1817.
Huschke, E.: Ueber Craniosklerosis rachitica und verdickte Schädel überhaupt, Jena, 1858.
Ilg, J. G.: Einige anatomische Beobachtungen, enthaltend eine Berichtigung der seitherigen Lehre vom Bau der Schnecke des menschlichen Gehörorgans nebst einer anatomischen Beschreibung und Abbildung eines durch ausserordentliche Knochenwucherung sehr merkwürdigen Schädels, Prag, 1821.
Jadelot: Description anatomique d'une tête humaine extraordinaire, Paris, 1799.
Kilian: **Anatomische Untersuchungen über das neunte Gehirnnervenpaar, Pest, 1822, S. 133.**
Malpighi: Opera posthuma, Londini, 1697, p. 49.
Otto: Neue seltene Beobachtungen aus der Anatomie, Physiologie und Pathologie, Berlin. 1824.
Prince, M.: Americ. Neurol. Association, 1895, June 6, The Journ. of Nerv. and Ment. Disease, 1895, p. 504.
Putnam, G. J.: Hyperostosis Cranii (cephalomegaly), with Illustrations, The Journ. of Nerv. and Ment. Disease, 1895, p. 500.
Starr, Allen: Megalo-Cephalic or Leontiasis ossea, The Amer. Journ. of Medic. Sciences, 1894, Vol. CVIII., p. 676.
Vrolik, G.: Specimen anatomico-pathologicum inaugurale de hyperostosi cranii, Dissertatio, Amstelodami, MDCCCXLVIII.

MULTIPLE TUMOUR-LIKE HYPEROSTOSES.

Baumgarten, F.: La léontiasis ossea (hyperostose des os de la tête), Thèse de Paris, 1892.
Virchow, R.: Die krankhaften Geschwülste, Bd. II., Berlin, 1864, S. 22

In addition Surgical Handbooks.

CONGENITAL PARTIAL MACROSOMIA, CONGENITAL AND PROGRESSIVE PARTIAL MACROSOMIA.*

* Only some of the most important works are quoted.

Adams, J.: Pathologic. Soc. of Dublin, 1854, April 8 (Referred to in The Monthly Journ. of Medicine, Edinburgh, Vol. XX., 1855, p. 170.)
— Singular Case of Hypertrophy of the Right Lower Extremity with Superficial Cutaneous Nævus, The Lancet, 1858, II., Aug. 7.
Albert, E.: Fälle von Makrodactylie. Wiener med. Presse, 1872, S. 10.
Baginsky, A.: Berliner medicinische Gesellschaft, 27 Nov., 1895, Berliner klin. Wochenschr., 1895, S. 1079.
Bessel-Hagen. F.: Ueber Knochen- und Gelenksanomalien, insbesonders bei partiellem Riesenwuchs und bei multiplen cartilaginösen Exostosen, Langenbeck's Archiv für klin. Chirurgie, Bd. XLI.
Burchardt: Vorstellung eines Falles von halbseitiger Akromegalie, Gesellschaft der Charité-Aerzte, 27 October, 1892; Berliner klin. Wochenschr., 1893, S. 580.
Busch, W.: Beitrag zur Kenntniss der angeborenen Hypertrophie der Extremitäten, Langenbeck's Archiv für klin. Chirgurie, Bd. VII., 1866, S. 174. (Much literature information.)
Cénas: Sur un cas d'acromégalie probablement congénitale, Loir médical, St. Etienne, 1890. (Referred to by Collins.)
Ewald, A.: Angeborene und fortschreitende Hypertrophie der linken Hand Virchow's Archiv, Bd. LVI., S. 421.

Fischer: Der Riesenwuchs, Deutsche Zeitschr. für Chirurgie, Bd. XII., 1880, S. 1, (Much literature information.)
Friedberg, H.: Riesenwuchs des rechten Beines, Virchow's Archiv, XLVI., 1867, S. 353.
Goldscheider, A.: Bemerkungen über einen Fall von Riesenwuchs, Du Bois-Reymond's Archiv für Physiologie, 1889, S. 154.
Hahn: Schmidt's Jahrbücher, V., 1835, S. 139.
Higginbotham: Petersburger med. Zeitschr., 1863, S. 205. (Referred to by Fischer.)
Hornstein, S.: Ein Fall von halbseitigem Riesenwuchs, Virchow's Archiv, CXXXIII., 1893, S. 440.
Jacobson, D.: Ein seltener Fall von universellem angeborenem fortschreitendem Riesenwuchs, Virchow's Archiv, CXXXIX. 1895, S. 104.
Kantback, A. A.: A Case of Acromegaly, The Brit Med. Journ., 1891, II., p. 188.
Koehler, A.: Angeborener Riesenwuchs des linken Mittelfingers mit Polysarcie der Finger und Hohlhand, Berliner klin. Wochenschr., 1888, Nr. 1.
Lewin, G.: Studien über die bei halbseitigen Atrophien und Hypertrophien, namentlich des Gesichtes vorkommenden Erscheinungen, mit besonderer Berücksichtigung der Pigmentation, Charité-Annalen, 1884, Bd. IX., S. 619. (Much literature information.)
Machenhauer: Fall von angeborenem, particllem Riesenwuchs mit Berücksichtigung der Aetiologie desselben und verwandter Wachsthumsabnormitäten, Centralbl. für innere Medicin, 1896, Nr. 43.
Morton, T. S.: Two Cases of Congenital Hypertrophy of the Fingers, The Medical News, 1894, Vol. LXIV., p. 294.
Osler, W.: Case of Congenital and Progressive Hypertrophy of the Right Upper Limb, The Journ. of Anatomy and Physiology, Vol. XIV., 1879, p. 18.
Rake, Beaven: A Case of Acromegaly, The Brit. Med. Journ., 1893, I., p. 518.
Shoemaker, G. E.: Congenital Hypertrophy of the Foot, The Medical News, 1894, Vol. LXIV., p. 296.
True, H., et Marmejan: Des hypertrophie du corps latérales totales ou particlles, Montpellier médical, 1888. 16 mars.
Wagner: Hypertrophie der rechten Brust und der rechten oberen Extremität, besonders der Hand und der Finger, Med Jahrbücher der k. k. österr. Staaten, Wein, 1839, Bd. XIX., S. 378.
Wagner, P.: Ueber angeborenen und erworbenen Riesenwuchs, Berichte der med. Gesellschaft zu Leipzig, 14 Juni, 1887, Schmidt's Jahrb., CCXVI., S. 191.
— Zur Casuistik des angeborenen und erworbenen Riesenwuchses, Deutsche Zeitschr. für Chirurgie, Bd. XXVI., 1887, S. 281.
Wittelshöfer, R.: Ueber angeborenen Riesenwuchs der oberen und unteren Extremitäten, Deutsches Archiv für klin. Chirurgie, Bd. XXIV., 1879, S. 57.
Wulff, F.: Ueber Makrodactylie, Petersburger med. Zeitschr., Bd. I., 1861, S. 280.

ACQUIRED PARTIAL MACROSOMIA.

Ascher: Berliner Gesellschaft für Psychiatrie und Nervenkrankheit, 21 Mai, 1894, Neurol Centralbl., 1894, S. 429.
Barilli, G.: Historia cuiusdam discriminis inter accrementum partis dextrae et sinistrae corporis in muliere quadam, quae gravi etiam Elephantiasi laborabat. Novi commentarii Instituti Bononiensis, Tomus VII., 1814, p. 63.
Eastes: Pathological Society of London, Medical Times and Gazette, 1867, p. 22.
Mosler: Ueber die sogenannte Akromegalie (Pachyacrie), Festschr. Rud. Virchow gewidmet zur Vollendung seines 70. Lebensjahres, Bd. II., Berlin, 1891, S. 143.

Schlesinger. H.: Zur Kenntniss der Akromegalie und der akromegalieähnlichen Zustände (partielle Makrosomie), Wiener klin. Wochenschr., 1897, S. 445.

Wagner, P.: Zur Casuistik des angeborenen und erworbenen Riesenwuchses, Deutsche Zeitschr. für Chirurgie, Bd. XXVI., 1887, S. 281.

SYRINGOMYELIA *

* Only some of the more important works are quoted.

Bernhardt, M.: Ueber die sogenannte " Morvan'sche Krankheit," Deutsche med. Wochenschrift. 1891, S. 285.

Bier: Ein Fall von Akromegalie, Mittheil. aus der chirurg. Klinik in Kiel, 1888.

Chantemesse, M.: Sur un cas de syringomyélie à forme acromégalique, Le Progrès méd., 1895, I., p. 273.

Charcot, J. M., und E. Brissaud: Sur un cas de syringomyélie observé en 1875 et 1890. Le Progrès méd., 1891, p. 73.

Fischer. H.: Beitrag zur Casuistik der Akromegalie und Syringomyelie, Dissertation, Kiel, 1891.

Hoffmann: Zur Lehre von der Syringomyelie, Deutsche Zeitschr. für Nervenheilkunde, III., S. 51.

Holschewnikoff: Ein Fall von Syringomyelie und eigenthümlicher Degeneration der peripheren Nerven, verbunden mit trophischen Störungen (Akromegalie), Virchow's Archiv für patholog. Anatomie, etc., CXIX., S. 10.

Karg: Zwei Fälle von ausgedehnten neurotischen Knochen- und Gelenkserkrankungen, Arch für klin. Chirurgie, XLI., 1891, S. 101.

Lonazel: Contribution à l'étude de la maladie de Morvan, Thèse de Paris, 1890.

Marie, P.: Un cas de syringomyélie à forme pseudo-acromégalique, Bull. et Mémoires de la Soc. méd. des Hôpit., Paris, 6 avril, 1894.

Peterson, F.: A Case of Acromegaly combined with Syringomyelia, The Medical Record, 1893, Vol. XLIV., p. 391.

Schlesinger. H: Die Syringomyelie, Leipzig und Wien, 1895.

— Zur Kenntniss der Akromegalie und der akromegalieähnlichen Zustände (partielle Makrosomie), Wiener klin. Wochenschr., 1897, S. 445.

VARIOUS FORMS OF NEUROTIC HYPERTROPHY.

Gasne, G., und Souques A.: Un cas d'hypertrophie des pieds et des mains avec troubles vasomoteurs des extrémités chez un hystérique, Nouvelle Iconographie de la Salpêtrière, 1892.

Rendu: Soc. méd. des Hôpit. de Paris, 12 juillet, 1895, La Semaine méd. 1895, p. 305.

Sarbó, A: Az akromégaliarol, Orvosi Hetilap, 1892, No. 12—13.

Wagner. P.: Zur Casuistik des angeborenen und erworbenen Riesenwuchses, Deutsche Zeitschr. für Chirurgie, XXVI., 1887, S. 281.

ERYTHROMELALGIA.

Lewin, G., und Benda, Th.: Ueber Erythromelalgie, Berliner klin, Wochenschr., 1894, S. 53. (Much literature information.)

Meyer, G.: Elephantiasisartige Anschwellung beider Unterschenkel nebst eigenartigen vasomotorischen Störungen an Händen und Füssen, Deutsche med. Wochenschr., 1894, S. 519.

HYPERTROPHIC OSTEOARTHROPATHY.*

* Only the works quoted in the text are cited.

Bamberger, E. v.: Sitzung der k. k. Gesellschaft der Aerzte in Wien, 8 März, 1889, Wiener klin. Wochenschr., 1889, p. 225.
— Ueber Knochenveränderungen bei chronischen Lungen- und Herzkrankheiten, Zeitschrift für klin. Med., XVIII., S. 193.
Elliot, G. F.: Multiple Sarcoma Associated with Osteitis deformans, The Lancet 1888, I., p. 170.
Field, F. A.: Acromegaly and Hypertrophic Pulmonary Osteoarthropathy, The Brit. Med. Journ., 1893, II., p. 14.
Fraentzel: Ueber Akromegalie, Deutsche med. Wochenschr., 1888, S. 651.
Gerhardt, C.: Ein Fall von Akromegalie, Berliner klin. Wochenschfr , 1890, S. 1183.
Gessler, H.: Ueber Akromegalie, Med. Correspondenzblatt des Württemberger, ärztl. Landesvereines, 1893, 6 Juni.
Godlee, Rickman J.: Clinical Lectures on Bone and Joint Changes in Connection with Thoracic Disease, The Brit. Med. Journ., 1896, II., p. 57.
Gourand: Un cas d'acromégalie, Bull. de la Soc. méd. des Hôpit., Paris, 21 août, 1889.
Marie, P.: De l'ostéo-arthropathie hypertrophiante pneumique, Revue de méd., 1890, p. 1.
Recklinghausen, F. v.: Naturw. med. Verein in Strassburg, 12 Juni, 1896.
Redmond: Acromegaly, Roy. Acad. of Medicine of Ireland, 1890, Nov. 21. The Brit. Med. Journ., 1890, II., p. 1481.
Saundby, R.: A Case of Acromegaly, Illustrated Med. News, 1889.
Teleky, L.: Beiträge zur Lehre von der "Ostéoarthropathie hypertrophiante pneumique," Wiener klin. Wochenschr., 1897, S. 143. (Much literature information.)
Waldo: Case of Acromegaly, Bristol Medico-chirurgical Society, The Brit. Med. Journ., 1890, I., p. 301.

VARIOUS ENLARGEMENTS OF THE EXTREMITIES RESEMBLING ACROMEGALY.

Dercum, F. X.: Three Cases of a hitherto Unclassified Affection, Resembling in its Grosser Aspects Obesity but associated with Special Nervous Symptoms— Adiposis dolorosa, The Amer. Journ. of the Med. Sciences, 1892, CIV., p. 521.
Hersmann, C. F.: A Case of Progressive Enlargement of the Hands, Internat. Medical Magazine. Vol. III , 1894, p. 602.
Whittaker, J. T.: A Case of Multiple Osteo-Enchondroma, Internat. Medical Magazine, Vol. III , 1894, p. 1.

The following references to cases of Acromegaly have appeared since Dr. Sternberg's monograph was published:—

Banks, L.: A Case of Acromegaly, Lancet. 1897, I., p. 27.
Dalton, N.: Pathological Society of London, Lancet, 1897, I., p. 1113.
Furnivall, P.: Pathological Society of London, Brit. Med. Journ., 1897, II., p. 1337.
Rolleston, H. D.: Pathological Society of London, Brit. Med. Journ., 1897, II., p. 1337.

D'Esterre, J. N.: Notes on a case of Acromegaly, Brit. Med. Journ., 1897, II., p. 1630.
Hunter, W.: Pathological Society of London, Lancet, 1898, I., p. 789.
Fraser, D., and Napier, A.: Glasgow Pathological and Clinical Society, Brit. Med. Journ., 1898, I., p. 889.
Kauffmann: Midland Medical Society, Brit. Med. Journ., 1898, I., p. 950.
Thompson, W. J.: Midland Medical Society, Brit. Med. Journ., 1898, I., p. 950.
McCausland: Royal Academy of Medicine in Ire'and, Brit. Med. Journ., 1898, I., p. 951.
Bewley, H. T.: Royal Academy of Medicine in Ireland, Brit. Med. Journ., 1898, I., p. 954.
Matignon: La Médecine Moderne Nov. 6th, 1898 (quoted in Brit. Med. Journ., 1898, I., p. 49, Supplement.)
Neal, J. B., and Jackson Smyth. E.: A Case of Acromegaly, Lancet, 1898, II., p. 193.
Shattock, S. G.: Pathological Society of London, Brit. Med. Journ., Vol. II., p. 1253.
Cyon: Progrès Méd., Nov. 26th, 1898 (quoted in Brit. Med. Journ., 1898, II., p. 96, supplement).

(Translator).

THE

FORTY-FIRST ANNUAL REPORT

OF THE

NEW SYDENHAM SOCIETY

WITH

*BALANCE SHEET FOR 1898, LIST OF OFFICERS FOR 1899-1900,
AND LIST OF PUBLISHED WORKS.*

AGENT AND DEPÔT FOR THE PUBLICATIONS,
H. K. LEWIS, 136, GOWER STREET, LONDON.

OFFICERS FOR 1899–1900.

President.
HENRY POWER, Esq., M.B.

Vice-Presidents.

THEODORE D. ACLAND, M.D.
THOMAS BARLOW, M.D.
R. L. BOWLES, M.D.
T. LAUDER BRUNTON, M.D., F.R.S.
Sir W. H. BROADBENT, Bart., M.D.
W. WATSON CHEYNE, Esq., F.R.S.
W. S. CHURCH, M.D., Pres. R.C.P.
*J. WARD COUSINS, M.D. (Southsea).
JULIUS DRESCHFELD, M.D. (Manchester).
Sir W. TENNANT GAIRDNER, M.D. (Glasgow).
G. E. HERMAN, M.D.
W. ALLAN JAMIESON, M.D. (Edinburgh).
P. W. LATHAM, M.D. (Cambridge).
Lord LISTER, P.R.S.
STEPHEN MACKENZIE, M.D.
Sir RICHARD DOUGLAS-POWELL, Bart., M.D.
R. SAUNDBY, M.D. (Birmingham).

Council.

*JAMES BARR, M.D. (Liverpool).
BYROM BRAMWELL, M.D. (Edin.).
H. RADCLIFFE CROCKER, M.D.
W. CLEMENT DANIEL, M.D. (Epsom).
*CLEMENT DUKES, M.D. (Rugby).
THOMAS EASTES, M.D. (Folkestone).
T. R. FRASER, M.D. (Edinburgh).
JAMIESON B. HURRY, M.D. (Reading).
T. VINCENT JACKSON, Esq. (Wolverhampton).
W. WARD LEADAM, M.D.
D. J. LEECH, M.D. (Manchester).
BEVAN LEWIS, M.D. (Wakefield).
*STEWART LOCKIE, M.D. (Carlisle).
DONALD MACALISTER, M.D. (Cambridge).
FREDERICK MANSER (Tunbridge Wells).
JOHN W. MOORE, M.D. (Dublin).
HUBERT M. MURRAY, M.D.
*WILLIAM NEWMAN, M.D. (Stamford).
*GEORGE OLIVER, M.D.
VIVIAN POORE, M.D.
J. J. PRINGLE, M.B.
R. J. PYE-SMITH, Esq. (Sheffield).
*GUTHRIE RANKIN, M.D. (Warwick).
*EDMUND W. ROUGHTON, M.D.
G. H. SAVAGE, M.D.
*ALFRED W. SHEEN, M.D. (Cardiff).
E. MARKHAM SKERRITT, M.D. (Bristol).
GILBART SMITH, M.D.
R. SHINGLETON SMITH, M.D. (Clifton).
T. P. TEALE, Esq., F.R.S. (Leeds).
J. ROBERTS-THOMSON, M.D. (Bournemouth).
T. W. THURSFIELD (Leamington).
WILLIAM WHITLA, M.D. (Belfast).
ALFRED WINKFIELD, Esq. (Oxford).

Treasurer.
W. SEDGWICK SAUNDERS, M.D., F.S.A., 13, Queen Street, Cheapside, E.C.

Auditors.
E. CLAPTON, M.D. | A. E. SANSOM, M.D.
WAREN TAY, Esq.

Hon. Secretary.
JONATHAN HUTCHINSON, Esq., F.R.S., LL.D., 15, Cavendish Square, W.

---

* *Those marked with an asterisk were not in office last year.*

REPORT

PRESENTED TO THE FORTY-FIRST ANNUAL MEETING OF THE NEW SYDENHAM SOCIETY, HELD IN PORTSMOUTH, WEDNESDAY, AUGUST 2ND, 1899.

The works which have been published for the year 1898 are the following:—

  I. Fasciculus XII. of the Atlas of Pathology. Coloured Portraits illustrating Hodgkin's disease or Lymphadenoma.
  II. Helferich's Hand-Atlas of Fractures and Dislocations, with added notes.
  III. The Twenty-fourth part of the Lexicon of Medical Terms.

For the current year only one volume has as yet been issued—the Twenty-fifth and concluding part of the Lexicon of Medical Terms.

Among those which are in forward preparation are:—

  I. Sternberg's Monograph on Acromegaly. Translated by Dr. Atkinson.
  II. Schlersinger's Monograph on Syringo-myelia.
  III. A volume of Selected Monographs from foreign sources. This volume will contain, with others, Lectures on the following subjects:—
   Erb on the Etiology of Tabes.
   Erb on the Treatment of Tabes.
   Lasch on Visceral Affections in the Early Stages of Syphilis.
   Marschalko on Tertiary Syphilis in reference to the Early Treatment of the Disease.
   Fournier on Recurring Syphilitic Eruptions.

Ehlers on Syphilis and General Paralysis in Iceland.
Nasse on Gonorrhœal Inflammation of Joints.
Ziemssen on the Open-air Treatment of Phthisis.
Ehlers on Statistics of Tertiary Syphilis.
Nielsen on Melanosis and Keratosis Arsenicalis.
Jadassohn on the Dermatoses produced by Drugs.

IV. A Volume of Selected Papers by English Authors. This volume will comprise, with others :—

Several Papers on Gynecological subjects, by the late Dr. Braxton Hicks, with a portrait of the author.
Some Papers by the late Sir G. M. Humphrey, with a portrait.
The Original Paper "On Certain Diseases of the Lymphatic Glands," by the late Dr. Hodgkin, with a portrait.

Dr. Limbech's *Treatise on the Pathology of the Blood* has been adopted for publication. The translation will, with the author's consent and assistance, be somewhat condensed from the original. Dr. Arthur Latham and Dr. Nachbar have jointly undertaken the translation and editing, and the work will probably be issued next year.

The Lexicon of Medical Terms has been brought to a conclusion by the publication of the Twenty-fifth part. A considerable quantity of material for an Appendix, dealing exclusively with the first half of the work, has already been collected by Mr. Power and Dr. Sedgwick and will shortly be published. In the meantime the preparation of Appendices for the remainder of the work will be proceeded with, with a view to their appearance in the course of a few years. Notices of words omitted will be thankfully received by the Editors.

It has been decided to allow new members to procure full sets of the Lexicon at the cost of about three pounds (varying with the binding).

It having been repeatedly suggested to the Council that a Companion Index to the whole of the Society's works would be a great convenience to those who possess them, it has been decided to prepare such a work. Its compilation, upon a plan which has been sketched out, has been entrusted to Dr. Dynes Parker, and it is hoped that it may constitute one of the volumes for the current year. It is anticipated that this Companion Index will, by facilitating reference to the Society's Library, give it more permanent value. This Library now comprises a hundred and seventy issues, and, after allowing for the fact that in this number repeated fasciculi of single works, such as the Lexicon, the two Atlases, &c., are counted, there still remain about one hundred bound volumes. Very few indeed of these were of merely temporary value, the great majority being such as will never be out of date, and many of them classics.

With the object of facilitating the making up of complete sets, the Council has arranged for the sale to members of back volumes at very much reduced prices, the details of which may be ascertained from the Society's agent. See also pp. 33 to 38 of this Report.

The Council much hopes that the members of the Society will, alike in their own interest and in that of sound medical literature, exert themselves to procure new members. It is also very desirable to assist the sale of the stock in hand. During the last forty years of the Society's life a large quantity of surplus stock has gradually accumulated, and its disposal and dissemination would be a gain both to the Society and the profession.

The Society's accounts were as usual audited at the end of 1898. The Treasurer's balance sheet is appended, and it will be seen that for the first time since its foundation the year closed with a debt. This has since been cleared off. It is hoped that the next audit will present a more satisfactory record. There is however every reason for effort on the part of the members to increase the income.

Dr. THE NEW SYDENHAM SOCIETY.—BALANCE SHEET FOR 1898. Cr.

Receipts.	£	s.	d.	Expenditure.	£	s.	d.
Balance in hand brought forward from last account	63	6	0	Artists, Editors and Translators; Printers, Paper, and Bookbinders	1422	15	0
	£	s.	d.				
Subscriptions—10 for 1896 to 1893	10	10	0	Warehousing of Stock	30	0	0
" 14 " 1894	14	14	0	Expenses of Management:—			
" 17 " 1895	17	17	0		£	s.	d.
" 65 " 1896	68	5	0	Agent's Salary and Commission	197	11	1
" 399 " 1897	418	19	0	Disbursements (chiefly carriage of books)	112	13	5
" 868 " 1898	911	8	0	Advertisements	91	11	0
" 11 " 1899	11	11	0	Fire Insurance	14	1	3
				Treasurer's Expenses	2	15	0
Say 1381 Subscriptions	1453	4	0	Assistant Secretary	54	5	6
Back Volumes	48	7	6				472 17 3
Repayment of postage, &c., charged in Agent's Disbursement Account	44	11	0				
	1546	2	6				
Less deductions by Local Secretaries	16	17	11				
	1529	4	7				
Contribution from the family of the late Dr. Braxton Hicks towards the cost of publishing selections from his works	50	0	0				
Balance overpaid	283	1	8				
	£1925	12	3		£1925	12	3

W. SEDGWICK SAUNDERS, *Treasurer*.

Examined, compared with vouchers and found correct, the balance overpaid to December 31st, 1898, being £283 1s. 8d., at an Audit held this 12th day of July, 1899.

EDWARD CLAPTON
A. ERNEST SANSOM } *Auditors*.
WAREN TAY

LONDON, *July, 1899.*

CLASSIFIED LIST

OF THE

SOCIETY'S PUBLICATIONS.

Medicine.

A TREATISE ON CHOLELITHIASIS. By Dr. B. NAUNYN. Translated by ARCHIBALD E. GARROD, M.A., M.D.

"This volume is a worthy companion to its illustrious predecessors."—*New York Medical Journal*, July 10, 1897.

"This is one of those masterly books in which German literature is rich. It is well worthy of the choice of the New Sydenham Society, and it has received justice at the hands of the translator."—*Practitioner*, Nov. 1897.

"The New Sydenham Society have been happy in the selection of Professor Naunyn's work for translation, as it undoubtedly contains in small compass one of the best studies of Cholelithiasis available."—*British Medical Journal*, Jan. 30, 1897.

LECTURES ON PHARMACOLOGY. By Dr. C. BINZ. Vol. I. Translated from the second German edition by ARTHUR C. LATHAM, M.A., M.B., OXON. Vol. II. Translated by PETER W. LATHAM, M.A., M.D.

"Will be welcomed by English readers."—*Lancet*, March 28, 1896.

"We are very glad indeed that the New Sydenham Society has published Dr. Binz's well-known 'Lectures on Pharmacology,' and we may at once say we have rarely read a more interesting book."—*Practitioner*, Aug. 1896.

"It is with great pleasure that the appearance of an English translation of Professor Binz's admirable Lectures on Pharmacology is welcomed. In their original language they are well known and highly appreciated by many readers in this country, and the present excellent translation will do much to extend their usefulness."—*Pharmaceutical Journal*, June 13, 1896.

"The Sydenham Society deserves the thanks of the medical profession in Great Britain for selecting these Lectures on Pharmacology for translation; they are valuable alike for the student, the practitioner, and the professed pharmacologist. . . . . . The main feature of the work is the admirable skill with which the author has, in accordance with this view, set forth the essential facts relating to the properties of drugs—physical, chemical, and physiological." *Brit. Med. Journal*, May 1, 1897.

"The appearance of the second volume of these Lectures will without doubt be welcomed by all members of the medical profession, for it is a book which will appeal equally to the practitioner and to the student."—*Lancet*, May 15, 1897.

A CONTRIBUTION TO THE STUDY OF SYRINGO-MYELIA. By Dr. ISAAC BRUHL. Translated, with notes and additions, by JAMES GALLOWAY, M.D., and LINDLEY SCOTT, M.D.

"This monograph is well known as comprising one of the most detailed and accurate accounts of a condition of which symptomatology is especially marked by sensory and trophic disturbances, and at the same time so well defined as to admit of clinical diagnosis."—*Lancet*, Jan. 15, 1898.

PALUDISM. By Dr. A. LAVERAN. Translated by J. W. MARTIN, M.D., F.R.C.P.E.

"We think the members of the medical profession in the United Kingdom and English-speaking countries generally are under a debt of gratitude to the New Sydenham Society for bringing under their notice one of the freshest and ablest monographs of recent years."—*Dublin Medical Journal*.

"The New Sydenham Society has done well in issuing a translation of the monograph by Dr. Laveran, in which the whole subject is treated with remarkable lucidity and scientific precision."—*Lancet*.

A COLLECTION OF THE PUBLISHED WRITINGS OF SIR WILLIAM WITHEY GULL, Bart., M.D., F.R.S., Physician to Guy's Hospital. Vol. I. Medical Papers. Vol. II. Memoir and Addresses. Edited and Arranged by THEODORE DYKE ACLAND, M.D.

MONOGRAPHS ON MALARIA:—

On Summer-Autumn Malarial Fevers. By Dr. E. Marchiafava and Dr. A. Bignami. Translated from the first Italian Edition by J. Harry Thompson, M.A., M.D.; and

The Malarial Parasites. A Description based upon observations made by the author and other observers. By Julius Mannaberg, M.D. Illustrated by four Lithographic Plates and six Charts. Translated from the German by R. W. Felkin, M.D., F.R.S.E.

"This important volume is well worthy of the attention of the English reader. . . . . . (It) will prove a valuable addition to the admirable series with which the New Sydenham Society is enriching medical literature."—*Lancet*.

"A knowledge of the facts these works describe is indispensable for teachers of medicine and pathology everywhere, and for all practitioners in malarial countries."—*Brit. Medical Journal*.

MICRO-ORGANISMS, WITH SPECIAL REFERENCE TO THE ETIOLOGY OF THE INFECTIOUS DISEASES. By Dr. C. FLÜGGE, O. O. Professor and Director of the Hygienic Institute at Göttingen. Translated by W. WATSON CHEYNE, M.B., Surgeon to King's College Hospital. With 144 Drawings.

This volume forms an important addition to English medical literature, Flügge's book being justly considered one of the best standard text-books."—*British Medical Journal*.

"This translation is a most important addition to the English literature concerning Bacteria, and well deserves a place beside the most important volumes hitherto issued by the New Sydenham Society."—*Dublin Medical Journal.*

VACCINATION AND ITS RESULTS. A Report based on the evidence taken by the Royal Commission, 1889–1897. Vol. 1. The text of the Commission Report.

LECTURES ON GENERAL PATHOLOGY. 3 Vols. By JULIUS COHNHEIM. Translated from the Second German Edition by ALEXANDER B. McKEE, M.B., Dublin.

"The excellence of the author's work is retained by the care and ability with which the Lectures are done into English by Dr. McKee, and the volumes form a useful and welcome addition to the list of valuable books provided for the profession by the New Sydenham Society."—*Medical Press.*

LECTURES ON CHILDREN'S DISEASES. 2 Vols. By Dr. C. HENOCH. Translated from the Fourth Edition (1889) by JOHN THOMSON, M.B., F.R.C.P. Edinb.

"The clinical types are depicted with the hand of a master, and the remarks upon etiology and treatment are exhaustive and precise. It is long since we have read any book with more pleasure and profit than we have experienced in perusing Prof. Henoch's work in its English dress." — *Glasgow Med. Journal.*

"It is an exceedingly valuable work, reflecting as it does the very best clinical opinion in Germany. Useful hints may be gathered on almost every page; few authorities are quoted, the author mainly relying on his own varied clinical experience, which has now extended over forty-five years. Dr. Thomson has done his work as a translator well, and has succeeded in producing a readable English version of a most valuable text-book."—*British Medical Journal.*

RECENT ESSAYS BY VARIOUS AUTHORS ON BACTERIA IN RELATION TO DISEASE. Selected and Edited by W. WATSON CHEYNE, M.B., F.R.C.S.

"This is a valuable collection of some of the most important papers on Bacteriology which have appeared in Germany, including Koch's papers on the investigation of Pathogenic Organisms, the Etiology of Tuberculosis, and the Etiology of Cholera; Frieländer's paper on the Micrococci of Pneumonia; and others on Leprosy, Enteric Fever, Glanders, &c., by well-known bacteriologists."—*Birm. Med. Review.*

DISEASES OF DIGESTIVE ORGANS. 2 vols. By Dr. C. A. EWALD. Translated from the Third German Edition (1890) by ROBERT SAUNDBY, M.D.

"The New Sydenham Society has been the means of bringing before the notice of the English reader many works of high merit which have appeared in foreign countries. The selection of Professor Ewald's classical treatise upon digestion has been no less happy than many others that have preceded it, whilst the assignment of the task of translating it to Dr. Saundby was fitting and could not have been better."—*Lancet.*

GEOGRAPHICAL AND HISTORICAL PATHOLOGY. Three vols. By Dr. Aug. Hirsch. Translated from the Second Edition by Charles Creighton, M.D.

    Vol. I. "The book is indeed a marvel of industry and erudition, and one which ought to be consulted by every writer on Medicine; no summary will, however, suffice to indicate the wealth of material so laboriously collected and so skilfully arranged, and our readers must turn to the volume itself, which will well repay perusal."—*Lancet.*

    Vol. II. "It is a deep mine of facts and information combined, and judiciously arranged by the learned author; and Dr. Creighton has admirably performed his part in presenting it in an attractive English dress."—*Dublin Medical Journal.*

ON THE TEMPERATURE IN DISEASE: A MANUAL OF MEDICAL THERMOMETRY. By Dr. C. A. Wunderlich. (Leipzig.) Translated by Dr. Bathurst Woodman. With forty Woodcuts and seven Lithographs.

LECTURES ON CLINICAL MEDICINE, delivered at the Hôtel Dieu, Paris. By Professor Trousseau. Five Volumes. Vol. 1, translated, with notes and appendices, by the late Dr. Bazire. Vols. 2 to 5, translated from the third edition, revised and enlarged, by Sir John Rose Cormack.

LATHAM'S COLLECTED WORKS. 2 vols. Edited by Dr. Robert Martin. With Memoir of Latham by Sir Thomas Watson.

LOCAL ASPHYXIA AND SYMMETRICAL GANGRENE OF THE EXTREMITIES. By Maurice Raynaud. Translated by Dr. Thomas Barlow.

ON THE NATURE OF MALARIA. By Professors Edwin Klebs and C. Tommasi-Crudeli; and Alterations in the Red Globules in Malaria Infection; and On the Origin of Melanæmia. By Professor Ettore Marchiafava and Dr. A. Celli. Translated by Dr. E. Drummond, of Rome.

CLINICAL LECTURES ON MEDICINE AND SURGERY. Translated from the German, and selected from Professor Volkmann's Series. Three Volumes.

    (Third Series.) "This volume is replete with interesting clinical details. ..... The work is one well worthy of close and attentive study."—*Dublin Medical Journal*, Aug. 1894.

MEMOIRS ON DIPHTHERIA; containing Memoirs by Bretonneau, Trousseau, Daviot, Guersant, Bouchet, Empis, &c. Selected and Translated by Dr. R. H. Semple.

RADICKE'S PAPERS ON THE APPLICATION OF STATISTICS TO MEDICAL INQUIRIES. Translated by Dr. Bond.

LECTURES ON PHTHISIS. By Professor Niemeyer. Translated by Professor Baumler.

THE COLLECTED WORKS OF DR. ADDISON. Edited, with Introductory Prefaces to several of the Papers, by Dr. Wilks and Dr. Daldy. Portrait, and numerous Lithographs.

A GUIDE TO THE QUALITATIVE AND QUANTITATIVE ANALYSIS OF THE URINE. By Dr. C. Neubauer and Dr. J. Vogel. Fourth edition, considerably enlarged. Translated by William O. Markham, F.R.C.P.L. With four Lithographs, and numerous Woodcuts.

MEMOIRS ON ABDOMINAL TUMOURS AND INTUMESCENCE. By Dr. Bright. Reprinted from the "Guy's Hospital Reports," with a Preface by Dr. Barlow. Numerous Woodcuts.

A CLINICAL ACCOUNT OF DISEASES OF THE LIVER. By Prof. Frerichs. 2 vols. Translated by Dr. Murchison. Coloured Lithographs, and numerous Woodcuts.

CZERMAK ON THE PRACTICAL USES OF THE LARYNGOSCOPE. Translated by Dr. G. D. Gibb. Numerous Woodcuts.

A HAND-BOOK OF PHYSICAL DIAGNOSIS, COMPRISING THE THROAT, THORAX, AND ABDOMEN. By Dr. Paul Guttmann, of Berlin. Translated by Dr. Napier, of Glasgow.

ESSAYS ON ACROMEGALY. By Drs. Pierre Marie and Souza Leite. Translated by Procter S. Hutchinson, M.R.C.S.

AN ATLAS OF ILLUSTRATIONS OF PATHOLOGY, COMPILED (CHIEFLY FROM ORIGINAL SOURCES) FOR THE SOCIETY.

The Committee in charge of this work consists of Dr. Gee, Dr. Green, Mr. Holmes, and Mr. Hutchinson.

TWELVE FASCICULI have been published.

"Of the many valuable works published by this great Society, none are more acceptable to us than the 'Atlas of Pathology.'.... Such a vast and desirable undertaking as the publishing of this work is worthy of the Society named after the greatest English physician."—*Medical Press and Circular.*

The following subjects have been illustrated :—

FIRST FASCICULUS.
DISEASES OF THE KIDNEY.

Scrofula; Syphilis; and Lymph-Adenoma.—Plate I.
5 Figures.

Nephritis after Diphtheria; Scarlet Fever; and Burns.—Plate II.
7 Figures.

The Granular Kidney in different stages.—Plate III.
8 Figures.

Embolism; Infarction Processes from Pyæmia; Jaundice and Purpura; Scrofula.—Plate IV.
6 Figures.

SECOND FASCICULUS.
DISEASES OF THE KIDNEY, SUPRARENAL CAPSULES, AND SPLEEN.

Amyloid Disease and Cancer of the Kidney.—Plate V.
5 Figures.

Various Diseased Conditions of the Spleen.—Plate VI.
5 Figures.

Diseases of the Suprarenal Capsules and Spleen.—Plate VII.
9 Figures.

Microscopic Pathology of Kidneys.—Plate VIII.

20 Figures.—Lardaceous Disease, Contracted Granular Kidney, Catarrhal Nephritis, Casts.

Microscopic Pathology of the Kidney and Spleen.—Plate IX.

23 Figures.—Scarlatinal Nephritis, Fatty and Cystic Degeneration, Interstitial Nephritis, &c., Spleen in Hodgkin's Disease, Adenoma of Suprarena Capsule, &c.

Microscopic Pathology of Spleen and Suprarenals.—Plate X.

15 Figures.—Leucocythæmic Spleen, Muscular Hypertrophy, Tubercle of Spleen, Addison's Disease of Suprarenals.

With Essay on the Pathology of the Kidney, by Dr. Greenfield. Essay on the Pathology of the Spleen and Suprarenals, by Dr. Goodhart.

THIRD FASCICULUS.
DISEASES OF THE LIVER.

Lymph-Adenoma of Liver.—Plate XI.

Plate XII.

Fig. 1. Dilatation of the Bile Ducts in the Liver from pressure of a gall stone in cystic duct.

Fig. 2. Cancer of the Liver, with dilatation of the ducts and staining of the hepatic tissue.

Plate XIII.
Syphilitic Cirrhosis of the Liver.

Plate XIV.
Fig. 1. Red Atrophy, with acute Yellow Atrophy of the Liver.
Fig. 2. Microscopical appearances of the yellow swollen parts of the Liver (Acute Yellow Atrophy).
Fig. 3. Microscopical appearances of Red Atrophy of the Liver.

Plate XV.
Fig. 1. Lardaceous Liver.
Fig. 2. Lardaceous Liver, showing the iodine reaction.

Plate XVI.
Fig. 1. Cancer of the Liver.
Fig. 2. Nutmeg Liver, Chronic Congestion, and Atrophy of the Liver from mitral disease.

"We look on this Pathological Atlas, in all its three fasciculi, as one of the best things that the Society has as yet done. The illustrations are nearly life size; the colouring is beautiful and true to nature; and we have not seen in this or any other country any work of this kind that satisfied us so much. Taken alone, it would be well worth the annual guinea; and will, when finished, constitute a treatise which every practising physician should possess."
—*Medical Press and Circular.*

FOURTH FASCICULUS.
DISEASES OF THE LIVER, including one Figure of Spleen.

Diseases of the Liver and Spleen.—Plate XVII.
Fig. 1. Cirrhosis of the Liver resembling the Nutmeg Liver.
Fig. 2. Brown Atrophy of the Liver.
Fig. 3. Cirrhosis of the Liver.
Fig. 4. Lymph-Adenoma of the Spleen (Hodgkin's Disease).

Diseases of the Liver.—Plate XVIII.
Fig. 1. Fatty Liver from Poisoning by Phosphorus.
Fig. 2. Cirrhosis of the Liver.
Fig. 3. Tubercular Liver.
Fig. 4. Cirrhosis of the Liver.

Diseases of the Liver.—Plate XIX.
Cystic Disease of the Liver.

Microscopic Pathology of the Liver.—Plate XX.
Fig. 1. Lardaceous Disease of the Liver. Fig. 2. Fatty Liver. Fig. 3. Early Cirrhosis. Figs. 4 & 5. Cirrhosis of the Liver (after Hamilton). Fig. 6. Cirrhosis of the Liver. Fig. 7. A Vegetation from the surface of the Liver. Fig. 8. Spindle-cell Sarcoma of the Liver. Fig. 9. Disseminated Growths of Fibrous Nature in the Liver. Fig. 10. Lardaceous Disease of the Liver. Fig. 11. Cavernous Tumour in the Liver. Fig. 12. Acute Yellow Atrophy of the Liver. Fig. 13. Cavernous Tumour in the Liver. Fig. 14. Early Cirrhosis. Fig. 15. Columnar Epithelioma of the Liver.

Microscopic Pathology of the Liver.—Plate XXI.

Fig. 1. Cirrhosis of the Liver. Fig. 2. Cirrhosis of the Liver. Fig. 3. Monolobular Cirrhosis. Fig. 4. The Nutmeg Liver (Romose Atrophy of Moxon). Fig. 5. Tubercular Liver. Fig. 6. The Nutmeg Liver. Fig. 7. Miliary Gummata. Fig. 8. Idiopathic Anæmia. Figs. 9 & 10. Cancer of the Bile Ducts. Fig. 11. Cancer spreading from the Biliary Ducts. Fig. 12. Early Gummatous Infiltration of the Liver. Fig. 13. "Common" Cirrhosis. Fig. 14. Tubercular Liver. Fig. 15. Idiopathic Anæmia.

Microscopic Pathology of the Liver.—Plate XXII.

Fig. 1. "Pericellular" Cirrhosis. Fig. 2. Cirrhosis of the Liver. Fig. 3. Nutmeg Liver. Fig. 4. Cystic Liver. Fig. 5. Cystic Liver. Fig. 6. Early Cancer of the Liver. Fig. 7. Extreme Tubercular Disease of the Liver. Fig. 8. Brown Atrophy of the Liver. Fig. 9. Extreme Tubercular Disease. Fig. 10. Myxœdematous Liver. Figs. 11, 12 & 13. "Contracting Scirrhus of the Liver simulating Cirrhosis." Figs. 14, 15 & 16. Varieties of Cell Vacuolation and Proliferation. Fig. 17. Primary Adenoma of the Liver. Fig. 18. Leukæmic Liver. Fig. 19. Primary Adenoma of the Liver.

FIFTH FASCICULUS.

DISEASES OF THE LIVER (chiefly of the Gall-Bladder and Larger Bile Ducts).

Syphilitic and Lardaceous Disease of the Liver.—Plate XXIII.

Diseases of the Liver.—Plate XXIV.
Fig. 1. Abscesses in the Liver.
Fig. 2. Papilloma of the Gall-Bladder.

Diseases of the Liver.—Plate XXV.
Cancer of Gall-Bladder and Liver.
Gall-stones, with Obstruction and Dilatation of the Cystic Duct.

Diseases of the Liver.—Plate XXVI.
Cancer of the Stomach extending to the Cystic Duct.

SIXTH FASCICULUS.
Hydatid Cysts of the Liver.—Plate XXVII.
Urinary Calculi.—Plates XXVIII. to XXXI.
Comprising 46 Figures.

"Of the many valuable works published by this great Society, none are more acceptable to us than this Atlas of Pathology, of which we have received the sixth fasciculus. Such a vast and desirable undertaking as the publishing of this work is worthy of the Society named after the greatest English physician. . . . . We think that no medical man will be consulting his best interests if he hesitates to become a member of the Society. He certainly will have no more useful books than those bearing the medallion of the immortal Sydenham."—*Medical Press and Circular.*

SEVENTH FASCICULUS.
Urinary Calculi and Gall Stones.—Plate XXXII.
Enlargement of the Prostate Gland.—Plate XXXIII.
Enlargement of Prostate, Urinary Calculi.—Plate XXXIV.
Osteitis Deformans (Paget's Disease).—Plate XXXV.
Comprising 30 Figures.

EIGHTH FASCICULUS.

Diseases of Brain and Spinal Cord.

Plate XXXVI.

Fig. 1. Hydatid in the Posterior Corner of the Right Lateral Ventricle.
Fig. 2. Abscess on the Under Surface of the Right Cerebellar Hemisphere, close to the Petrous Portion of the Temporal Bone.

Plate XXXVII.

Fig. 1. Hæmorrhage into the Right Hemisphere and Median Lobe of the Cerebellum.
Fig. 2. Tubercles of various sizes situated on the Upper Surface of the Cerebellar Hemispheres.
Fig. 3. A Tuberculous Tumour situated between the left side of the Pons Varolii, the Medulla Oblongata, and the adjacent surface of the Cerebellar Hemisphere.

Plate XXXVIII.

Fig. 1. A severely crushed Spinal Cord.
Fig. 2. The Cervical Spinal Cord of a Man who had died under almost precisely similar conditions to those specified in the preceding case.
Fig. 3. Hæmorrhage external to the Vertebral Theca.

Plate XXXIX.

Figs. 1, 2, & 3. A Tuberculous Tumour on the Spinal Dura Mater.

Plate XL.

Fig. 1. Cartilaginous Deposits on the Spinal Arachnoid.
Fig. 2. Myelitis after Concussion of the Spine.

Plate XLI.

Fig. 1. Tubercle in Pia Mater of Cord.
Fig. 2. A Fibrous Tumour lodged in the Cauda Equina.

"The New Sydenham Society is doing good service in issuing a series of pathological drawings, which are extremely well executed and faithful. . . . . The explanatory text is clear and concise; and indeed the whole production is highly creditable to the Society, and will be much appreciated by its members."
—*Lancet*, Jan. 2, 1893.

NINTH FASCICULUS.

Diseases of the Testis. (Part I.)

Plate XLII.

Fig. 1. Hydrocele of the Spermatic Cord.
Fig. 2. " " Epididymis.
Fig. 3. Pedunculated Cartilaginous Body attached to the Globus Major.
Fig. 4. A Calcareous Plate in the Tunica Vaginalis, that portion immediately covering the Testis.
Fig. 5. A number of Calcareous and Cartilaginous Bodies formed in the Visceral Layer of the Tunica Vaginalis, and on the Globus Major of the Epididymis.
Fig. 6. A Multilocular Cyst developed between the Tunica Vaginalis and the Tunica albuginea.

Fig. 7. A Hydrocele of the upper part of the Tunica Vaginalis, the lower part having become obliterated by adhesion to the Testicle, which is seen in section.

Plate XLIII.

Fig. I. The Common Hydrocele of the Tunica Vaginalis.
Fig. II. A Varicocele of moderate size unravelled.
Fig. III. A large Varicocele.

Plate XLIV.

Fig. I. Undescended and Atrophied Testis.
Fig. II. Atrophy (extreme) of one Testicle and Epididymis.
Fig. III. Cystic Disease (? Sarcoma) of the Testis.

Plate XLV.

Syphilis of the Testicle.

Fig. 1. Breaking down Gumma in the Testis.
Fig. 2. Gumma of the Testis due to Inherited Syphilis.
Figs. 3 & 4. Gummatous Disease of Testis and Lung.
Fig. 5. Gummatous deposit in Testis and Epididymis from acquired Syphilis.
Fig. 6. Gummatous Disease of the Testis, with great enlargement of the Organ.

Plate XLVI.

Tumours of the Testicle (3 figs.); Gumma of the Testicle (1 fig.)

Fig. 1. Medullary Cancer.
Fig. 2. Cystic Chondro-Sarcoma.
Fig. 3. Gumma of Testicle, with Hydrocele.
Fig. 4. A Sarcoma involving the whole Testicle, and spreading up the Spermatic Cord.

TENTH FASCICULUS.

Diseases of the Testis. (Part II.)

Plate XLVII.

Fig. 1. Sarcoma (Round-celled or Lympho-Sarcoma) of the Testicle.
Fig. 2. View of an Anterior-posterior Section of the above Tumour, showing a greyish-brown surface obscurely divided into Lobes.
Fig. 3. A slowly-growing Tumour of the Testicle, probably of Sarcomatous nature.

Plate XLVIII.

Fig. 1. Hydrocele of the Tunica Albuginea.
Fig. 2. Malignant Tumour of the Testis, from a boy aged two years.
Fig. 3. Hæmorrhagic Sarcoma of Testicle.

Plate XLIX.

Misplaced Testicle in the Perineum.

"This is an interesting fasciculus of the New Sydenham Society's 'Atlas of Pathology.' . . . . . . Mr. Hutchinson, jun., gives an account of the chief diseases of the Testis, especially those which have been illustrated in the present and preceding fasciculi. His article is a valuable monograph on the Pathology of the Testis."—*Dublin Medical Journal*, March, 1896.

"We congratulate the New Sydenham Society on the continuation of their useful 'Atlas of Pathology.' The illustrations are, as they always have been, most excellent."—*British Medical Journal*, May 30, 1896.

"This set of Plates well maintains the reputation gained by the preceding fasciculi of the New Sydenham Society's Atlas, and that is saying a great deal."—*Birmingham Medical Review*, July, 1896.

ELEVENTH FASCICULUS.

A Treatise on the Pathology, Diagnosis, and Treatment of Neuroma. By ROBERT W. SMITH, M.D. (Plates L. to LXIV.)

"We feel we need do no more than chronicle the reappearance of Smith's masterpiece, and draw the attention of the younger generation of pathologists to a work which fifty years have not succeeded in rendering a whit antiquated."—*Medical Press*, July 6, 1898.

TWELFTH FASCICULUS.

INFECTIVE DISEASE OF THE LYMPHATIC SYSTEM: Lymph-Adenoma, or Hodgkin's Malady. (Plates LXV. to LXVIII.)

"The twelfth fasciculus offers four excellent coloured plates of Lymph-Adenoma, or Hodgkin's Disease. The illustrations have a certain interest of their own in that they are reproductions, now for the first time published, of original water-colour drawings made by Sir Robert Carswell."—*British Medical Journal*, March 11, 1899.

ON THE DISEASES OF OLD AGE. By Prof. CHARCOT. Translated by Mr. WILLIAM TUKE.

THE DIAGNOSIS AND TREATMENT OF DISEASES OF THE CHEST. By Dr. STOKES. A Reprint Edited by Dr. HUDSON, of Dublin.

THE COLLECTED WORKS OF DR. WARBURTON BEGBIE. Edited by Dr. DYCE DUCKWORTH. With a Memoir and Portrait.

SELECTIONS FROM THE CLINICAL WORKS OF DR. DUCHENNE (of Boulogne). Translated and Edited by Dr. VIVIAN POORE.

CLINICAL LECTURES ON THE PRACTICE OF MEDICINE. Vols. I. and II. By the late ROBERT J. GRAVES, M.D. Reprinted from the Second Edition, Edited by Dr. NELIGAN.

ALBUMINURIA IN HEALTH AND DISEASE. By Dr. H. SENATOR. Translated by Dr. T. P. SMITH.

SOME CONSIDERATIONS ON THE NATURE AND PATHOLOGY OF TYPHUS AND TYPHOID FEVER. By the late Dr. P. STEWART, Edited by Dr. W. CAYLEY.

Surgery.

FRACTURES AND DISLOCATIONS. By Professor Dr. H. HELFERICH. Illustrated with sixty-eight Plates, and one hundred and twenty-six Figures in the Text. Translated from the Third Edition (1897), with Notes and additional Illustrations, by J. HUTCHINSON, Jun., F.R.C.S.

"Owing to the clearness of description and the beauty of the illustrations, this is a book that should meet with a cordial reception from practitioners and students, and to the latter especially it should prove a great aid in the study of a subject usually voted difficult and dry."—*Edin. Medical Journal*, July, 1899.

"The whole work is complete, and a great addition to any library."—*Canadian Practitioner*, May, 1899.

ESMARCH ON THE USES OF COLD IN SURGICAL PRACTICE. Translated by Dr. MONTGOMERY. Woodcuts.

"Esmarch's treatise is of high practical interest."—*British Medical Journal*.

BILLROTH'S LECTURES ON SURGICAL PATHOLOGY AND THERAPEUTICS. A Hand-book for Students and Practitioners. 2 vols.

INVESTIGATION INTO THE ETIOLOGY OF THE TRAUMATIC INFECTIVE DISEASES. By R. KOCH. Translated, with Lithographic Plates, by Mr. WATSON CHEYNE.

ON THE PROCESS OF REPAIR AFTER RESECTION AND EXTIRPATION OF BONES. By Dr. A. WAGNER, of Berlin. Translated by Mr. T. HOLMES.

CLINICAL LECTURES. Selected from Professor Volkmann's Series. 2 vols. (See "Medicine.")

THE WORKS OF ABRAHAM COLLES. Chiefly his Treatise on the Venereal Disease and on the Use of Mercury. Edited, with Portrait, by Dr. McDONNELL, of Dublin.

Gynæcology and Midwifery.

A TREATISE ON GYNÆCOLOGY, CLINICAL AND OPERATIVE. By S. POZZI. 3 Vols.

"It is a good work on Gynæcology, well translated; and authors, translators, and the New Sydenham Society are all to be congratulated on its successful completion."—*Edin. Med. Journal*.

"This, the third volume, completes Professor Pozzi's splendid work on Gynæcology. In our notices of the two former volumes we freely expressed our admiration of the book, and on reading the present volume, we find that the same care and trouble has been expended as in the preceding volumes. Whilst such monographs are produced by the New Sydenham Society, there are many and strong inducements to those members of the medical profession who are not members to join. They will consult their own interests by doing so."—*Med. Press.*

A TEXT-BOOK OF MIDWIFERY. By OTTO SPIEGELBERG. Translated from the Second German Edition by Dr. J. B. HURRY. 2 vols.

"It would be difficult to speak too highly of the book as a general text-book of Midwifery; it is neither too long nor too difficult for the student, while the practitioner wishing to read up the authorities on some special point will find ample information of a practical kind."—*British Medical Journal.*

"The New Sydenham Society has done much good work and conferred many benefits upon the English student and practitioner, but it has not done better than by giving Spiegelberg's great book on Midwifery to the English reader."—*Lancet.*

HISTORY AND ETIOLOGY OF SPONDYLOLISTHESIS. By Dr. FRANZ LUDWIG NEUGEBAUER, of Warsaw. Translated by Dr. FANCOURT BARNES.

ON THE MORE IMPORTANT DISEASES OF WOMEN AND CHILDREN, with other Papers, by Dr. GOOCH. Reprinted; with a Prefatory Essay by Dr. ROBERT FERGUSON. With woodcuts.

CLINICAL MEMOIRS ON DISEASES OF WOMEN. By Drs. BERNUTZ and GOUPIL. 2 vols. Translated and abridged by Dr. MEADOWS.

MOVEABLE KIDNEY IN WOMEN. By Dr. LEOPOLD LANDAU. Translated and Edited, with notes, by FRANCIS HENRY CHAMPNEYS, M.A.

SMELLIE'S TREATISE ON THE THEORY AND PRACTICE OF MIDWIFERY. 3 vols. Edited and Annotated by Dr. McCLINTOCK, of Dublin. With Portrait of SMELLIE.

Diseases of the Eye and Ear.

ON THE ANOMALIES OF ACCOMMODATION AND REFRACTION OF THE EYE, with a PRELIMINARY ESSAY ON PHYSIOLOGICAL DIOPTRICS. By F. C. DONDERS, M.D., Professor of Physiology and Ophthalmology in the University of Utrecht. Written expressly for the Society. Translated from the Author's Manuscript by W. D. MOORE, M.D.

THREE MEMOIRS ON GLAUCOMA AND ON IRIDECTOMY AS A MEANS OF TREATMENT. By Professor Von Græfe. Translated by Mr. T. Windsor, of Manchester.

ON THE MECHANISM OF THE BONES OF THE EAR AND THE MEMBRANA TYMPANI. (Pamphlet.) By Professor Helmholtz. Translated by Mr. Hinton.

THE AURAL SURGERY OF THE PRESENT DAY. By W. Kramer, M.D., of Berlin. Translated by Henry Power, Esq., F.R.C.S., M.B. With two Tables and nine Woodcuts.

VON TROELTSCH'S TREATISE ON DISEASES OF THE EAR. Translated, with Notes, by Mr. Hinton.

Forensic Medicine.

A HANDBOOK OF THE PRACTICE OF FORENSIC MEDICINE, BASED UPON PERSONAL EXPERIENCE. By J. L. Casper, M.D., late Professor of Medical Jurisprudence in the University of Berlin. Translated by G. W. Balfour, M.D. 4 vols.

Diseases of the Nervous System.

PIERRE MARIE'S LECTURES ON DISEASES OF THE SPINAL CORD. Translated by Dr. Montagu Lubbock.

"These Lectures will well maintain the high reputation of their author, and, thanks to the excellent rendering of Dr. Montagu Lubbock, they may be read with as much pleasure in English as in the original."—*British Medical Journal*, Jan. 18, 1896.

"Dr. Pierre Marie has in these Lectures, which the New Sydenham Society has done well to place in its series, followed the lines laid down by his master, and has produced a work which is worthy to rank with those of Charcot."—*Lancet*, Nov. 23, 1895.

SCHRŒDER VAN DER KOLK ON A CASE OF ATROPHY OF THE LEFT HEMISPHERE OF THE BRAIN. Translated by Dr. W. Moore, of Dublin. Four Lithographs.

ON THROMBOSIS OF THE CEREBRAL SINUSES. By Professor Von Dusch. Translated by Dr. Whitley.

LECTURES ON DISEASES OF THE NERVOUS SYSTEM. By Professor CHARCOT. (First, Second, and Third Series.) Translated by Dr. SIGERSON, of Dublin. With woodcuts.

A MANUAL OF MENTAL PATHOLOGY AND THERAPEUTICS. By Professor GRIESINGER. Translated by Dr. LOCKHART ROBERTSON and Dr. JAMES RUTHERFORD.

ON EPILEPSY. By Professor SCHRŒDER VAN DER KOLK.

CHARCOT'S TREATISE ON THE LOCALISATION OF CEREBRAL AND SPINAL DISEASE. Translated by Dr. HADDEN.

Anatomy, Physiology, and General Pathology.

A MANUAL OF HUMAN AND COMPARATIVE HISTOLOGY. By S. STRICKER. 3 vols. Translated by Mr. POWER.

EXPERIMENTAL RESEARCHES ON THE EFFECTS OF LOSS OF BLOOD IN PRODUCING CONVULSIONS. By Drs. KUSSMAUL and TENNER. Translated by Dr. BRONNER, of Bradford.

A MANUAL OF PATHOLOGICAL HISTOLOGY, intended to serve as an introduction to the study of Morbid Anatomy. By Professor RINDFLEISCH. (Bonn.) 2 vols. Translated by Dr. BAXTER.

AN ATLAS OF ILLUSTRATIONS OF PATHOLOGY. (See "Medicine," page 11.)

ON THE MINUTE STRUCTURE AND FUNCTIONS OF THE SPINAL CORD. By Professor SCHRŒDER VAN DER KOLK. Translated by Dr. W. D. MOORE. Numerous Lithographs.

ON THE MINUTE STRUCTURE AND FUNCTIONS OF THE MEDULLA OBLONGATA, AND ON EPILEPSY. By Professor SCHRŒDER VAN DER KOLK. Translated by Dr. W. D. MOORE. Numerous Lithographs.

Retrospects, and Works of General Reference.

A LEXICON OF MEDICAL TERMS. Edited by Mr. POWER and Dr. SEDGWICK. Parts I. to XXV. This Lexicon is based upon the well-known work of Dr. MAYNE, the copyright of which was purchased by the Society. It is, however, entirely rewritten by the present Editors, and very much enlarged. (See bindings and prices on p. 37.)

"The work is carefully and elaborately done, and comprehends every reference which the medical or scientific inquirer could possibly require."—*Medical Press and Circular.*

"When complete, the work will be a most valuable addition to the library, not only of medical men, but of those scientists who are interested in Medicine and the allied sciences."—*R. Neale, M.D., in London Medical Recorder.*

"When finished, the Lexicon will be a credit to British Medicine, and worthy of the great Physician whose name the Society bears."—*Dublin Medical Journal.*

A YEAR-BOOK OF MEDICINE AND SURGERY, AND THEIR ALLIED SCIENCES, for each of the Years 1859 to 1864.

A BIENNIAL RETROSPECT OF MEDICINE, SURGERY, AND THEIR ALLIED SCIENCES, for the Years 1865-66, 1867-68, 1869-70, 1871-72, 1873-74.

THE MEDICAL DIGEST. Being a means of ready reference to the principal contributions to Medical Science during the last Thirty years. By Dr. RICHARD NEALE.

BIBLIOTHECA THERAPEUTICA; OR BIBLIOGRAPHY OF THERAPEUTICS. By E. J. WARING, M.D. 2 vols.

Diseases of the Skin and Syphilis.

PRIZE ESSAYS ON LEPROSY (Series I. and II.):—

On the History of the Decline and final Extinction of Leprosy as an Endemic Disease in the British Islands. By George Newman, M.D.

Conditions under which Leprosy has declined in Iceland. By Edward Ehlers, M.D.

Leprosy in South Africa. By S. P. Impey, M.D., M.C.

On Spontaneous Recovery from Leprosy. By S. P. Impey, M.,D. M.C.

A Contribution to the History of Leprosy in Australia. By J. Ashburton Thompson, M.D., D.P.H.

Report on the Conditions under which Leprosy occurs in China, Indo-China, Malaya, the Archipelago, and Oceania. Compiled chiefly during 1894. By James Cantlie, M.A., M.B., F.R.C.S.

"The essays are supplemental to each other, and form the most valuable contribution to the study of the disease that we have."—*Medical Press*, Aug. 24, 1898.

"The present volume is no exception to the rule that all the publications of the New Sydenham Society are of great interest and value. . . . . . A most valuable contribution to our knowledge on the subject of leprosy."—*New York Medical Journal*, Nov. 19, 1898.

SELECTED MONOGRAPHS ON DERMATOLOGY:—

Selections from the Dermatological Writings of Dr. P. G. UNNA. (Translations, chiefly in abstract. Edited by Phineas S. Abrahams, M.A., M.D., B.Sc., F.R.C.P.I.)

On the appearance of Herpes Zoster during the administration of Arsenic. By Ludwig Nielsen, M.D.

A collection of Dr. Duhring's Papers on Dermatitis Herpetiformis.

The Sensation of Itching. By Edward Bennet Bronson, M.D.

Report of a case of the Mycosis Fongoïde of Alibert. By Henry W. Blanc, M.D.

Pellagra. By Ludwig Berger, M.A. (Translated and abridged by Frank H. Barendt, M.D. Lond., F.R.C.S. Eng.)

Drug Eruptions. A Clinical Study of the Irritant Effects of Drugs upon the Skin. By Prince A. Morrow, A.M., M.D. (Edited by T. Colcott Fox, M.B. Lond., F.R.C.P.)

Researches on Psoriasis. By Ludwig Nielsen, M.D. (Translated by Frank H. Barendt, M.D.)

"The whole forms a most useful and instructive volume to all who are interested in dermatological subjects."—*Lancet*.

"All the papers composing the volume are well worth reprinting in a work of this kind, and Dr. Duhring's and Dr. Morrow's papers alone, as not being otherwise readily accessible, would constitute ample justification for its publication."—*British Medical Journal*.

SELECTED ESSAYS AND MONOGRAPHS. (Translations and Reprints from Various Sources.)

"The volume thus contains chiefly subjects of dermatological and syphilographic character, and is perhaps most to be valued by reason of the opportunity it affords to the English reader of the study of the characters of a tropical malady the nature of which has often been debated."—*Lancet*, Jan. 15, 1898.

"The Sydenham Society is to be congratulated upon the selection of essays and monographs contained in this volume. The essays cover a wide range of subjects, mostly of great pathological and clinical interest, though necessarily of varying importance."—*Glasgow Med. Journal*, April, 1898.

"The entire book is replete with valuable information."—*New York Med. Journal*, June 4, 1898.

ON SYPHILIS IN INFANTS. By Paul Diday. Translated by Dr. Whitley.

ON DISEASES OF THE SKIN, INCLUDING THE EXANTHEMATA. By Professor Hebra. 5 vols. Translated and Edited by Dr. Hilton Fagge, Dr. Pye-Smith, and Mr. Waren Tay.

LANCEREAUX'S TREATISE ON SYPHILIS. 2 vols. Translated by Dr. Whitley.

The Society's Atlas of Diseases of the Skin.

In seventeen Fasciculi comprising the following subjects. Unless otherwise indicated, the Plates are original.

	PLATE
Favus. From Hebra.	I.
Tinea Tonsurans. From Hebra.	II.
Lupus Exulcerans. From Hebra.	III.
Psoriasis Diffusa. From Hebra.	IV.
Lupus Serpiginosus; Alopecia Areata. From Hebra.	V.
Ichthyosis. From Hebra.	VI.
Lupus Vulgaris et Serpiginosus (Cicatrising). From Hebra.	VII.
Herpes Zoster Frontalis (affecting the Frontal and Trochlear Branches of the Fifth Nerve).	VIII.
Molluscum Contagiosum, A, on a Child's Face; B, on the Breast of the Child's Mother; C, Anatomical Characters of the Tumours; D, Microscopic Characters.	IX.
Leucoderma.	X.
Morbus Addisonii.	XI.
Pemphigus.	XII.
Pityriasis Versicolor.	XIII.
Psoriasis Inveterata..	XIV.
Eczema Impetiginodes on Face of Adult.	XV.
Eczema on the Face, &c., of Infant; Eczema Rubrum on Leg of Adult.	XVI.
Psoriasis of Hands and Finger-nails; Syphilitic Psoriasis of Finger-nails; Congenito-Syphilitic Psoriasis of Finger- and Toe-nails; Onychia Maligna; Chronic General Onychitis..	XVII.

	PLATE
Molluscum Fibrosum seu Simplex.	XVIII.
Psoriasis-Lupus (Lupus non Exedens, in numerous Symmetrical Patches).	XIX.
Porrigo Contagiosa (e pediculis).	XX.
Erythema Nodosum.	XXI.
Morbus Pedicularis.	XXII.
Herpes Zoster (with scars of a former attack).	XXIII.
Erythema Circinatum.	XXIV.
Eczema (from Sugar).	XXV.
Acne Vulgaris.	XXVI.
Scabies (on Hand of Child). Scabies (with Œdema, &c.) Scabies Norvegica.	XXVII.
Porrigo Contagiosum after Vaccination. Circinate Eruptions in Congenital Syphilis.	XXVIII.
True Leprosy (Tubercular Form). True Leprosy (Anæsthetic Form).	XXIX.
Pityriasis Rubra.	XXX.
Papular Syphilitic Eruption, with Indurated Chancre on the Skin of the Abdomen.	XXXI.
Pruriginous Impetigo after Varicella.	XXXII.
Eruption produced by Iodide of Potassium.	XXXIII.
Lichen of Infants.	XXXIV.
Kerion of Scalp after Ringworm.	XXXV.
Tinea Circinata.	XXXVI.
Rupia-Psoriasis (from inherited Syphilis).	XXXVII.
Prurigo Adolescentium.	XXXVIII.
Purpura Thrombotica.	XXXIX.
Syphilitic Rupia, with Keloid on Scars	XL.
Framboesia (Endemic Verrugas).	XLI.
Lupus Erythematosus.	XLII.
Morphæa, or Addison's Keloid.	XLIII.
Ulcerating Eruption from Bromide of Potassium.	XLIV.
Purpura Hæmorrhagica.	XLV.
Molluscum Contagiosum.	XLVI.
Pemphigus Foliaceus.	XLVII.
Inherited Syphilis.	XLVIII.
Syphilitic Tubercular Lupus.	XLIX.

A CATALOGUE OF THE PORTRAITS COMPRISED IN THE SOCIETY'S ATLAS OF SKIN DISEASES. Prepared, at the request of the Council, by Mr. HUTCHINSON. Parts 1 and 2.

LIST OF PUBLISHED WORKS

Arranged according to the Year of Issue.

Vol.   1859.   (*First Year.*)

1. Diday on Infantile Syphilis.
2. Gooch on Diseases of Women.
3. Memoirs on Diphtheria.
4. Van der Kolk on the Spinal Cord, &c.
5. Monographs (Kussmaul and Tenner, Graefe, Wagner, &c.)

1860.   (*Second Year.*)

6. Dr. Bright on Abdominal Tumours.
7. Frerichs on Diseases of the Liver. Vol. I.
8. A Yearbook for 1859.
9. Atlas of Portraits of Skin Diseases. (1st Fasciculus.)

1861.   (*Third Year.*)

10. A Yearbook for 1860.
11. Monographs (Czermak, Dusch, Radicke, &c.)
12. *Casper's Forensic Medicine. Vol. I.
14. *Atlas of Portraits of Skin Diseases. (2nd Fasciculus.)

1862.   (*Fourth Year.*)

13. *Frerichs on Diseases of the Liver. Vol. II.
15. A Yearbook for 1861.
16. Casper's Forensic Medicine. Vol. II.
17. Atlas of Portraits of Skin Diseases. (3rd Fasciculus.)

1863.   (*Fifth Year.*)

18. *Kramer on Diseases of the Ear.
19. A Yearbook for 1862.
20. Neubauer and Vogel on the Urine.

Vol.   1864. (*Sixth Year.*)
21. Casper's Forensic Medicine. Vol. III.
22.*Donders on Accommodation and Refraction of the Eye.
23. A Yearbook for 1863.
24. Atlas of Portraits of Skin Diseases. (4th Fasciculus.)

1865. (*Seventh Year.*)
25. A Yearbook for 1864.
26. Casper's Forensic Medicine. Vol. IV.
27.*Atlas of Portraits of Skin Diseases. (5th Fasciculus.)

1866. (*Eighth Year.*)
28. Bernutz and Goupil on the Diseases of Women. Vol. I.
29. Atlas of Portraits of Skin Diseases. (6th Fasciculus.)
30.*Hebra on Diseases of the Skin. Vol. I.
31. Bernutz and Goupil on Diseases of Women. Vol. II.

1867. (*Ninth Year.*)
32. Biennial Retrospect of Medicine and Surgery.
33. Griesinger on Mental Pathology and Therapeutics.
34.*Atlas of Portraits of Skin Diseases. (7th Fasciculus.)
35. Trousseau's Clinical Medicine. Vol. I.

1868. (*Tenth Year.*)
36. The Collected Works of Dr. Addison.
37. Hebra on Skin Diseases. Vol. II.
38. Lancereaux's Treatise on Syphilis. Vol. I.
39. Atlas of Portraits of Skin Diseases. (8th Fasciculus.)
40. Catalogue of Atlas of Skin Diseases. (First Part.)

1869. (*Eleventh Year.*)
41. Lancereaux's Treatise on Syphilis. Vol. II.
42.*Trousseau's Clinical Medicine. Vol. II.
43. Biennial Retrospect of Medicine and Surgery.
44. Atlas of Portraits of Skin Diseases. (9th Fasciculus.)

1870. (*Twelfth Year.*)
45. Trousseau's Lectures on Clinical Medicine. Vol. III.
46. Niemeyer's Lectures on Pulmonary Consumption.
47. Stricker's Manual of Histology. Vol. I.
48. Atlas of Portraits of Skin Diseases. (10th Fasciculus.)

VOL.   1871.   (*Thirteenth Year.*)
49. WUNDERLICH's Medical Thermometry.
50. BIENNIAL Retrospect of Medicine and Surgery.
51. TROUSSEAU's Clinical Medicine. Vol. IV.
52. ATLAS of Portraits of Skin Diseases. (11th Fasciculus.)

1872.   (*Fourteenth Year.*)
53. STRICKER's Manual of Histology. Vol. II.
54. RINDFLEISCH's Pathological Histology. Vol. I.
55. TROUSSEAU's Clinical Medicine. Vol. V.
56. ATLAS of Portraits of Skin Diseases. (12th Fasciculus.)

1873.   (*Fifteenth Year.*)
57. STRICKER's Manual of Histology. Vol. III.
58. RINDFLEISCH's Pathological Histology. Vol. II.
59. BIENNIAL Retrospect of Medicine and Surgery.
60. ATLAS of Portraits of Skin Diseases. (13th Fasciculus.)

1874.   (*Sixteenth Year.*)
61. HEBRA on Skin Diseases. Vol. III.
62. Von TROELTSCH on Diseases of the Ear.
     HELMHOLTZ on Membrana Tympani, &c. (In one Vol.)
63. ATLAS of Portraits of Skin Diseases. (14th Fasciculus.)
64. HEBRA on Skin Diseases. Vol. IV.

1875.   (*Seventeenth Year.*)
65. BIENNIAL Retrospect of Medicine and Surgery.
66. CATALOGUE of Atlas of Skin Diseases. (Second Part.)
67. ATLAS of Portraits of Skin Diseases. (15th Fasciculus.)
68. CLINICAL Lectures by various German Professors. Vol. I.
69. LATHAM's Works. Vol. I.

1876.   (*Eighteenth Year.*)
70. SMELLIE's Midwifery, by McClintock. Vol. I.
71. CLINICAL Lectures by various German Professors. Vol. II.
72.*CHARCOT's Diseases of the Nervous System. Vol. I.
73. BILLROTH's Lectures on Surgical Pathology. Vol. I.

1877.   (*Nineteenth Year.*)
74. SMELLIE's Midwifery, by McClintock. Vol. II.
75. THE Medical Digest, by Dr. Neale.
76. BILLROTH's Lectures on Surgical Pathology. Vol. II.
77. ATLAS of Illustrations of Pathology. (Fasciculus I.)

Vol.   1878.   (*Twentieth Year.*)

78. BIBLIOTHECA Therapeutica, by Dr. Waring. Vol. I.
79. SMELLIE'S Midwifery, by McClintock. Vol. III.
80. LATHAM'S Works. Vol. II.
81. LEXICON of Medical Terms. (First Part.) *Issued with Part II. only, as Vol. 83.*

1879.   (*Twenty-first Year.*)

82. BIBLIOTHECA Therapeutica, by Dr. Waring. Vol. II.
83. LEXICON of Medical Terms. (Second Part.) *Including re-issue of First Part.*
84. MANUAL of Physical Diagnosis, by Dr. Guttmann.
85. ATLAS of Illustrations of Pathology. (Fasciculus II.)

1880.   (*Twenty-second Year.*)

86. HEBRA on Diseases of the Skin. Vol. V.
87. LEXICON of Medical Terms. (Third Part.)
88. KOCH'S Researches on Wound Infection.
89. LEXICON of Medical Terms. (Fourth Part.)
90. CHARCOT'S Diseases of the Nervous System. Vol. II.
91. ATLAS of Illustrations of Pathology. (Fasciculus III.)

1881.   (*Twenty-third Year.*)

92. SELECTIONS from the Works of Abraham Colles.
93. LEXICON of Medical Terms. (Fifth Part.)
94. BILLROTH'S Clinical Surgery.
95. CHARCOT on Diseases of Old Age.
96. LEXICON of Medical Terms. (Sixth Part.)
97. ATLAS of Illustrations of Pathology. (Fasciculus IV.)

1882.   (*Twenty-fourth Year.*)

98. STOKES on Diseases of the Chest.
99. ATLAS of Portraits of Skin Diseases. (16th Fasciculus.)
100. THE Collected Works of Dr. Warburton Begbie.
101. LEXICON of Medical Terms. (Seventh Part.)
102. CHARCOT on Localisation of Cerebral and Spinal Disease.
103. LEXICON of Medical Terms. (Eighth Part.)

1883.   (*Twenty-fifth Year.*)

104. ATLAS of Illustrations of Pathology. (Fasciculus V.)
105. SELECTIONS from the Works of Dr. Duchenne.
106. HIRSCH on Geographical and Historical Pathology. Vol. I.
107. LEXICON of Medical Terms. (Ninth Part.)

Vol.   1884.   (*Twenty-sixth Year.*)
108. ATLAS of Portraits of Skin Diseases.   (17th Fasciculus.)
109. GRAVES's Clinical Medicine. Vol. I. (Reprinted.)
110. SELECTED Monographs (Senator, Stewart, Landau).
111. LEXICON of Medical Terms.   (Tenth Part.)

1885.   (*Twenty-seventh Year.*)
112. HIRSCH on Geographical and Historical Pathology. Vol. II.
113. GRAVES's Clinical Medicine. Vol. II.
114. LEXICON of Medical Terms.   (Eleventh Part.)

1886.   (*Twenty-eighth Year.*)
115. SELECTED Essays on Micro-Parasites in Disease. Edited by W. Watson Cheyne.
116. LEXICON of Medical Terms.   (Twelfth Part.)
117. HIRSCH on Geographical and Historical Pathology. Vol. III.
118. LEXICON of Medical Terms.   (Thirteenth Part.)

1887.   (*Twenty-ninth Year.*)
119. SPIEGELBERG's Midwifery. Vol. I.
120. LEXICON of Medical Terms.   (Fourteenth Part.)
121. SELECTED MONOGRAPHS:— Raynaud's Disturbances of Circulation in the Extremities; Klebs and Tommasi-Crudeli on the Nature of Malaria; Marchiafava and Celli on the Blood in Malaria-Infection; Neugebauer on Spondylolisthesis.
122. ATLAS of Pathology.   (Fasciculus VI.)

1888.   (*Thirtieth Year.*)
123. SPIEGELBERG's Midwifery. Vol. II.
124. LEXICON of Medical Terms.   (Fifteenth Part.)
125. HENOCH's Diseases of Children. Vol. I.
126. COHNHEIM's General Pathology. Vol. I.

1889.   (*Thirty-first Year.*)
127. ATLAS of Pathology.   (Fasciculus VII.)
128. CHARCOT's Diseases of the Nervous System. Vol. III.
129. COHNHEIM's General Pathology. Vol. II.
130. LEXICON of Medical Terms.   (Sixteenth Part.)
131. HENOCH's Lectures on Diseases of Children. Vol. II.

Vol.   1890.   (*Thirty-second Year.*)
132. FLÜGGE's Micro-Organisms.
133. COHNHEIM's General Pathology.   Vol. III.
134. LEXICON of Medical Terms.   (Seventeenth Part.)
135. ATLAS of Pathology.   (Fasciculus VIII.)

1891.   (*Thirty-third Year.*)
136. EWALD's Diseases of Digestive Organs.   Vol. I.
137. ESSAYS on Acromegaly.   By Drs. Pierre Marie and Souza Leite.
138. LEXICON of Medical Terms.   (Eighteenth Part.)
139. EWALD's Diseases of Digestive Organs.   Vol. II.
140. POZZI's Treatise on Gynæcology.   Vol. I.

1892.   (*Thirty-fourth Year.*)
141. LEXICON of Medical Terms.   (Nineteenth Part.)
142. LEXICON of Medical Terms.   (Twentieth Part.)
143. A VOLUME of Dermatological Papers.
144. POZZI on Gynæcology.   Vol. II.
145. POZZI on Gynæcology.   Vol. III.

1893.   (*Thirty-fifth Year.*)
146. LAVERAN on Paludism and its Organism.
147. THE Works of Sir William Gull.   Vol. I.
148. MONOGRAPHS and Lectures from German Sources.
149. LEXICON of Medical Terms.   (Twenty-first Part.)

1894.   (*Thirty-sixth Year.*)
150. Two Monographs on Malaria and the Parasites of Malarial Fevers.
151. ATLAS of Pathology.   (Fasciculus IX.)
152. PIERRE MARIE's Diseases of Spinal Cord.

1895.   (*Thirty-seventh Year.*)
153. ATLAS of Pathology.   (Fasciculus X.)
154. BINZ's Lectures on Pharmacology.   Vol. I.
155. LEXICON of Medical Terms.   (Twenty-second Part.)
156. THE Works of Sir William Gull.   Vol. II.

Vol.   1896.   (*Thirty-eighth Year.*)

157. PRIZE Essays on Leprosy. (Newman, Ehlers, Impey.)
158. NAUNYN on Cholelithiasis.
159. BINZ's Lectures on Pharmacology. Vol. II.
160. LEXICON of Medical Terms. (Twenty-third Part.)
161. SELECTED Lectures and Papers from Foreign Sources.

1897.   (*Thirty-ninth Year.*)

162. PRIZE Essays on Leprosy. Series II. (Ashburton Thompson and Cantlie.)
163. ATLAS of Pathology. (Fasciculus XI.) Smith on Neuroma.
164. A REPORT on Vaccination and its results. Based on the Reports of the Royal Commission. Vol. I.

1898.   (*Fortieth Year.*)

165. LEXICON of Medical Terms. (Twenty-fourth Part.)
166. ATLAS of Pathology. (Fasciculus XII.) Hodgkin's Disease.
167. HELFERICH's Fractures and Dislocations.

1899.   (*Forty-first Year.*)

168. LEXICON of Medical Terms. (Twenty-fifth Part.)
169. STERNBERG's Monograph on Acromegaly.

Volumes marked * are now quite out of print.

LIST OF VOLUMES

ISSUED IN PAST YEARS,

REARRANGED IN SETS

FOR THE CONVENIENCE OF NEW SUBSCRIBERS.

The Subscription for each Set is One Guinea.

Subscribers taking Four or more of the following Sets at one time may have One extra Set Gratis.

SET I.—*Three vols.*
　Two Monographs on Malaria and the Parasites of Malarial Fevers.
　Laveran on Paludism.
　Selected Monographs, vol. 121, on Malaria, &c.

SET II.—*Five vols.*
　Pierre Marie's Diseases of Spinal Cord.
　Hirsch's Geographical and Historical Pathology.
　Koch's Researches on Wound Infection.

SET III.—*Five vols.*
　Binz's Lectures on Pharmacology, 2 vols.
　Naunyn on Cholelithiasis.
　Ewald's Disorders of Digestive Organs, 2 vols.

SET IV.—*Four vols.*
　Pozzi's Gynecology, 3 vols.
　Selected Monographs, vol. 110. (With illustrations).

SET V.—*Eight vols.*
　The Works of Sir William Gull, 2 vols.
　The Collected Works of Dr. Addison.
　Latham's Works, 2 vols.
　Selections from the Works of Colles.
　Warburton Begbie's Works.
　Graves's Clinical Medicine, 2 vols.

SET VI.—*Seven vols.*
　Selected Lectures and Papers from Foreign Sources.
　Clinical Lectures by various German Professors, series i., ii., & iii.
　Selected Monographs, vols. 5, 11, & 121.

SET VII.—*Six vols.*
　Selected Monographs on Dermatology (Unna, Nielsen, Duhring, Bronson, Blanc, Berger, Prince-Morrow).
　Essays on Acromegaly (Pierre Marie and Souza Leite).
　The Works of Sir William Gull, 2 vols.
　Monographs and Lectures from German Sources, series iii.
　Selected Monographs, vol. 110.

SET VIII.—*Seven vols.*
　Billroth's Clinical Surgery. (Illustrated).
　Essays on Micro-Parasites in Disease. Selected by Watson Cheyne. (Illustrated).
　Monographs and Lectures from German Sources, series iii., vol. 148.
　Essays on Acromegaly (Pierre Marie and Souza Leite).
　Memoirs on Diphtheria.
　Lancereaux's Syphilis, 2 vols.

SET IX.—*Six vols.*
　Selected Monographs on Dermatology (Unna, Nielsen, Duhring, Bronson, Blanc, Berger, Prince-Morrow).
　Neubauer and Vogel on the Urine. (Illustrated).
　Bernutz and Goupil's Diseases of Women, 2 vols.
　Henoch's Diseases of Children, 2 vols.

SET X.—*Eight vols.*
　Selected Lectures and Papers from Foreign Sources, vol. 161.
　Naunyn on Cholelithiasis.
　Hebra's Diseases of the Skin, vols. ii., iii., iv. and v.
　Griesinger on Mental Pathology.
　Niemeyer's Lectures on Pulmonary Consumption.

SET XI.—*Seven vols.*
　Naunyn on Cholelithiasis.
　Stricker's Histology, Human and Comparative, 3 vols. (Illustrated).
　Selections from the works of Dr. Duchenne.
　Koch's Researches on Wound Infection.
　Stokes on Diseases of the Chest.

SET XII.—*Five vols.*
　Selected Monographs on Dermatology (Unna, Nielsen, Duhring, Bronson, Blanc, Berger, Prince-Morrow).
　Cohnheim's General Pathology, 3 vols.
　Wunderlich's Medical Thermometry.

SET XIII.—*Five vols.*
　Pierre Marie's Diseases of Spinal Cord.
　Charcot's Diseases of the Nervous System, vols. ii. and iii., complete in themselves.
　Charcot's Localization of Cerebral Disease. (Illustrated).
　Charcot's Diseases of Old Age. (Illustrated).

SET XIV.—*Six vols.*
　Hirsch's Geographical and Historical Pathology, 3 vols.
　Waring's Bibliotheca Therapeutica, 2 vols.
　Selected Monographs, vol. 121. (With illustrations).

SET XV.—*Six vols.*
　Spiegelberg's Midwifery, 2 vols. (Illustrated).
　Smellie's Midwifery, 3 vols.
　Selected Monographs, vol. 121. (With illustrations).

LIST OF VOLUMES IN SETS. 35

SET XVI.—*Eight vols.*
    The Collected Works of Dr. Warburton Begbie.
    Billroth's Clinical Surgery.
    Von Troeltsch on Diseases of the Ear. (Illustrated).
    Charcot on Diseases of Old Age. (Illustrated).
    Selection from the Works of Colles.
    Graves's Clinical Medicine, 2 vols.
    Niemeyer's Lectures on Pulmonary Consumption.

SET XVII.—*Eight vols.*
    Sir William Gull's Works, 2 vols.
    Selected Monographs, vol. 110. (With illustrations).
    Latham's Works, 2 vols.
    Rindfleisch's Pathological Histology, 2 vols. (Illustrated).
    Selections from the Works of Colles.

SET XVIII.—*Five vols.*
    Ewald's Diseases of Digestive Organs, 2 vols.
    Henoch's Diseases of Children, 2 vols.
    Stokes on Diseases of the Chest.

SET XIX.—*Four vols.*
    Essays on Micro-Parasites in Disease. Selected by Watson Cheyne. (Illustrated).
    Flugge's Micro-Organisms.
    Selected Monographs, vol. 121. (With illustrations).
    Monographs and Lectures from German Sources, series iii., vol. 148.

SET XX.—*Seven vols.*
    Trousseau's Clinical Medicine, vols. i., iv. and v., complete in themselves.
    Stokes on Diseases of the Chest.
    Graves's Clinical Medicine, 2 vols.
    Selections from the Works of Colles.

SET XXI.—*Seven vols.*
    Selected Lectures and Papers from Foreign Sources, vol. 161.
    Waring's Bibliotheca Therapeutica, 2 vols.
    Billroth's Clinical Surgery. (Illustrated).
    Charcot's Diseases of Old Age. (Illustrated).
    Charcot's Cerebral Disease. (Illustrated).
    Griesinger's Mental Pathology.

SET XXII.—*Four vols.*
    Spiegelberg's Midwifery, 2 vols.
    Henoch's Diseases of Children, 2 vols.

SET XXIII.—*Five vols.*
    Binz's Lectures on Pharmacology, 2 vols.
    Cohnheim's General Pathology, 3 vols.

SET XXIV.—*Six vols.*
    Pierre Marie's Diseases of Spinal Cord.
    Billroth's Surgical Pathology, 2 vols.
    Billroth's Clinical Surgery.
    Diday's Infantile Syphilis.
    Van der Kolk on the Spinal Cord, &c.

N.B.—When several of the above Sets are taken by a subscriber, if they contain duplicate volumes, such duplicates can be exchanged for other volumes of equal value.

LIST OF SURPLUS VOLUMES,
With Prices.

N.B.—The prices affixed can be continued only for a limited period until surplus stock is disposed of.

ADDISON'S COLLECTED WORKS. 2s.

ATLAS OF PATHOLOGY. Bound in cloth, complete I. to XII. with Index. £3. 3s. Separate Fasciculi II. to XII. 10s. 6d. each.

ATLAS OF SKIN DISEASES. Fasciculi 4 and 7 to 17. 7s. 6d. each. Portfolio containing 35 plates (the remainder being out of print), £2 2s.

BERNUTZ AND GOUPIL'S DISEASES OF WOMEN. 2 vols. 5s.

BILLROTH'S CLINICAL SURGERY. 4s.

BILLROTH'S SURGICAL PATHOLOGY. 2 vols. 7s. 6d.

BINZ'S LECTURES ON PHARMACOLOGY. 2 vols. 10s.

BRIGHT ON ABDOMINAL TUMOURS. 2s.

CHARCOT'S DISEASES OF NERVOUS SYSTEM. Vols. II. and III. 7s. 6d.

CHARCOT'S DISEASES OF OLD AGE. 3s. 6d.

CHARCOT'S LOCALIZATION OF CEREBRAL DISEASE. 3s. 6d.

COHNHEIM'S GENERAL PATHOLOGY. 3 vols. 15s.

DERMATOLOGICAL PAPERS (UNNA, DUHRING, PRINCE-MORROW, &c.). 6s.

ESSAYS ON ACROMEGALY (PIERRE MARIE AND SOUZA LEITE). 3s. 6d.

EWALD'S DISORDERS OF DIGESTION. 2 vols. 10s.

FLUGGE'S MICRO-ORGANISMS. 7s. 6d.

GERMAN CLINICAL LECTURES. Series I., II., and III., each volume complete in itself. 3s. each.

GRAVES'S CLINICAL MEDICINE. 2 vols. 7s. 6d.

GRIESINGER'S MENTAL PATHOLOGY. 5s.

GULL'S WORKS. 2 vols. 7s. 6d.

GUTTMANN'S PHYSICAL DIAGNOSIS. 5s.

HEBRA'S DISEASES OF THE SKIN. Vols. II., III., IV., and V. 2s. 6d. each.

HENOCH'S DISEASES OF CHILDREN. 2 vols. 12s. 6d.

HIRSCH'S GEOGRAPHICAL AND HISTORICAL PATHOLOGY. 3 vols. 12s. 6d.

KOCH'S WOUND INFECTION. 2s. 6d.

LANCEREAUX'S SYPHILIS. 2 vols. 5s.

LATHAM'S WORKS. 2 vols. 5s.

LEXICON OF MEDICAL TERMS. Vols. I. to V. (in Parts), £2 10s.; bound in roan back, cloth sides, marbled edges, £3 3s.; half morocco, gilt top, £3 13s. 6d.

MEMOIRS ON DIPHTHERIA. 2s.

MICRO-PARASITES IN DISEASE (Edited by W. Watson Cheyne). 7s. 6d.

NAUNYN'S CHOLELITHIASIS. 3s. 6d.

NEUBAUER AND VOGEL ON THE URINE. 3s. 6d.

NIEMEYER'S LECTURES ON PULMONARY CONSUMPTION. 2s. 6d.

PIERRE MARIE'S DISEASES OF SPINAL CORD. 10s.

RINDFLEISCH'S PATHOLOGICAL HISTOLOGY. 2 vols. 6s.

SELECTED MONOGRAPHS (CZERMAK, DUSCH AND RADICKE, &c.). 3s.

SELECTED MONOGRAPHS (KUSSMAUL AND TENNER, GRAEFE, WAGNER, &c.). 2s. 6d.

SELECTED MONOGRAPHS (SENATOR, STEWART, AND LANDAU). 4s.

SELECTED MONOGRAPHS (RAYNAUD, KLEBS, AND TOMMASI CRUDELI, MARCHIAFAVA AND CELLI, NEUGEBAUER). 6s.

SELECTIONS FROM THE WORKS OF DUCHENNE. 5s.

SELECTIONS FROM THE WORKS OF COLLES. 2s. 6d.

SMELLIE'S MIDWIFERY. 3 vols. 7s. 6d.

SPIEGELBERG'S MIDWIFERY. 2 vols. 12s. 6d.

STOKES ON DISEASES OF THE CHEST. 3s.

STRICKER'S MANUAL OF HISTOLOGY. 3 vols. 10s. 6d.

TROUSSEAU'S CLINICAL MEDICINE. Vols. I., IV. and V. (complete in themselves). 5s. each.

VAN DER KOLK ON DISEASES OF SPINAL CORD. 2s.

VON TROELTSCH'S DISEASES OF THE EAR. 2s.

WARBURTON BEGBIE'S WORKS. 3s.

WARING'S BIBLIOTHECA THERAPEUTICA. 2 vols. 5s.

WUNDERLICH'S MEDICAL THERMOMETRY. 3s. 6d.

YEAR-BOOKS AND BIENNIAL RETROSPECTS, 1859-74. 11 volumes. 1s. 6d. each, or the set of 11 volumes for 12s. 6d.

LAWS OF THE NEW SYDENHAM SOCIETY.

I.—The Society is instituted for the purpose of supplying certain acknowledged deficiencies in the existing means of diffusing medical literature, and shall be called "THE NEW SYDENHAM SOCIETY."

II.—The Society shall carry out its objects by a succession of publications, of which the following shall be the chief:—1. Translations of Foreign Works, Papers, and Essays of merit, to be reproduced as early as practicable after their original issue. 2. British Works, Papers, Lectures, &c., which, whilst of great value, have become from any cause difficult to be obtained, excluding those of living authors. 3. Annual Volumes consisting of Reports in Abstract of the progress of the different branches of Medical and Surgical Science during the year. 4. Dictionaries of Medical Bibliography and Biography. Those included under Nos. 1 and 2 shall be held to have the first claim on the attention of the Society; and the carrying out of those under Nos. 3 and 4 shall be considered dependent upon the amount of funds which may be placed at its disposal.

III.—The Subscription constituting a Member shall be One Guinea, to be paid *in advance* on the 1st of January annually, and it shall entitle the subscriber to a copy of every work published for that year. *No books shall be issued to any Member until his subscription for the year has been paid.*

IV.—The Officers of the Society shall be elected from the Members, and shall consist of a President, sixteen Vice-Presidents, a Treasurer, a Secretary, and a Council of thirty-two, in whom the power of framing Bye-laws and of directing the affairs of the Society shall be vested. Twelve of the Council shall be provincial residents.

V.—Five Members of the Council shall form a quorum.

VI.—The Officers of the Society shall be elected by ballot at the General Anniversary Meeting of the Society. Balloting lists of Officers proposed by the Council, with blank places for such alterations as any Member may wish to make, shall be laid on the Society's table for the use of Members.

VII.—The President, Vice-Presidents, and Council, shall be eligible for re-election, except that of the Vice-Presidents four, and of the Council eight, shall retire every year.

VIII.—The Council shall appoint local Honorary Secretaries wherever they shall see fit.

IX.—The business of the President shall be to preside at the Annual and Extraordinary Meetings of the Society; in his absence one of the Vice-Presidents, or the Treasurer, or any Member of the Council chosen by the Members present, shall take the Chair.

X.—The Treasurer, or some person appointed by him, shall receive all moneys due to the Society.

XI.—The money in the hands of the Treasurer, which shall not be immediately required for the uses of the Society, shall be vested in such speedily available securities as shall be approved by the Council.

XII.—The Council shall select the Works to be published by the Society, and shall make all arrangements, pecuniary or otherwise, in regard to their publication. In the event of any Member of the Council being appointed to edit any Work for the Society, for which he is to receive pecuniary remuneration, he shall immediately cease to be a Member of the Council, and shall not be eligible for re-election till after the publication of the Work.

XIII.—The Council shall lay before the Members at each Anniversary Meeting a Report of their proceedings during the past year, and also an account of the Receipts and Expenditure of the Society; and shall further cause to be printed and circulated among the Members an abstract of such Report and Accounts immediately after such Anniversary Meeting.

XIV.—The annual Accounts of the Receipts and Expenditure of the Society shall be audited by a Committee of three Members, selected at the preceding Anniversary Meeting from among the Members at large.

XV.—The Secretary shall have the management of the general Correspondence of the Society, and of such other business as may arise in carrying out its objects.

XVI.—The local Secretaries shall further the objects of the Society in their respective districts, and shall be in communication with the metropolitan Secretary.

XVII.—The Anniversary Meeting shall be held in the same town as, and at the time of, the Annual Meeting of the British Medical Association, notice of it having been given to all Members at least a week before the day fixed on.

XVIII.—The Members generally shall be invited and encouraged to propose Works, &c., and to make any suggestions to the Council they may think likely to be useful.

XIX.—The Works of the Society shall be printed for the Members only.

XX.—No alteration in the Laws of the Society shall be made, except at a General Meeting. Notice of the alteration to be proposed must also have been laid before the Council at least a month previously.

XXI.—The Council shall have power to call a General Meeting of the Members at any time, and shall also be required to do so within three weeks, upon receiving a requisition in writing to that effect from not less than twenty Members of the Society.

XXII.—All Special General Meetings of the Society shall be held at such place as the Council may appoint.

XXIII.—The Council shall meet at least once in two months, unless by special resolution to the contrary.

GENERAL INFORMATION.

The SUBSCRIPTION is One Guinea annually, to be paid IN ADVANCE. The best mode of sending money is by Cheque, Post-office or Postal Order, payable to Mr. H. K. LEWIS; or by Cheque to the order of the Treasurer, Dr. SEDGWICK SAUNDERS. It is requested that in future all communications in reference to the payment of Subscriptions, or the issue of Books, may be made to Mr. LEWIS, the Society's Agent, and not to the Secretary.

IMPORTANT NOTICE TO NEW SUBSCRIBERS AND LOCAL SECRETARIES.—New Members who subscribe for the current year and not fewer than three past years at the same time, will be allowed to select volumes from the surplus stock to the value of one guinea without additional payment. The like privilege will be secured each year by any Local Secretary who has the subscriptions of all the members on his list (the number being not less than ten) paid before the end of March for the current year. Arrangements have been made by which new Members can obtain single Volumes, or sets of Volumes, from the Society's stock in hand. Some of the Volumes, of which a larger surplus exists than of others, can be purchased at fixed prices (for which see list). The Society's Agent is empowered to make special arrangements with new Members who may wish to obtain any of the past Volumes.

CARRIAGE, &c.—The Society's Works are supplied free of cost to any address in London, Edinburgh, or Dublin; but the expenses of Carriage to all other places must be borne by the members to whom they are sent. Members are requested to give detailed instructions respecting the mode by which they wish their Volumes to be forwarded, and also to remember that the Society's responsibility ceases when the Book has been delivered according to the instructions given. Members residing in the British Isles wishing to receive their Works by post can do so by prepaying the sum of 2s. for the year for postage.

BINDING CASES AND PORTFOLIOS.—The Society's Agent is prepared to supply, at fixed prices, CASES for binding the Lexicon, and PORTFOLIOS for the reception of the Plates of Skin Diseases, and for the Pathological Atlas.

To prevent misapprehensions as regards the punctual issue of each year's series, it seems desirable to reprint the following extract from the Report for the year 1882:—

"If the members would kindly understand that the Society's financial year is from January to December, its year of issue from June to June, and that its subscriptions are due in advance, the working of the Society would be much facilitated. From this point of view, the issue of volumes for each succeeding year has always in the past been punctually completed, and probably will be so in the future. The works promised are issued *for* the year specified, but are not all of them issued *in it*."

The Council will always be glad to receive suggestions from Members, particularly with regard to any recent foreign works which are thought suitable for publication by the Society (*vide* Law XVIII.). It is requested that such communications be forwarded to the Secretary in the first instance.

Hon. Secretary.
JONATHAN HUTCHINSON, Esq., F.R.S., 15, Cavendish Square, London, W.

Agent and Depôt for Books.
Mr. H. K. LEWIS, 136, Gower Street, London, W.C.

WEST, NEWMAN AND CO., PRINTERS, 54, HATTON GARDEN, LONDON, E.C.

www.ingramcontent.com/pod-product-compliance
Lightning Source LLC
Chambersburg PA
CBHW020252170426
43202CB00008B/339